Cultural Politics and the Mass Media

THE HISTORY OF COMMUNICATION

Robert W. McChesney and John C. Nerone, editors

A list of books in the series appears at the end of this book.

Cultural Politics
and the Mass Media

ALASKA NATIVE VOICES

Patrick J. Daley and Beverly A. James

UNIVERSITY OF ILLINOIS PRESS

URBANA AND CHICAGO

© 2004 by Patrick J. Daley and Beverly A. James

All rights reserved

Manufactured in the United States of America

C 5 4 3 2 1

∞ This book is printed on acid-free paper.

Library of Congress Cataloging-in-Publication Data

Daley, Patrick, 1950–

Cultural politics and the mass media : Alaska Native voices /
Patrick J. Daley and Beverly A. James.

p.   cm. — (The history of communication)

Includes bibliographical references and index.

ISBN 0-252-02938-0 (cloth : alk. paper)

1. Indian mass media—Alaska.

2. Indigenous peoples and mass media—Alaska.

3. Indians of North America—Alaska—Ethnic identity.

4. Indian radio stations—Alaska.

I. James, Beverly A. (Beverly Ann), 1947–

II. Title.

III. Series.

E78.A3D13   2004

302.23'44'089970798—dc22   2003024633

CONTENTS

ACKNOWLEDGMENTS

Permission to use material previously published elsewhere in different form is gratefully acknowledged:

A version of chapter 1 was published in the *Journal of Communication Inquiry* 22.4 (October 1998): 365–84. © 1998 by Sage Publications, Inc. Used by permission of Sage Publications, Inc.

A much-abbreviated version of chapter 2 was published as "The *Alaska Fisherman* and the Paradox of Assimilation: Progress, Power, and the Preservation of Culture" in *Native Press Research Journal* 5 (Summer 1987): 2–15. Used by permission of the American Native Press Archives, University of Arkansas at Little Rock.

A much-abbreviated version of chapter 3 was published as "An Authentic Voice in the Technocratic Wilderness: Alaskan Natives and the *Tundra Times*" in *Journal of Communication* 36.3 (Summer 1986): 10–30. Used by permission of Oxford University Press.

An abbreviated version of chapter 4 was published in *Javnost/The Public* 5.2 (Summer 1998): 49–60. Used by permission of *Javnost/The Public*.

A quite different and much-abbreviated version of chapter 5 was published as "Origination of State-Supported Entertainment Television in Rural Alaska" in *Journal of Broadcasting and Electronic Media* 31.2 (Summer 1987): 169–

80. Used by permission of the Broadcast Education Association (<http://www.beaweb.org>). That article underwent a philosophical sea change and appeared as "Ethnic Broadcasting in Alaska: The Failure of a Participatory Model" in *Ethnic Minority Media: An International Perspective,* ed. Stephen Harold Riggins (Thousand Oaks, Calif.: Sage Publications, 1992), 23–43. © 1992 by Sage Publications, Inc. Used by permission of Sage Publications, Inc.

ABBREVIATIONS

AAIA	Association on American Indian Affairs
AAPBS	Associated Alaska Public Broadcasting Stations
ACS	Alaska Conservation Society
AEBC	Alaska Educational Broadcasting Commission
AEC	Atomic Energy Commission
AFN	Alaska Federation of Natives
AIM	American Indian Movement
ANB	Alaska Native Brotherhood
ANCSA	Alaska Native Claims Settlement Act
ANILCA	Alaska National Interest Lands Conservation Act
ANM	"Alaska Native Magazine"
APBC	Alaska Public Broadcasting Commission
ARCS	Alaska Rural Communications Service
ASNA	Arctic Slope Native Association
ASOSS	Alaska State Operated School System
ATS	Applied Technology Satellite
AVCP	Association of Village Council Presidents
BBI	Bethel Broadcasting Incorporated
BIA	Bureau of Indian Affairs
CMP	Central Maine Power
CNER	Center for Northern Educational Research
CNI	Committee for Nuclear Information
COMSAT	Communications Satellite Corporation
CPB	Corporation for Public Broadcasting

DEW	Distant Early Warning
DOE	Department of Education
DRC	Development and Resources Corporation
DTIP	Division of Territories and Island Possessions
FAA	Federal Aviation Administration
FCC	Federal Communications Commission
GOT	Governor's Office of Telecommunications
KBI	Kotzebue Broadcasting Incorporated
LKSD	Lower Kuskokwim School District
NANA	Northwest Alaska Native Association
NPR	National Public Radio
NSHEC	North Slope Higher Education Center
NWREL	Northwest Regional Educational Laboratory
OEO	Office of Economic Opportunity
PBS	Public Broadcasting System
RATNET	Rural Alaska Television Network
REAB	Rampart Economic Advisory Board
SATVDP	Satellite Television Demonstration Project
TAF	The *Alaska Fisherman*
WAMCATS	Washington-Alaska Military Cable and Telegraph System
YPA	Yukon Power for America

Cultural Politics and the Mass Media

INTRODUCTION: Alaska Natives' Mass-Mediated Challenges to Euro-American Cultural Hegemony

THIS BOOK is about indigenous communication and cultural politics in Alaska. It presents a critical but sympathetic examination of the ways in which the indigenous peoples in Alaska have used various forms of mass media and community media for purposes of cultural expression and self-determination. Arranged chronologically, the chapters present a series of case studies of how Alaska Natives have responded to threats to their land and to their power to define their own cultural realities. In the episodes that we describe, the political establishment either attempted to control valuable resources or to steer major economic projects through territorial, state, and federal legislatures, using its ability to command the media stage at the territorial, and later, the state level. Political and economic leaders, supported by mainstream journalists, defined these economic resources and projects through the unexamined lens of the dominant culture, thus ignoring the indigenous groups whose economic and cultural patterns of living were at stake. We contend that this "whitening" of the public sphere by default was a racial marker naturalizing the dominant ethnicity and silencing other ethnic groups.

As with indigenous settlements elsewhere, most of Alaska's 278 villages are traditional communities with land-based cultures and close-knit kinship systems where people have constructed an enduring sense of solidarity around a clearly articulated ideal of home. Nearly 70 percent of Alaska's 98,000 indigenous peoples live in rural areas where the maintenance of their community lives—the production and reproduction of their cultural beliefs—is inextricably linked to subsistence practices, which, in turn, are dependent on the land. Subsistence as a whole way of life is captured eloquently in the words of a Yup'ik Eskimo: "We . . . the Eskimos . . . are very proud of one thing, that is our culture and our Native way of life, to live off the land, because we know culture and our traditional way of life cannot be bought, cannot be taken away from us no matter what happens. We live through this life, thick and thin . . . and that is . . . our way of life through our culture . . . given to us by our forefathers and elders" (Axel Johnson cited in Berger 1985, 51).

From a cultural studies perspective, this Yup'ik Eskimo's definition of culture as a whole way of life resonates with the democratic conception of the term culture in Raymond Williams's genealogy in *Keywords* (1985, 87–93). At the same time, it hints at the stresses and strains traditional ways of life have undergone when outside capital has intervened to exploit resources on Native lands and waters. Historically, globalization reached the shores of Alaska in the eighteenth century when Russian capitalists forced Aleuts into catching the valuable sea otter and dislocated Tlingits by exporting the colonial catch from one of their traditional sites around present-day Sitka to St. Petersburg, Russia, and eventually on to the Chinese market (Gibson 1976, 33–34). Shortly after the sale of Alaska by Russia to the United States, Seattle– and San Francisco–based fishing corporations wrested control of rich salmon areas in southeastern Alaska from Native subsistence fishermen and, together with Presbyterian missionaries and educators, reconfigured Tlingit and Haida cultures in fundamental ways. Since then, gold mining, cold war geopolitics, and the discovery of oil have brought more White settlers to Alaska, resulting in a clash of cultures whereby a capitalist ethos of competitive individualism has been met by political and cultural resistance from seven diverse Alaska Native groups.

In all of these Native and non-Native contacts, two problematic issues have always been at stake. The first has to do with the disruption of place, where stable relationships and social interactions were threatened, first by imperial reconfigurations, and later by corporate and state impositions. By understanding place in terms of stable relationships and ongoing subsistence practices, we are emphasizing the structure of feelings that indigenous peoples have for place as a symbolic guarantee of cultural belongingness (Hall 1995, 180; Morley 2000, 9; Berger 1985, 51; Widders and Noble 1993, 101; Rose 1995, 88). In the words of a recent Alaska Native report, one has to understand the actual practices of subsistence "'on the ground' in the lives of real people" (Alaska Natives Commission 1994, 3:3). Subsistence activities link extended families into a complex network of associations where, as a judge who collected evidence on subsistence puts it, the network "recreates the

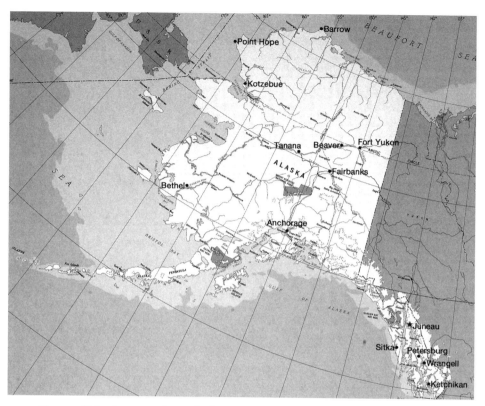

Figure 1. This place map shows the location of several Alaska Native villages, most of which are accessible only by plane, boat, snowmobile, or dog sled.

social order and gives meaning and value to each person's contributions and rewards" (Berger 1985, 52).

The second problematic issue has to do with the disruption of systems of meaning—the way in which competing cultures have "fought" to make sense of the physical environment and their relationship to it. In Alaska, Aleuts, Yup'ik and Inupiat Eskimos, and Athabascan, Tlingit, Haida, and Tsimshian Indians occupy and use distinct homelands where they have a sense of belonging with the land and with nature that partially constructs their differing senses of identity. In fact, for them, the political economy of subsistence is not only an important means of sustenance, but it is also a cultural way of life whose everyday practices subsume and transcend economic arguments for its legitimation, and constitute a cultural imperative for survival (Alaska Natives Commission 1994, 2:58). This cultural rootedness and the respect indigenous peoples express for all the animate and inanimate things that this place holds goes to the heart of their cultural identities. As one Yup'ik Eskimo mother puts it, "how firm we stand and plant our feet upon our land determines the strength of our children's heartbeats" (Koutchak cited in Berger 1985, 47). Over the past century, these cultural expressions have increased in frequency, volume, and intensity in indigenous settlements scattered over hundreds of thousands of square miles in Alaska because of disruptions in place, in subsistence practices, and in peoples' sense of who they are. As Stuart Hall notes, the correlation of culture and place for traditional peoples is the very meaning of ethnicity: "When shared meaning systems are underpinned by long, historical settlement of a population and 'shaping' in one physical environment, with strong kinship links as a result of continuous intermarriage over generations, we get a *very* strong and *strongly bounded* idea of culture and identity. . . . We call this very strong, well-bounded version of identity *ethnicity*. . . . Place, in short, is one of the key discourses in the systems of meaning we call culture and it functions to help stabilize cultural patterns and fix cultural identities, as they say, 'beyond the play of history'" (1995, 181). In Alaska, these different ethnic groups hold in common an ongoing political economy of subsistence practices, investing the rhythms of these seasonal activities with ritualized communal exchanges, sharing ceremonies, and spiritual storytelling.

Each case study in this book examines disruptions to place and shared meaning systems by focusing on mass mediated struggles Alaska Natives have mounted to resist capitalist and racist discourses that underpinned White man's physical incursions. Our understanding of this counterhegemonic process follows the notion of "resistance as cultural persistence" developed by indigenous communication scholar Gail Guthrie Valaskakis. According to Valaskakis, the adoption and use of new media by indigenous groups can be understood as a set of cultural practices that reinforce and amplify the group's own creative roots and dynamism (1993, 293; also cited in Bennett and Blundell 1995, 4). As she puts it, for indigenous groups in North America, their rootedness and sense of belonging constitutes the discourse of Indian Country [where] "the struggle over land is told and re-told in the stories of survival that reconstruct, imagine, and most of all, assert, Indian experience permeating the memorized past and the politicized future" (Valaskakis 1996, 156). Her concept of resistance as cultural persistence thus elegantly accounts for the ways traditional oral societies appropriated the new media of mass communication on their terms without being blindly consigned to the culturally limiting Euro-American bipolar opposites of assimilationism or some essentialized other—the noble savage or the "primitive" Alaska Native.

Clearly, then, for indigenous peoples in general, and for Alaska Native groups in particular, what has long been at stake is not only the right to occupy and use their homelands but also their right to control their means of communication. In this sense, freedom for indigenous peoples is premised on control over their political economy and control over capacity to tell their own stories. Anything less than the fulfillment of these two premises will result either in continued cultural subjugation at best or cultural genocide at worst. Nancy Fraser's work on justice and alternative public spheres is useful for articulating a conception of cultural politics applicable to indigenous peoples. Fraser takes issue with a preponderant tendency in both academic and everyday political discourse to see the struggle for recognition in the form of group identity as the paradigm of political conflict in the late twentieth century. The problem with identity politics, she says, is that it has too often decoupled political recognition from questions of political economy (1997, 2). As a way of reconstituting the false separation of the material and the symbolic, she proposes a critical theory of recognition that has two components: socioeconomic justice rooted in political economy and symbolic justice "rooted in patterns of representation, interpretation, and communication" (14). She makes it clear that the economic and the cultural are always already intertwined since "material economic institutions have a constitutive, irreducible cultural dimension to them" in their normative framing, and that cultural practices are always "underpinned by material supports" (15).

As we have noted, for Alaska Natives, economies of subsistence are not understood capitalistically as some external land base to be exploited as an objective material resource, but instead they are a complex fusion of the material and the cultural. Valaskakis says that "this expression of a relationship with the material environment is multi-faceted, including not only words and sounds, but a range of signs that . . . emerge from the shadowed recesses of oral traditions . . . the reconstruction of animals, mythical characters, and features of the physical environment as *persons*—named and equally involved with people of the past and the present—which, like sacred places, situates Native American identity and locality" (1996, 164). By conjoining a social politics of redistribution with a symbolic politics of expression, Fraser's concept of cultural politics opens up alternative public spheres for ethnic groups marginalized by capitalist economic norms that privilege individual possession and competition rooted in exploitation of natural resources. One of the enduring lessons of the case studies in this book is that when sociopolitical ideas must compete in a singular public sphere, those ideas that already fit into the dominating value structure will have an unfair advantage over those that do not.

As communication scholar David Morley notes, "the need for a variety of public spheres is premised on the recognition that public spheres themselves are not spaces of zero-degree culture, equally hospitable to any form of cultural expression" (2000, 117). In order to create alternative public spheres and achieve Fraser's notion of symbolic justice, control over communication systems in rural Alaska must be placed in the hands of those who live there. In articulating what a democratic system of communication might look like, Raymond Williams writes that "communication is something that belongs to the whole society." Furthermore, he maintains that we need to rid ourselves of the false ideology that sees communication only as a way of controlling people or making money from them; instead, he says that ordinary people should have that control in their own hands (1989, 29).

As this book shows, there have been some positive historical movements in these directions in indigenous settlements in rural Alaska, but there have also been some serious reversals. In this introduction we will explicate some of the most recent advances and reversals in terms of the relationship between political economy, place, and mediated resistance as cultural persistence; we will explain how we came to an understanding of these issues as communication researchers; we will offer synopses of the book's chapters; and we will explain the terminology we use to refer to various Alaska Native groups. The biggest reversal in Alaska Natives' efforts to control their material and symbolic lives took place in 1971 when Congress passed the Alaska Native Claims Settlement Act (ANCSA), extinguishing aboriginal land rights, placing subsistence in jeopardy, and upsetting the indigenous peoples' understandings of place as a generator of cultural belongingness. Thomas Berger, a Canadian judge and advocate for Native rights, has argued that members of the U.S. Congress treated ANCSA as a piece of social engineering to extend capitalism to the tundra because they did not wish to acknowledge the legitimacy of Native ways of life (1985, 90–95).

In a 1973 letter to the editor of the *Tundra Times*, Alaska Native Fred Bigjim expressed dismay over the cultural conundrums embodied in ANCSA's capitalistic corporate land selection process and dissatisfaction with its reconfiguration of the common aboriginal relationship to place where land and its bounty are shared in trust by villagers:

Joe Ayagtug and I took a week's trip into the territory surrounding our village to see how the land selection will work here. We covered our traditional hunting and fishing grounds where our people have lived for centuries. Although everyone knew the area, we never put up markers, fences, or boundaries because there were enough resources for everyone to survive.

What we found was large areas that had been marked off by others, especially the Federal Government. Some of it is in National Parks, Wildlife Refuges, Bird Sanctuaries; while other areas are held by the State of Alaska and private corporations. That means that land available to us to choose is smaller because of all these others who are outsiders as far as we Natives are concerned. (Bigjim and Ito-Alder 1974, 29–30)

In addition to the sacred qualities that the land holds for them, indigenous peoples also express a historical awareness of the land from which their tribal group has come since time immemorial (Widders and Noble 1993, 102–4). A southeastern Alaska Native woman expressed this sense of belonging to the country with custodial responsibilities and obligations to look after the land, saying "the land we hold in trust is our wealth. It is the only wealth that we could possibly pass on to our children . . . with all her bounty and rich culture" (Helmer cited in Berger 1985, n.p. [between 47 and 48]).

Instead of conveying land title to self-governing communities or tribes, ANCSA conveyed fee title to Alaska Natives organized into thirteen private, profit-making corporations. In order to "profit" from the land, Alaska Natives would have had to control the land and exploit its resources in a manner inconsistent with their traditional values, their consensus forms of decision making, and their cultural identities. In another letter to the *Tundra Times,* Bigjim wrote about the new corporate leaders emerging among Alaska Natives, warning that they might fall into the gap between the White world and the Native way of life. As he claims, "they may . . . end up representing the White world in the Native village rather than representing the Native villages in the White world. . . . We don't want to become better White men or beat them at their own game. We just want a chance to develop our traditional values into a satisfying way of life that we can understand" (Bigjim and Ito-Adler 1974, 82). His letter recognized ANCSA's threat to cultural identity, its disruption of traditional forms of leadership, and its economic shift from the pursuit of game to the pursuit of dollars. As he understood it, "nobody wants to know about the leadership we used to have . . . respected men in the villages who knew how to do the necessary things . . . to deal with the forces of nature and the relationships between the Native people in the villages" (81–82).

While ANCSA remains a major reversal with its disastrous implications for political economies of subsistence and for its production of incongruent cultural senses of place, it also engendered, as Bigjim's many letters to the *Tundra Times* indicated, mass-mediated resistance as cultural persistence. In keeping with the communicative practices of resistance as cultural persistence, by the time all of Bigjim's letters had been published, Alaska Native groups had established two noncommercial, Native-owned-and-operated radio stations in northwestern and southwestern Alaska. The stations' originators saw them as part of a communicative return to their roots where they could address Native problems in their own self-constituted public spheres and give voice to the traditional values of their elders.

However, the symbolic dimensions of the cultural politics of representation have also been complicated by the latest encounters with globalization whereby transnational systems of mass communication compress time and elide space. In village Alaska, more than two hundred satellite dishes have dotted the tundra since the late 1970s, inviting Alaska Natives to watch on television a consumer global culture much different than their own. Speaking of Americans in general, communication scholar Joshua Meyrowitz argues that the electronic media have deterritorialized us as spectators, leaving us with "no sense of place" (1985, 308). Similarly, John Durham Peters asks whether the mass media have altered the relevance of place as a marker of intelligibility in social description (1997, 79).

The seductiveness of these messages beamed in from afar raises the question of what happens to the sense of place in indigenous settings. What happens to the texture of community life when a culture of competitive individualism and consumption invades the spaces and complex patterns of subsistence where a culture of sharing has always persisted? Our empirical investigations show that Alaska Natives have displayed a resilient sense of place in culturally materialist ways—a resiliency that can be partially read off of their own mediated cultural productions. Along these lines, then, for indigenous peoples, Meyrowitz's claim (1985, 117) that "electronic messages steal into places" without invitation needs to be resituated in the context of a strong sense of place where the social terrain of the receiving culture shapes its peoples' "reading practices."

Paraphrasing human geographer Gillian Rose (1995, 99), we suggest that future investigators of indigenous cultural reception need to ask, "whose sense of place is more powerful in a particular situation?" In indigenous settings, place serves as a rich container of culture and offers a primary filter against the traveling cultures embedded in global messages. In Alaska, a strong sense of place was also related to the origination and control over electronically mediated cultural production. In southwestern Alaska, Yup'ik Eskimos had historically suffered fewer disruptions of place at the hands of Western entrepreneurs because their lands contained fewer exploitable resources than other parts of the state. As part of a determined effort to address shared political, economic, and cultural problems among an association of village councils, Yup'ik Eskimos pioneered the introduction of electronic communication as community media—both radio and television. These community media were partially responsible for a growing political consciousness in the 1970s among villagers in the region. In the early 1980s, fourteen Yup'ik tribal governments joined together to form Yupiit Nation as part of a full-fledged sovereignty movement to replace a Western-oriented political hegemony and its accompanying forms of cultural domination.

Our own education on Native sovereignty, tribal rights, and the political economies of subsistence began late in 1983 when we first heard about Yupiit Nation. Interested in questions of culture, communication, and self-determination, we were inspired by news of Yupiit Nation to get a better understanding of what seemed to be a budding revolution on the tundra. Let us briefly explain how our ideas came together, how we arrived at our research problems, and how we developed a communicative framework for situating these problems historically. After this explanation, we will give a synopsis of each chapter and conclude with remarks on Native terminology.

Soon after moving to Alaska in the early 1980s to assume academic positions in a university journalism and broadcasting program, we were struck by the highly charged political and economic atmosphere that pervaded the state's rich cultural landscape. Much of this political tension was generated by economic developers and sport hunting and fishing enthusiasts whose interests were fundamentally at odds with those of Alaska Natives and a small body of environmentalists. As communication scholars, we noted that mainstream news accounts concerning development, hunting, fishing, and other uses of the land invariably reproduced a deep-seated majoritarian interest in individual rights to the exclusion of the cultural practices of subsistence or the environmental practices of conservation. The mainstream print media, the airwaves, and even bumper stickers resonated with a fiercely anticonservationist discourse and scarcely concealed venom for the architects of the 1980 Alaska National Interest Lands Conservation Act (ANILCA), former president Jimmy Carter and Representative Morris Udall. At issue was access to the newly established 104 million acres of protected park lands, wildlife refuges, and wilderness areas. Fulfilling a congressional promise going back to the Alaska Native Claims Settlement Act (ANCSA) of 1971, ANILCA provided for the subsistence hunting and fishing rights of Alaska Natives.

Yet Alaska's economic and political elite, including the owners of the
mainstream mass media, were almost uniformly of one voice, decrying the
"lock-up" of the "state's" resources by the federal government. Alaska's congressional delegation, its governor, the vast majority of its legislature, corporate mining and oil interests, and sourdough miners constituted an enduring bloc whose hegemony commanded the terms of on-again, off-again,
state-sponsored subsistence laws that sought to enshrine hunting and fishing
rights on the grounds of possessive individualism. Believing that the land can
support intensive resource exploitation, most non-Native Alaskans sought
access to the land for purposes of economic development (McBeath and
Morehouse 1994, 24–26). The state's legislative efforts at individualizing access to the land did the ideological work of denying the communal meaning
subsistence rights have for Alaska Natives. To this day, subsistence remains a
highly charged term whose meaning takes on the connotations of its "primary" definers.

Northern studies scholar George Wenzel (1991, 57–60) argues that many
economists and anthropologists mistakenly understand subsistence as a self-
contained system of material production for the hunter's own use. Besides
reducing subsistence to individual acts of putting food on the table, this conception freezes Natives into an ahistorical past and denies the reality of intercultural contact and historical change. In other words, according to this
discourse, the use of snowmobiles and high-powered rifles by Alaska Natives
disqualifies their claim to be practicing a "privileged" form of subsistence
because these technologies are not "authentic" or "traditional." In effect, the
argument from authenticity freezes indigenous cultures into the logically
indefensible position that other cultures can change but theirs cannot. Thus,
the dominant discourse on subsistence either extends the concept to apply
to any hunter or fisherman operating outside the cash economy, or it relegates the practice to a romanticized past of skin kayaks and ivory fishhooks
that now exists only in museums. This dominant discourse on subsistence
is part of the essentialist trap set by the nineteenth-century imperialist mindset that remains alive and well today.

The Australian Aboriginal scholar Mudrooroo counters this essentialism
with his reminder that "all cultures and societies change and adapt and it is
in a dynamic and shifting environment of adaptation that the political claims
of indigenous peoples are situated" (cited in Ashcroft, Griffiths, and Tiffin
1995, 214). Valaskakis calls the dynamic blending of the modern with the tra-

ditional "innovative traditionalism." Applied to subsistence, innovative traditionalism accounts for the fact that modern instruments of the harvest,
transportation, and storage of wild foods may have changed but the human
and cultural needs of subsistence remain the same (cited in Bennett and Blundell 1995, 4–5). Alaska Native groups have also addressed this misguided,
ahistorical view of modern subsistence, decrying the fact that many policy-
makers see it as nothing more than a "cultural antique." They point out that
the technologies of subsistence have changed profoundly, but that the fundamental goals remain the same and that the harvests are as dynamic and
productive as ever. In fact, a 1987 study revealed that the vast majority of rural
residents chose to practice subsistence and that almost half of ninety-eight
communities surveyed reported a median per capita harvest of 252 pounds
of wild foods each year (Alaska Natives Commission 1994, 3:5; McBeath and
Morehouse 1994, 12).

After learning about the cultural complexity and sophistication of political economies of subsistence, we reexamined how these fourteen Yup'ik
Eskimo villages in southwestern Alaska were shifting the grounds of the ideological struggle by declaring their citizens members of Yupiit Nation with
fundamental rights to political and cultural self-determination, including
control over subsistence. The Yup'ik's declaration of democratic citizenship
was a fundamental assertion of their right to take control over outside forces.
Investigating whether there were earlier efforts by Alaska Natives to shift the
ideological terrain, we found numerous historical examples of cultural resistance effected either by particular indigenous groups or by alliances of
indigenous groups to implement their own systems of mass communication
and to construct their own public spheres as bulwarks against physical and
cultural annihilation. These historical examples comprise the book's stories
whereby Alaska Native voices struggled to articulate a cultural politics of self-
determination and cultural vitalization through a sometimes-uneasy control
over community and mass media.

In chapter 1, we examine the construction of a Western, Christian, and
capitalistic ideology articulated by Presbyterian missionaries who collabo-
rated closely with government officials in Juneau and Washington, D.C., to
establish religious and vocational education for Tlingit and Haida youth. The
missionaries' vocational pedagogy sought to foster individual discipline and
adherence to the rhythms of the industrial clock, but as the *North Star,* the
Presbyterian newspaper published at the Sitka Industrial Training School
indicated, classroom attendance fell off drastically at the height of subsistence
seasons. The establishment of Presbyterian schools in southeastern Alaska

in the 1880s coincided with the federal government's assimilationist policies and the reigning "progressive" notion of a universal, Christian civilization. Sheldon Jackson's Sitka Industrial Training School followed the educational philosophy of Lieutenant Richard Pratt's Carlisle Indian Industrial School in Pennsylvania, where the operative principle was to "kill the Indian in him and save the man" (cited in Adams 1995, 52). With his English-only policy, Jackson substituted cultural violence for physical brutality. He complemented his cultural assimilationism with a salvage anthropology aimed at collecting artifacts for display of the "vanished Natives" as residual signs for them of their former practices. Jackson's museum culture safely ensconced Tlingit and Haida Natives in what one Native scholar calls "the stasis box of the 19th century . . . a thinly disguised coffin" where change is over and "their story is complete" (Weaver 1997, 18).

In the first chapter, we pay close textual attention to Jackson's newspaper as a means to further his Christianizing mission and to control the arena of cultural production. In the *North Star,* Jackson told stories of Alaska Natives for outside consumption while providing instruction for Native youth in printing processes, a pedagogical tactic that would later backfire on the political establishment and pierce the armor of its supposed cultural superiority. But for nearly a decade Jackson's journalistic work yielded philanthropic contributions and delivered a nascent tourist trade to Alaska for Easterners curious to see the beauty of the land and Jackson's work in redeeming the "savages." To paraphrase Robert Berkhofer (1978), the dominant stories became those of "the White man's" Alaska Native, packaging the grand narrative of Western Christianity in scientific wrapping and advancing a belief in the irreducible difference between the "primitive" and modern mind (Carey 1989, 62). As Hall aptly describes the process, a basic distinction was drawn between the "West and the Rest" (1992).

In the second chapter, we first document the disruptions faced by Tlingit and Haida Indians in dealing with colonial usurpation of traditional salmon fishing rights by absentee oligopolistic salmon packers. Second, we describe both the power of and the resistance to the Presbyterian ideology. Some Natives indigenized Christianity in a way that allowed them to keep salient aspects of their traditional religious practices under cover, while others practiced Russian Orthodoxy because of its tolerance for Native languages and customs. When commercial fishing interests were at their strongest, a seemingly conservative Christian fraternal organization, the Alaska Native Brotherhood (ANB), started the *Alaska Fisherman,* the territory's first Native-owned-and-operated newspaper, in 1923. The economic and political battles waged in its pages are the subject of the second chapter.

In particular, we show how the *Alaska Fisherman* constructed its primary argument against the corporate use of fish traps. Under the editorship of William Paul, a Tlingit Indian, the *Alaska Fisherman* fought for Native citizenship rights, delivered the "canoe vote," and underscored the cultural significance of fish for southeastern Alaska Natives with its claim that the issue was always about fish *and* people. As a man who had spent much of his life maneuvering through White religious, educational, business, and legal institutions in the contiguous forty-eight states, part of Paul's editorial and political success derived from what Hall has called the "in-between" of different cultures where Paul learned to negotiate and translate between cultures (1995, 206).

Using a narrative of Raven, the culture hero and trickster/cultural transformer for southeastern Alaska Native peoples, Paul articulated his philosophy of communication with the assertion that "a group of people without the power of telling what they have done can be robbed." His argument for the Natives' right to tell their own stories was articulated principally against the hegemony constructed by John Troy in his *Alaska Daily Empire* (Juneau). Troy's powerful paper supported the colonial structure of outside canning and mining interests. As the paper's editorial voice, Troy was a racist spokesman attacking Tlingit and Haida Indians whenever they challenged these established powers. Paul's counterhegemonic project articulated in the *Alaska Fisherman* was a prime example of resistance as cultural persistence, an effort underlining the centrality of civil rights and the cultural practices of subsistence.

While the *Alaska Fisherman* was an early victim of the Depression, the poor economic times had the paradoxically beneficial effect of weakening outside interests, leaving Alaska Natives relatively undisturbed in their lands and cultural practices. However, Alaska's geopolitical importance during World War II ended this quiet period, bringing in new money and new settlers. Except for a brief period during the late-nineteenth-century gold rush, this marked the first time that census figures showed more settlers than Alaska Natives. After the war, new pressures for statehood went hand-in-glove with new economic schemes that, more often than not, infringed on the fundamental aboriginal land rights of Alaska Natives. Despite these infringements, traditional histories of Alaska pay scant attention to these Native concerns; instead, they approach the prestatehood period from the perspective of Alaska as a settler colony, neglected by the federal government and controlled by outside economic interests (see Nichols 1924 and Gruening 1954).

In the third chapter, we examine three critical, technocratic challenges to the physical and cultural integrity of Alaska Natives: first, a plan by the Atomic Energy Commission (Project Chariot) to use atomic bombs, ostensibly to create a harbor in northwestern Alaska; second, the U.S. Fish and Wildlife Service's enforcement of an international migratory bird treaty forbidding Alaska Natives from taking eider ducks for subsistence purposes during the only time period they were in northern flyways; and third, a proposal to construct the world's largest hydroelectric facility, Rampart Dam, a project that would have flooded seven Athabascan villages and created a reservoir larger than Lake Erie. In response to the first two challenges, Inupiat Eskimos met in Barrow in late 1961 and called for a Native newspaper to counter the Alaska mainstream press's celebration of technocratic fixes to the state's struggling economy and to assert their right to feed themselves in traditional ways. Originally conceived as an outlet for the news and views of Inupiat Eskimos, the *Tundra Times* strategically aligned all Alaska Native groups under the banner of a pan-Native medium in the early 1960s. As with the example of Paul and the *Alaska Fisherman,* at least part of the success of the *Tundra Times* can be attributed to its editor, Howard Rock, a man who had come "home." Having spent the better part of two decades outside of Alaska, Rock was the product of different cultures, learning to think and write from *difference* (Hall 1995, 206). Perhaps Rock and the *Tundra Times*'s greatest contribution to Alaska Native self-determination was giving voice to Native opposition to the Rampart Dam plan—the gargantuan hydroelectric project that threatened to inundate millions of acres of Native homelands rich in subsistence fish and game. Spurred by indigenous opposition, the *Tundra Times* facilitated the organization of the Alaska Native lands claim movement.

Up until the advent of the *Tundra Times,* the print media in Alaska's largest cities had commanded an inordinately important role in formulating a political and economic hegemony in a territory and state continually oscillating between economic boom and bust. In the territorial period, this media hegemony generally served either the interests of corporations in the contiguous forty-eight states or the self-interests of Alaska's often transient "rugged individualists." In either case, their sense of public responsibility and obligation—their solicitude and respect for the original inhabitants—was about as wide as a flake of gold dust. After Alaska's economic wartime boom brought settlers and money to the territory and reinvigorated the statehood movement in the late 1940s and early 1950s, Robert Atwood, publisher of the *Anchorage Daily Times,* and C. W. Snedden, publisher of the *Fairbanks Daily News-Miner,* led the symbolic charge. Since Alaska's transient White population was one stumbling block to statehood and since that obstacle could be overcome with better long-term job opportunities, Atwood and Snedden were quick to push the economic buttons of the latest business boosters.

With statehood approved by Congress in 1958 and officially effective in 1959, the state was granted the right to take more than 103 million acres of land from the public domain, despite the fact that aboriginal land rights were still unresolved. These land selections were seen as potential economic engines for a state badly in need of revenue (McBeath and Morehouse 1994, 79, 108). As publishers of the state's two largest newspapers, Atwood's and Snedden's successful leadership in the statehood movement shifted to promotion of the Atomic Energy Commission's Project Chariot in 1958 and to Yukon Power for America's Rampart Dam in the early 1960s. In particular, the Rampart Dam project was "sold" to the public as an economic benefit to all Alaskans. Its sales effort was predicated on its promoters' belief in an assimilated and integrated society. Thus, this culturally ideological blind spot enabled seemingly enlightened political leaders such as Senator Ernest Gruening to devalue all that was dear to Natives, calling their lands ugly and worthless and labeling their subsistence practices as welfare traps. These descriptions were articulated ad nauseam in the battle to detonate six atomic bombs at Point Hope, ostensibly for harbor construction, and to build a gargantuan dam at Rampart Canyon for hydroelectric power. While these threats to the material and cultural integrity of Alaska Natives were instrumental in raising their political consciousness, in giving birth to the *Tundra Times,* and in prompting Native groups to organize in regions all over the state in defense of their land claims, the economic discovery that greased the wheels of Congress in "finally" settling the aboriginal land claims of Alaska Natives was Atlantic Richfield's discovery of oil on Alaska's North Slope in 1967.

With the achievement of the land claims settlement in late 1971, a new medium of communication among Yup'ik Eskimos in southwestern Alaska in 1971 would return the focus of Alaska Natives to their local concerns and their particular cultures. In chapter 4, we describe how the development of Alaska Native community radio owes its legacy to the organizing efforts of the lands claim movement, particularly to federal funding programs in rural areas available to them under President Lyndon Johnson's War on Poverty programs in the 1960s. The broadcasting efforts that emerged here were fundamentally aimed at collective cultural cohesion. Our analysis leans heavily on James Carey's ritual view of communication. Indeed, his definition of communication as culture (1989) resonates strongly with the Yup'ik Eskimos' self-identification of their traditional culture as one that emphasizes "speaking out to create, maintain, and perpetuate a well-governed society" (Fienup-Riordan 1990, 198).

But after the first decade of Alaska Natives' experience with the community-building efforts of local radio, shifts in federal and state communication policies threatened to turn the medium into a transmission belt for "neutral information" and commodified popular culture. In particular, with the leaner federal budgets during the Reagan years, community radio had to make compromises on questions of control and programming in order to survive. Fortunately for Yup'ik Eskimos in southwestern Alaska, these struggles resulted in a resurgence of cultural self-awareness, in employment of radio as an extension of oral traditions, and in a heightened willingness to engage in collective actions to advance their political and cultural goals. Despite these advances, we contend that the cultural integrity and vitality of Alaska Natives requires a concerted effort to strengthen local control over radio. As Carey maintains in his ritual view of communication, what is at stake is not the extension of messages in space so much as it is the maintenance of society in time, those meaningful practices that draw people together in fellowship and commonality (1989, 43).

The birth of electronic communication over the radio airwaves was quickly complemented in widely scattered areas of Alaska in the mid-1970s by the introduction of televisual communication distributed over satellite technology. In chapter 5, we examine how the space-binding biases of satellite technology have had deleterious consequences for the cultural politics of community television in Alaska. We analyze federal/state health- and education-oriented experiments in the satellite delivery of information to rurally isolated Native communities with a critical, theoretical perspective informed by Carey and John Quirk's (1970) creative interpretations of the tendencies and limitations of communication technologies as first articulated by Canadian economic historian Harold Adams Innis. While these well-intentioned bureaucratic projects sought to tread the fine line between the efficient delivery of messages and cultural and democratic relevance, they always erred on the side of bureaucratic imperatives.

Nevertheless, with the technological and visual genie of television now out of the bottle in remote areas of Alaska, the state committed itself to the delivery of a combination of entertainment and educational television programming after initial federal experiments had run their course. We situate the state's guidelines for the provision of television against Native-oriented efforts to use technology to produce and show their own programming. We argue that the former paled in its satisfaction of the diverse cultural needs of Alaska Native citizens when compared to some of their own efforts.

In the conclusion, we ask what kinds of cultural stories might make a beneficial difference in the lives of Alaska Natives. Following up on historian Calvin Martin's claim that we all live by a story, we concur in his contention that too many Alaska Natives have lost their stories and suggest that the mass media are often at fault for these losses. Martin reminds us that facts only make sense within a certain paradigm of reality and that there are now at least two very different realities percolating in North America, one Western and one Aboriginal (1999, 82, 121, 128). Martin's poignant insights provide us with our final point of departure, a close reading of a detailed set of notes of a North Slope higher education class on "broadcasting and the news." A small culturally diverse class of students in Barrow, Alaska, struggled with the Western journalistic paradigm of objectivity. The notes reveal that, for them, this paradigm signaled cultural pain and dislocation. Interrogating Western news values from an indigenous perspective, they began to see objectivity as a poseur—a masquerader hiding a storyteller's perspective as if its teller were everywhere and nowhere. For Alaska Native storytellers, the important point is to narrate stories from those places where their understandings of nature are part and parcel of their cultural milieus.

In short, then, this book is organized as a selective series of historically informed case studies of the experiences of Alaska Natives as they have fought to give voice to their cultural representations through their own media. These struggles were fundamentally ideological clashes, with Alaska Natives articulating counterhegemonic discourses through a wide range of media as they asserted their rights to cultural expression. As an investigation of indigenous cultural politics, the book's inescapable starting point is the connection between indigenous peoples' territorial groundedness, their subsistence cultural practices, and their needs and desires to communicate their cultural identities in wide-ranging ways, including their articulation through the media of mass communication. With intercultural contact, new technologies have been introduced into the cultural milieus of Alaska Natives, altering both their subsistence and communicative patterns. Part of their ongoing struggle turns on the cultural prerogative of benefiting from technological developments without the imposition of ethnocentric judgments about what these changes mean for their so-called authentic selves.

Alaska has a diverse population with the highest percentage of indigenous peoples in the country—more than 98,000 Alaska Natives and American Indians or 15.6 percent of the state's total population (U.S. Census Bureau 2000). As we noted, seven major groups comprise most of this population: Aleuts; Inupiat Eskimos; Yup'ik Eskimos; and Athabascan, Tlingit, Haida, and Tsimshian Indians (see figure 2). Our personal, archival, and mass-mediated encounters with Alaska Natives indicated to us their great pride in their cultural heterogeneity, their cultural differences. In fact, they persistently resisted pan-Native artifices and were very careful to avoid any conflation of cultural identities. However, as we will see, the cultural diversity of Alaska Native peoples found political unity—a kind of strategic essentialism—in their fight to retain their ancestral lands and their subsistence practices. In order to understand these "culture wars," one has to begin with an appreciation for the inseparability of Alaska Natives' everyday cultural lives with land and nature.

As a book focused on the intersection of a number of indigenous cultures with a dominating White culture, we have tried to adopt the terms of self-designation acceptable to the indigenous peoples of Alaska. As is the custom in Alaska when referring to the indigenous peoples as a whole, we use Alaska as an adjective, as in Alaska Natives (Berger 1985, viii). With respect to individual Native groups, we refer to the Aleuts and to the Athabascan, Tlingit, Haida, and Tsimshian Indians, for these are the accepted self-designations for these cultural groups in Alaska. There are numerous "tribes," or geographic units, in the vast interior of Alaska whom we have chosen to group together under the commonly accepted spelling of Athabascan rather than the more precise designation of Koyukon, Kutchin, Ingalik, and Tanaina Indians, to name just a few (Nelson 1983, 3). Occasionally, we refer to these Indian groups by using regional adjectives. For example, we refer to the Tlingit and Haida Indians as southeastern Alaska Natives. Other times we make reference to the similarities of these people with other Northwest Pacific Coast peoples by designating them in that way. Alaska Indian groups tend to bear a greater physical and cultural similarity to other Northwest Pacific Coast cultures or to Indians in the contiguous forty-eight states than they do to Aleuts and Eskimos.

The popular conception of Eskimos as the principal group of Arctic peoples obscures some significant differences among the "Eskimo family." Indeed, the popular and etymological references to the Eskimos have been in error. The *Oxford English* and *Webster's New World* dictionaries have incorrectly traced the term Eskimo to the proto-Algonquian root meaning "eaters of raw flesh" (Fienup-Riordan 1990, 5). Fienup-Riordan maintains that the word is properly derived from a Montagnais form meaning "snowshoe-setter." Thus, many Canadian and Greenlandic Natives have taken umbrage at this designation and preferred the term "Inuit," a designation meaning "people" (1990,

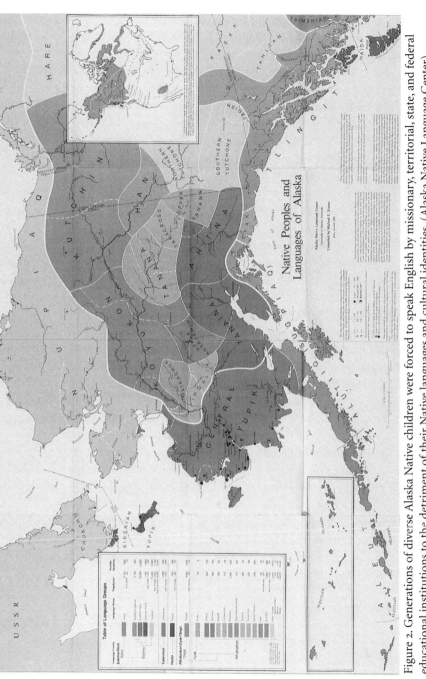

Figure 2. Generations of diverse Alaska Native children were forced to speak English by missionary, territorial, state, and federal educational institutions to the detriment of their Native languages and cultural identities. (Alaska Native Language Center)

5). In Alaska, the northwestern and southwestern Natives of the larger Eskimo family have not adopted the designation of Inuit, but they have chosen designations that conform closely to the linguistic branches to which they belong. So from southern Norton Sound to the Bristol Bay area of southwestern Alaska, the Yup'ik speaking branch of Eskimos prefer to be called Yup'ik Eskimos from the Yup'ik word *yuk,* for person, and *pik,* for genuine or real. Hence, we refer to them as Yup'ik Eskimos (Fienup-Riordan 1990, 5). The family of Eskimos residing from Norton Sound upward all along the northwestern and northern Alaskan coastlines speak Inupiaq and prefer the designation Inupiat Eskimos. That is the designation we follow in this book.

In contradistinction to Alaska Natives, we frequently refer to Whites or non-Natives. Here we follow the definition outlined by Judge Thomas Berger in his *Village Journey,* a book commissioned by the Inuit Circumpolar Conference, an international organization of Eskimos from Alaska, Canada, and Greenland to review the Alaska Native Claims Settlement Act. Berger used the term Whites to refer to Western man and the representatives of industrialized society generally because this was the way the Alaska Natives from whom he gathered testimony used the expression (1985, viii).

Finally, we use the term indigenous peoples frequently, especially in this introduction. We do so to link together original inhabitants of lands whose sense of place and locality has given them shared meanings, beliefs and values, political economies of subsistence, and a deep and abiding feeling of cultural belongingness. Unlike Native Americans in the contiguous forty-eight states, Alaska Natives have not been displaced by a settler class, although they continue to be threatened by loss of control over their political economies and over their own narratives. While Alaska Natives still have a long way to go to establish control in these domains, we offer these historical stories of spirited examples of resistance as cultural persistence to indigenous peoples around the globe who constitute a Fourth World from Alaska to Tierra del Fuego, including the Ainu of Japan, the Aborigines of Australia, the Maori of New Zealand, the Sami of Scandinavia, the Inuit in Canada and Greenland, and the tribal peoples of Russia, China, India, and Southeast Asia.

1   Missionary Voices as the Discursive Terrain for Native Resistance

IN RECENT YEARS a spate of images and narratives of Alaska Natives has flooded the national media landscape. But this "northern exposure" is neither new nor culturally transparent. Euro-Americans have long been enchanted with images of the "Far North" and her exotic others, portrayed as happy dancing heathens in Robert Flaherty's documentary of Canadian Eskimos, *Nanook of the North,* or cast as savages in Jack London's naturalistic, survival-of-the-fittest novels. Predating both of these image-makers and storytellers, the *National Geographic* made Alaska a popular staple in its "scientific" coverage right from its inception in 1888.

Less well known are stories of how Alaska Natives have struggled to preserve their cultures on their own terms, adapting certain technologies and practices from the West while simultaneously resisting the appropriation of their aboriginal rights and resources. Throughout this book, we show how Alaska Natives, beginning in 1923, adopted modern mass media in the pursuit of what Gail Guthrie Valaskakis calls resistance as cultural persistence (1993, 293; see also Valaskakis cited in Bennett and Blundell 1995, 4). In this chapter, we demonstrate how her notion of resistance as cultural persistence is useful for thinking about the responses of indigenous peoples to cultural and territorial imperialism, for it offers a conceptual alternative to romantic images of some essentialized other on the one hand, and the assimilationist rhetoric of the melting pot metaphor on the other.

In Alaska, indigenous cultural persistence has been exercised against the backdrop of a Euro-American discursive hegemony. At an 1898 hearing in Juneau convened by Governor John Brady to hear the grievances of Tlingit

leaders, Chief Kadashan acknowledged the White man's self-designated position of superiority as he pled for the restoration of indigenous lands: "White
people are smart; our people are not as smart as white people. They have a
very fine name; they call themselves white people. Just like the sun shining
on this earth. They are powerful. . . . It is not right for such powerful people
as you are to take away from poor people like we are, our creeks and hunting grounds" (Hinckley 1970, 272).

To understand how Alaska Natives have maintained and/or recovered
symbolic boundaries in their struggles for self-determination, then, we need
to open the mouths of the imperialistic ventriloquists who purported to
speak for them (see Martin 1987, 33). We need to articulate the symbolic terrain against which the indigenous peoples of Alaska have had to respond in
order to resist cultural annihilation. The purpose of this chapter, therefore,
is to show the construction of a Western hegemony in its Alaskan foci—the
development of what Stuart Hall has called the "discourse of the West and
the Rest" (1992).

Specifically, we will examine conceptions of indigenous cultures advanced
by the nineteenth-century Presbyterian missionary, Sheldon Jackson, through
the *North Star* (1887–92, 1895–98), the first long-running missionary newspaper in Alaska.[1] Jackson presents a particularly interesting figure for analysis as a driving force behind Protestant efforts to evangelize and educate Alaska Natives and as a master publicist. In the late nineteenth century, the two
most characteristic features of America's colonial manifest destiny were commercial opportunities and possibilities for Christianizing "savages" (Torgovnick 1990, 27). Alaska and its abundant resources were well known by the
time Jackson and fellow missionary William Kelly started the *North Star* at
Sitka, in Alaska's southeastern archipelago, in December 1887. Russian explorers and fur hunters had arrived nearly 150 years earlier. English explorers and
traders visited Alaska in the late eighteenth century and Yankee traders arrived early in the nineteenth century, followed by Yankee whalers in the 1840s.
These far from innocent economic encounters of Western powers with Alaska
Natives contributed to the articulation of the "discourse of the West" as it
gets represented in the *North Star*. It is important, therefore, to set the historical context of Native/non-Native relationships prior to the establishment
of the newspaper.

We will thus begin with an account of contacts between Alaska Natives
and Russians in the eighteenth century. Following a short review of the Russian period, we briefly sketch the twenty-year period between the purchase
of Alaska by the United States and the advent of the *North Star*. We then pro-

vide a short description of the missionary path that led Sheldon Jackson to Alaska, followed by an analysis of his evolutionary theories of indigenous cultures. Finally, we offer a critical reading of the cultural, economic, and educational discourse of the *North Star.*

The Russian Period

Traditional histories treat the development of the frontier in the "New World" as moving from east to west, culminating at least momentarily at the shores of the Pacific. However, what makes the conquest of Alaska peculiar is that, as James Clifford notes, Western history arrived from the wrong direction: from the seat of imperial power in St. Petersburg eastward across Siberia and the Bering Sea to Alaska (1997, 303). Shortly before he died in 1726, Tsar Peter the Great commissioned the Danish captain Vitus Bering to sail east to the Siberian peninsula of Kamchatka and then on to America to claim the land for Russia (McBeath and Morehouse 1994, 33). In his second great expedition eastward, Bering set sail on June 4, 1741. By mid-summer, his crew had spotted Mount St. Elias in southeast Alaska, and had then headed west toward the Aleutian Islands where they settled in for the winter. Bering did not survive the winter, but a member of his crew, the naturalist George Wilhelm Steller, discovered the sea otter while off in search of food. That discovery led to the development of a lucrative fur trade and to what Hubert Bancroft called "the swarming of the promyshleniki," or professional fur hunters, to the coastline of Alaska (1886, 36–99).

The "landlubberish Russians" relied on the Aleuts' skill in handling the kayak and harpoon for the hunting of sea otters (Gibson 1976, 7–8). When the cooperation of the Aleuts could not be secured through trifling gifts, they were forced to hunt. Often, the men were taken great distances from their villages, and, in their absence, the Russians assaulted the Aleut women. Charges of gross brutalities were brought against the crew of one ship in 1762, resulting in an imperial edict that cautioned future companies against kidnapping and murder (Bancroft 1886, 121–26). This behavior was not exceptional. The Aleuts' cultural subsistence patterns were severely disrupted, and their population declined dramatically in the second half of the eighteenth century (Gibson 1976, 8; Krauss 1980, 14).

By the 1780s, the depletion of the sea otter forced the Russian traders to move east to Prince William Sound. After serious resistance by the Koniags, Grigori Shelikhov, considered the founder of Russian colonies in Alaska, established a settlement, Three Saints Harbor, on Kodiak Island in 1784. Two years later he set up a school to teach the Natives how to read and write in Russian, and more fundamentally, to sow the seeds of Christianity (Bancroft 1886, 227–29). The greatest Russian influences occurred during the nineteenth century. Of particular importance was the arrival in the Aleutians in 1824 of Ioann Veniaminov, a Russian Orthodox bishop who opened a school in Unalaska. Veniaminov worked with an Aleut chief to adapt the Slavonic alphabet to Aleut, and in 1834 they produced an Aleut catechism, the first book published in an Alaska Native language (Krauss 1980, 15). The school operated for more than thirty-five years with much of the instruction in Aleut (Bancroft 1886, 708–9).

Over the years, Alaska became less lucrative. By the 1850s, the sea otter was practically extinct as a result of the reckless hunting practices of the previous decades. Furthermore, Russia's treasury was nearly depleted as a result of the Crimean War, and therefore, by around 1860, the tsar began to explore the possibility of selling Alaska to the United States (Bancroft 1886, 591–92). On March 30, 1867, the Treaty of Cession was signed, as Secretary of State William Seward acted out his fantasy of manifest destiny.

At the time of purchase, the population of Alaska was almost exclusively Native. Jeannette Nichols lists the population at the time as 26,483 Natives, 1,421 Creoles or "half-breeds," 483 Russians and Siberians, 200 foreigners from other nations, and 150 Americans (1924, 38). The Treaty of Cession recognized the citizenship rights and land claims of "private and individual property holders," with the specific exception of "uncivilized Native tribes" (Federal Field Committee 1968, 56). This term apparently referred to those people who lived beyond the pale of Russian occupation, that is to say, the vast majority of Alaska Natives (McNickle 1973, 61).

The change in colonial administrations did not ease relations among Whites and Natives, particularly for the Tlingits of southeast Alaska. A Treasury Department agent in 1869 reported that "dissatisfaction among the tribes on account of the sale of the territory did not arise from any special feeling of hostility, but from the fact that it was sold without their consent, they arguing that their fathers originally owned all the country but allowed the Russians to occupy it for their mutual benefit, in that articles desired by them could be obtained from the Russians in exchange for furs; but the right of the Russians to sell the territory, except with the intention of giving them the proceeds is denied" (Arnold 1976, 62–63).

When the United States took possession of Alaska, the Army established headquarters in the former facilities of the Russian American Company in

Sitka, and set up outposts in other Russian settlements. Throughout the late 1860s and 1870s, the Army had sporadic run-ins with the Tlingits and Haidas, and it became apparent that the Army was strategically ill equipped to exercise control, particularly following troop cutbacks in the aftermath of the Civil War. As a result, the Navy was sent in to reassert political authority and to buttress the efforts of the missionaries who were making inroads in establishing "moral" authority. At this historical juncture, the assertion of authority by Protestant missionaries was the greatest threat to Native lands, languages, and subsistence practices. The story of this "moral expansion" begins with the arrival of Sheldon Jackson at Fort Wrangell, Alaska, in August 1877.

Sheldon Jackson

Standing just five feet tall, Sheldon Jackson, the "Napoleon"[2] of the Presbyterian missionaries in Alaska, was a well-intentioned but authoritarian architect of a Western discursive hegemony that sought to render the "rest" of Alaska's Native cultures to the dustbin of history. Jackson's missionary ideas were far from unique; indeed, they meshed well with the zeitgeist of the times. In particular, they articulated the conjunction of anthropological and cultural views of civilization then au courant in elite intellectual circles. They also converged with the federal government's haphazardly evolving Indian policy. To set the stage for our analysis of these anthropological and cultural discourses in the pages of the *North Star*, let us take a cursory look at the path that led Jackson to Alaska.

The Presbyterian Church's commitment to frontier ministrations went back to a resolution adopted by the Presbytery of Philadelphia in 1707, which said that its ministers "should supply 'desolate places where a minister is wanting'" (Goodykoontz 1939, 74). Jackson's contribution to the "winning of the West" began at a Choctaw mission in Indian Country, but ill health forced him to accept a reassignment to Minnesota. After ten years of service in Minnesota, in which he often stretched the geographic range of his assignment, Jackson convinced the Board of Home Missions to allow him to extend his work to the far west (Miller 1989, 2). In 1869 he was appointed superintendent of missions for western Iowa, Nebraska, Dakota, Idaho, Montana, Wyoming, and Utah (Goodykoontz 1939, 319).

Jackson's hagiographic biographer explains that according to the terms of his new assignment, Jackson was responsible for the territories cited "or as far as our jurisdiction extends." For Jackson, this clause included "the almost unknown province of Alaska, to which this dauntless missionary explorer longed to go" (Stewart 1908, 101). Jackson's ambitions were realized in 1877, when the Board of Home Missions assigned him to Alaska. Together with Amanda McFarland, an experienced missionary among the Indians of the Southwest, Jackson traveled to Fort Wrangell where he took control of a Methodist school run by a Tsimshian Indian.[3] The following spring, Jackson established a second Presbyterian school in Sitka (Stewart 1908, 296–302; Hinckley 1982, 28).

From the moment Jackson arrived in Alaska he embarked on the twin tasks of educating the Natives and collecting their artifacts. Indeed, Jackson's approach to Native education was closely tied to his interest in what is today called cultural anthropology. In a letter in 1887 announcing the establishment of a museum of natural history and ethnology, formally named the Sheldon Jackson Museum and Library in 1892, Jackson explained that its purpose was to "procure and have on hand for the study of the students the best specimens of the old works of their Ancestors; otherwise, in a few years there would be nothing left to show the coming generation of [N]atives how their fathers lived" (cited in Hulbert 1987, xi). Let us spend a moment examining Jackson's penchant for collecting Native artifacts as a way of unearthing the foundations of his philosophy of indigenous cultures.

Jackson accumulated more than three thousand items in Alaska over a twenty-five year period, relying mainly on traders and fellow missionaries as collectors. In a festschrift to Jackson on the centennial year of the Sheldon Jackson Museum, Bette Hulbert notes that "the concept of collecting cultural materials to be studied by future generations of that particular culture was unique at that time," given that the usual purpose of anthropological collecting was to further "the knowledge of peoples far removed from the culture area" (1987, xi). Hulbert and other contributors to the festschrift express admiration for Jackson's energy as a collector, but at the same time express exasperation with the paucity of information he recorded about the cultures that produced the objects. In an "open letter to Sheldon Jackson," Peter Corey, the editor of the festschrift and the curator of the museum, asks: "Why didn't you collect more background information on the artifacts you gathered? (A funny word—artifacts. It has come to connote items of antiquity, though it specifically denotes any item manufactured by man. The artifacts in the museum were items of everyday usage when you visited the people in their home villages. . . .) How I wish they could talk to me! . . . I know you were busy on these trips aboard the *Bear,* and we do appreciate the information you did record, but there was so much to be gotten! . . . I keep hoping that someday someone will find a diary or journal of yours that expresses your philosophy and method of collecting" (xiii).

What can we make of the apparent paradox that Jackson's collecting presents—a wealth of objects and a dearth of cultural information? As Corey wonders, what was Jackson's philosophy of collecting? Recent scholarship on the politics of exhibition in nineteenth-century ethnographic museums offers some insight into these questions (see, e.g., Coombes 1994; Stocking 1985). With the nascent discipline of anthropology providing scientific legitimacy, objects made and used by "primitive," "savage" peoples were collected by the very agents whose activities were transforming, and in some cases, eradicating those cultures—traders, explorers, colonial governors, and missionaries. Henrietta Lidchi emphasizes the point that the practices of collecting, identifying, classifying, and displaying such objects were important mechanisms historically in the cultural construction of the West and the Rest. In other words, she writes, anthropology, like all sciences, "is not primarily a *science of discovery*, but a *science of invention*" that discursively supported the political and economic exploitation of "exotic," "pre-literate" peoples (1997, 161). The ethnographic objects Jackson and his contemporaries collected contributed to the prevailing sense of ethnology and anthropology as discovery, in that the artifacts were seemingly plucked from natural settings and categorized according to purportedly neutral, objective systems of classification.

In keeping with the late-nineteenth-century notion that museums should preserve the material traces of "vanishing races," Jackson wanted to salvage the objects but to let the cultures die. Jackson's implicit philosophy of collecting thus fits the trope of salvage ethnography associated with the image of the vanishing red man.[4] He was no doubt familiar with the work of one of the most celebrated scholars of his time, fellow Union College alumnus Lewis Henry Morgan, whose 1877 book, *Ancient Society, or Researches in the Lines of Human Progress from Savagery through Barbarism to Civilization,* "stressed the dire need to salvage anthropological information on Native Americans before it was too late" (Berkhofer 1978, 54).

Morgan saw human history as an evolutionary process in which all peoples progress through three main stages—savagery, barbarism, and civilization—with each stage reflecting a close correlation between economic and cultural achievements. Morgan further broke these stages down into subperiods and classified economies characterized by fishing—the mainstay of life in southeast Alaska—as belonging to the second subperiod of savagery (Barnard 1967, 393–94). Consistent with Morgan's evolutionary determinism,

Jackson often referred to progressive developmental stages in talking about indigenous peoples, calling the Eskimos "low in the scale of humanity," or referring to the "barbarous lands" of Alaska. Along these same lines he praised the Aleuts for having achieved a "state of civilization" through the introduction of schools and churches by the Russians (Jackson 1880, 71–72, 118).

Jackson's adherence to a Morgan-like philosophy is transparently clear when we look at the development of missionary educational efforts in Alaska. The first step in acculturating Alaska Natives was the practice of homogenizing diverse Indian languages and habits. Reverend S. Hall Young, one of Jackson's first recruits, writes in 1880 of his work at the Tlingit Training Academy in Fort Wrangell: "One strong stand, which so far as I know I was the first to take, was the determination to do no translating into the Thlingit [sic] language or any other of the [N]ative dialects of that region. When I learned the inadequacy of these languages to express Christian thought, . . . I wrote to the mission Board . . . that we should let the old tongues with their superstition and sin die—the sooner the better—and replace these languages with that of Christian civilization, and compel the [N]atives in all our schools to talk English and English only" (cited in Krauss 1980, 23).

The board complied with Young's recommendation; English was the only language allowed at either the Fort Wrangell or the Sitka schools. The matter of eradicating Indian customs and routines was a more intractable problem. Reverend John G. Brady, another of Jackson's initial recruits, reasoned that if one were to regulate another's habits, one had to control that person's environment. This meant that having Native children in day schools was not enough. In a meeting with Jackson prior to a fifteen-month teaching stint in Sitka, Brady raised the issue, asking how he could "inculcate habits of 'civilized living' when his pupils daily returned to their 'demoralizing Indian village'" (Hinckley 1982, 44). From this point forward, Jackson's goal was the establishment of a boarding school with industrial training.

While a boarding school was started in Sitka in 1881, its cramped conditions and limited facilities did not satisfy Jackson's ambitions. His philosophy of Native education mirrored that of Lieutenant Richard Henry Pratt, whose 1879 founding of the Carlisle Indian Industrial School in Pennsylvania laid the groundwork for a national system of Native boarding schools (Hamley 1994, 3). For Pratt, education had nothing to do with the genius and wisdom of aboriginal cultures, and everything to do with "the knowledge, values, mores, and habits of Christian civilization" (Adams 1995, 18). Writing on Indian education, David Adams notes that Pratt believed Indian ways were inferior to those of Caucasians, and that Western civilization must triumph over savagery (1995, 51–52). Pratt put it a little more crassly when he said he subscribed to the principle, "Kill the Indian in him and save the man" (cited in Adams 1995, 52).

Jackson's similar goal of annihilating indigenous cultures through education is reflected in an 1883 letter he wrote to H. Price, Commissioner of Indian Affairs, arguing for the establishment of an industrial training school for Native children in Sitka, modeled along the lines of the Carlisle "experiment." He describes the unique environment of southeast Alaska, and argues that the training needed to make her people self-sufficient should draw upon the territory's rich fishing grounds. Writing about a civilization that had lived off the sea for centuries, Jackson artlessly places fishing at the forefront of his vision of industrial education in southeast Alaska: "The Training School needs to be on the coast where they can be taught navigation and steamship— the handling of boats and sails—improved methods of fishing and handling of fish nets—a copper shop—with the manufacture of barrels and casks in which to pack their fish—a sawmill—carpenter shop—boot and shoe shop" (Sheldon Jackson Papers). In keeping with the dominant philosophy of Native industrial education, Jackson clearly envisions fishing as a commercial practice that would lead to self-sufficiency in a cash economy.

Jackson was finally able to move ahead with his plans for industrial education when the Organic Act was passed in 1884. The act essentially established civil government in Alaska, and made provisions for the education of children regardless of race. Jackson had lobbied hard for this legislation, supported by John Eaton, U.S. Commissioner of Education, and Senator Benjamin Harrison, a fellow Presbyterian. Upon passage of the Organic Act, Jackson was appointed General Agent for Education in Alaska. About the same time, he was named pastor of the Sitka Presbyterian Church and superintendent of the Sitka Industrial Training School, setting in motion the wheels of his educational philosophy.

Responsible now for schools scattered over the vast, difficult terrain of Alaska, Jackson wanted to increase the size and scope of schools at Sitka and elsewhere. While some federal funds were channeled to the mission schools, he knew that the main financial route to missionary expansion originated in the homes of wealthy Presbyterians back East. Jackson was a master publicist and accomplished rhetor who knew how to entice the wealthy to contribute to his coffers.[5] He had acquired much experience as a fundraiser during his stint as superintendent of the Rocky Mountain district, where he had published the *Rocky Mountain Presbyterian* as part of his publicity apparatus. Over the years he had also written for such publications as the *Oc-*

cident, the *Chatauquan, Education,* and the *Illustrated Christian Weekly* (Hinckley 1965, 28). Clifford Drury, a historian of missions, maintains that Jackson "took second place to no one in his efficient use of the press to publicize his work" (1952, 208). We now turn to his work with the *North Star.*

The North Star, *1887–92, 1895–98*

The convergence of a couple of events led to the establishment of the *North Star* in 1887.[6] First, Jackson received a letter that spring from William Kelly, who had by that time replaced Jackson as head of the Sitka Industrial Training School. In his letter, Kelly outlined a plan to start a newspaper dedicated to missionary and educational news. Second, Jackson was one of a number of educators, scientists, and politicians who took part in a cruise that summer inaugurating passenger steamship tourism to Alaska.[7] Several members of that group approached Jackson about creating an organization to carry out scientific work on Alaskan natural history and culture, and a museum to house related artifacts. Jackson found the idea irresistible. That fall, the Society of Alaskan Natural History and Ethnology was founded, followed by the establishment of the museum in Sitka a year later. Jackson had come to believe that missionary work in Alaska might be funded through benefactors who would be courted as concerned, learned observers of a vanishing, primitive race. That is to say, Jackson envisioned the *North Star,* together with the museum, as tools for packaging and marketing exotic curiosities, the spectacular natural beauty of southeast Alaska, and the mission itself to potential donors.

Orienting the Reader

The *North Star* began publication in December 1887, under the editorship of Sheldon Jackson and William Kelly.[8] The first issue establishes the newspaper's tone through the presentation of a map of Alaska that takes up the entire first page. The map is credited to the U.S. Coast and Geodetic Survey, but the reader is told on the second page that the map has been corrected due to recent military explorations. Compositionally, the map is unusual for it had to be turned on its side to be read conventionally with north now at the top. Readers probably understood the seeming peculiarity because of late-nineteenth-century graphic reproduction restrictions. But the awkward placement of the map also heightens the notion of Alaska as a place of imposing size and geography in the spatial imagination of readers. And as readers learned that its physical boundaries had been corrected, they quite naturally must have thought about Alaska as uncharted land, empty terrain whose hazy contours awaited the clarity imposed by Arctic explorers.

But this map, as with all maps, has been invested with symbolic boundaries. So we need to ask, as postmodern geographers do (Soja 1989; Lefebvre 1991), whose map is this and what interests does it serve? Hall maintains that interests are occluded by a stereotyping strategy in which "the Rest becomes defined as everything that the West is not—its mirror image" (1992, 308). Along these lines, the map marks sites of "positive" value—the locations of mission schools. This implies that there are other sites of "negative" value, sites of heathenism or darkness needing Christian enlightenment (Goodall 1993, 66). The interests reflected in the *North Star,* then, are capitalist values of delineated property rights, carved into spheres of Christian influence.[9] The map conceals both the unmarked nomadic areas of influence characteristic of indigenous peoples, and the fact that the far north was indeed mapped by indigenous hunters (Brody 1982). In other words, the map functions as a manifesto for the erasure of vibrant, flourishing cultures.

Fully one-half of this first issue of the *North Star* is dedicated to tourist information. Readers learned of the visit of the cruise ship with its cargo of learned people and government officials, now referred to as "influential Christian tourists." Implicitly, the reader understood that these travelers were being enlisted as publicists for the mission among their circles of acquaintances at home. In addition, the reader was shown how the travelers were drawn into the civilizing and Christianizing efforts of the local missionaries, in that they stood as living object lessons for the Native students: "The presence of so many Americans of the better class has given the [N]atives a greater respect for the American people, and a higher conception of the power of the Gospel, which they think has made the difference between the good people they have seen and themselves in their ignorance and poverty" (*North Star* December 1887).

This focus on tourism would remain a staple in the *North Star*'s rhetoric throughout its existence, offering up exotic others in reconstructed ethnicity, contrasting the "degraded living zoos" of the Indian Village with the models of industrial training at the mission school, and selling Native curios with grudging acknowledgment of their aesthetic value. The touristic focus would become even more pronounced in the paper's second incarnation (1895–98), as potential donors were wooed in response to economic pressures—the nation's economic depression of 1893–94, and the Presbyterian Church's retrenchment of funding to its far northern posts, announced in one of the last issues of the paper before it suspended publication for the first time in 1892.

The paper's other major theme, education, was closely related to tourism. That is, once tourists were on the grounds of the industrial training school (in body or in spirit), they were canvassed for charitable contributions. The theme in this recurring narrative sought to address the question of what would become of the students once they had left the school. The answer—often posed weakly or defensively—was that education would teach them the values of Christian civilization and of capitalist individualism, thus freeing Native peoples from the dole.

The Tourist Theme

As a noncommercial publication, the only advertisement carried by the *North Star* in its first five years of existence was for the Northern Pacific Railroad, which linked up in Seattle with passenger steamships bound for Alaska. The coming and going of the five steamers that visited Sitka each month during the tourist season imposed a western temporal orientation on the community. In a March 1897 issue of the *North Star,* the editors write that "everybody's calendar begins and ends with the arrival of the steamer. When one wishes to make an appointment or do anything that can be postponed, it is always 'after the steamer.'"

While these observations were no doubt true for the mission faculty and other White citizens of Sitka, they ignored the indigenous peoples' rhythms of subsistence—the cyclical pattern of seasonal activities from berry picking to catching, salting, and drying fish—that structured the lives of most of the community. Indeed, an August 1895 article lamented the Natives' subsistence-centered temporal orientation as antithetical to industrial education with its forced discipline of the school bell. The *North Star* advanced a discursive formation of *time* that was tied to Western notions of discipline, accountability, and progress, and that was physically imposed through the technological apparatus of time clocks and factory whistles. The newspaper's misunderstanding of fundamental differences in cultural orientations toward time is indicative of the chasm between the Calvinist capitalism of the missionaries and the subsistence economies of the Alaska Natives.

Ironically, while the missionaries deplored the persistence of indigenous cultural practices, they were quite happy to exploit their potential for ethnic tourism. Valene Smith describes this form of tourism in *Hosts and Guests:* "*Ethnic tourism* is marketed to the public in terms of the 'quaint' customs of indigenous and often exotic peoples. . . . Destination activities that stimulate tourism include visits to [N]ative homes and villages, observation of dances and ceremonies, and shopping for primitive wares or curios, some of which may have intrinsic value to the art historian" (1989, 4). The *North Star* often promoted ethnic tourism, turning art, culture, and even people into commodities. In the September 1888 issue, Sheldon Jackson announces that the museum connected with the industrial training school "has come into possession of the largest and choicest assortment of celebrated stone carvings of the Hydah [*sic*] race that has ever been gathered together in Alaska." Seemingly a paean to high aesthetic values, Jackson's words go on to classify these objects into a kind of "rude-refined" opposition when he writes, "These figures, although made by a semi-civilized race with their rude [N]ative tools, as works of art will not suffer in comparison with carved stone mantel ornaments of the East" (*North Star* September 1888).

Hall discusses the "rude-refined" opposition of nations advanced by Enlightenment thinkers in their efforts to posit a universal path to civilization. Such models frequently held up the American savage as the lowest stage of social development in contrast to Western Europe as the summit (1992, 312–14). As embodied in the carvings, Native culture becomes both rude *and* refined, enhancing the value of the art as commodity. Jackson also plays on the ever-increasing scarcity of the commodity when he guilelessly informs the reader that the skill and art of stone carvings will soon be lost. A sample of these traces of a culture on its way out are listed for sale at prices ranging from fifteen to sixty dollars.

The children of the industrial training school were usually presented to tourists as budding industrial capitalists, as youngsters who had made "progress." However, during the three-month tourist season there were special occasions in which Native identity was commodified along the lines of what Dean MacCannell calls "reconstructed ethnicity." He defines this as "the process by which tourism promotes 'the restoration, preservation, and fictional recreation of ethnic attributes,' creating a museum-like commodity out of ethnic identity" (cited in Ross 1994, 87–88). The poster boy of reconstructed ethnicity for both the training school and the *North Star* was "Master Healey Wolf." A July 1892 article describes him as "a little Eskimo brought down to us from Point Barrow on the U.S. steamer *Bear* two years ago when Dr. Sheldon Jackson returned from his journey to the far north. . . .

He is very bright and speaks English as well as a Boston boy (American).[10] . . . Many of the tourists will remember him as one of the attractions of our Mission: When he appears in the Flag drill as the representative of Alaska, dressed in his reindeer suit, carrying a small American flag as he marches up to the Goddess of Liberty and asks that Alaska may be admitted into the Union." The article then implores readers to give to the missions so that children such as Healey can grow up to be missionaries.

Healey Wolf is reconstructed in a number of ways. In keeping with the rude-refined opposition, his first name was taken from the surname of the ship captain who took him to Sitka. And just as his identity is Anglicized, he is dressed in a reindeer wrap in the summer as a mark of his "Eskimoness."[11] And then "Healey" bears the American flag at a time when it was not possible for Alaska Natives to become U.S. citizens.

Although the tourist theme was almost never absent from the pages of the paper, it was amplified in the last couple of summers of the *North Star*'s publication. The front page of the July 1896 issue features a panoramic illustration of the school grounds, and the accompanying story is "a guide on how to use your time while at Sitka." A special tourist issue the following summer reiterates and extends these suggestions, offering a full itinerary for the cultural voyeur. Under the headline, "Tourists' Guide to Alaska," readers are supplied with a list of points of interest and a schedule by which to see them. Not surprisingly, the jewel in this tourists' showcase is the industrial training school with its various departments: carpenter and shoe shop, steam laundry, blacksmith shop, stable, museum and library, hospital, church, doctor's cottage, and storehouses.

The Native village, locally called the Ranch, is high on the editor's list of sights, but it is offered up as a contrast with the model cottages of the school. While the editor exercises enough public relations savvy not to play up the theme of destitution in the living zoo that is the village, the message is not lost on the inveterate reader. Images of the Ranch as decadent and barbaric had long been a staple in the *North Star*. In a March 1895 article, B. K. Wilbur describes the walk to the Ranch as beautiful until the visitor actually arrives: "Children but scantily clad run in and out with the babel of strange, and to our ears exceedingly ugly, sounds [and then] comes the odor, not of filth or putrefaction, but still the odor indescribable, the odor of the Ranch." In contrast, the reader is assured, the school's cottages—Boston houses—are clean and orderly. Native graduates who married were often sold these cottages to discourage them from living in traditional longhouses with extended families that, according to the pages of the paper, were sites of immorality. The editor of the tourist issue suggests that visitors get someone who knows the Ranch to guide them through it. They are encouraged not to restrict their gaze to the front row of houses, but to wander into the back street. Indeed, the editor advises visitors to go into the houses, stating that the Natives do not object and may even offer to sell them something.

Finally, on the last page of the special issue, there is an advertisement for the Millmore House, a hotel that specializes in the tourist trade. The advertisement mentions that guides are available for hunting, fishing, or sightseeing, and that the dining room serves game in season. Both sport and commercial fishing and hunting were beginning to make inroads into traditional subsistence waters and grounds in a colony without definitive recognition of aboriginal rights. As a federal district, lacking even territorial status in the nineteenth century, Alaska was not subject to the public land laws of the United States. As we noted in the introduction, to this day, conflicts rage over the use of the land for indigenous subsistence practices and for White sport or commercial hunting and fishing.

The Educational Theme

The conflict over who "owned" the land—indeed, competing definitions of the land—is at the heart of the historical relations between Natives and non-Natives in Alaska. As Chamberlin notes, missionary attitudes of evolutionary determinism required that indigenous peoples be weaned from nomadic ways (1975, 11–13). In 1887, Congress passed the General Allotment Act, designed to erase tribal consciousness and subsistence practices by dividing collectively held lands reserved for Native Americans into individual homesteads. According to the evolutionary theory behind this brutally disruptive act, Native Americans would move from the lower economic stage of subsistence to the higher stage of agriculture. As cruel and disastrous as this policy turned out to be in the contiguous forty-eight states, such tactics simply made no sense in Alaska, where, as Thomas Berger puts it, "Agricultural settlement throughout most of the area is out of the question: you cannot grow wheat on the tundra" (1991, 128).

The act did not pertain to Alaska, not for such logical reasons as Berger's, but simply because reservations had never been established in what was seen as *terra nullius,* a vast, icy emptiness. Nevertheless, the missionaries of Sitka made no bones about the need to break the back of subsistence economies, given their contradictions with Western-style schooling. They believed that subsistence practices encouraged indolence and detracted from their educational mission by fostering irregular school attendance. Consequently, the *North Star*'s editors were strong advocates for legally mandated school attendance. In the paper's first farewell issue, editor Alonzo Austin recounts the history of the mission and the problem of attendance: "Nearly every week their parents would take them away to fish and hunt . . . and we soon became convinced if we would do them any permanent good, we should need to have a boarding school where we could feed, clothe, and educate them. In such a school they would be removed from their environments of filth, vice, and crime and we could enforce a regular attendance at school" (*North Star* December 1892).

The perceived problem of school attendance points to a double inflection of the meaning of work in industrial education. Work not only meant engaging in the practices of a specific trade or vocation, it also reverberated with the Calvinist dictum that "idle hands do the devil's work." An unsigned article in January 1891 explaining missionary work brings out both of these inflections: "A lady is all the more efficient in Christian missionary work, who with other acquisitions takes pleasure in teaching [N]ative girls how to prepare a good dinner, how to tidy a room, and how to use the necessaries of life with economy. The gospel of industry," the writer adds, "must go hand in hand with the gospel of Christ."

In one attempt to answer the recurring question of what Native children would do upon graduation, a January 1897 article on the school's shoe shop also doubly inflects the meaning of work. Admitting that cobblers are not in demand in Alaska, the writer legitimizes the training by distinguishing between the occupation itself and the discipline associated with work in general. This front page story maintains that "it is far better for every young man to have mastered at least one good trade whether he works at it or not . . . besides it is but little more expense to teach the trades and they serve to cultivate steady habits of industry in the boys."

According to the *North Star*, the transformative act of graduating from the Sitka Industrial Training School would not only teach steady work habits, but it would also open up the possibility of buying a mission cottage, where education into civilized, Christian domesticity could last a lifetime. A teacher of the older students described the benefits of setting up housekeeping in a mission cottage: "The young people are removed from the temptations which a residence in the Indian Village would induce, and this buying a home and living in it alone is an object lesson to our people . . . to teach them to establish Christian homes; to abolish all their old customs and make of them intelligent citizens, willing and able to support themselves and those dependent upon them by honest industry (*North Star* September 1890). In short, the educational theme of the *North Star* is captured in the aphorism, attributed to Commissioner of Indian Affairs Thomas Morgan, that "the only good Indian is an educated Indian" (*North Star* March 1890).

Conclusion

As the United States jingoistically extended its empire into the southern Pacific in 1898, at the edge of the north Pacific, the *North Star*'s light was dimmed with the publication of its last issue in April. At the end of the year, as Tlingit leaders outlined their grievances at the aforementioned hearing in Juneau, Chief Kadashan expressed the kind of resistance to Western hegemony that would grow ever louder over the course of the next one hundred years:

> Long, long time ago before [W]hite people came to this country our people lived here at certain places where they went hunting and fishing. When the Russians were here, they did not have any stores in the interior, but they used to trade with our people here. . . . Then [after the purchase] the business men followed the soldiers. They commenced to trade with our people. Our people did not object, did not say anything to them. By and by they began to build canneries and take the creeks away from us, where they make salmon and when we told them these creeks belonged to us, they would not pay any attention to us and said all this country belonged to President, the big chief at Washington.
>
> We like to live like other people live. We make this complaint because we are very poor now. The time will come when we will not have anything left. The money and everything else in this country will be the property of the [W]hite man, and our people will have nothing. (Hinckley 1970, 270–71)

Clearly the chief's plea for the persistence of a way of life centered on communal subsistence activities was at variance with the message of the *North Star*. In their misguided opposition, educators such as Jackson at Sitka or Pratt at Carlisle represented the scientific, economic, and political attitudes of their times. Critics might argue that publications such as the *North Star* are of little consequence, for they merely mouthed the ideology of the times. But the point is, as Hall tells us, the idea of the West is not just the articulation of a set of ideas but it is productive of the very formation of that society (1992, 276).

Alaska Natives do not need to be salvaged like so many objectified others. Nor do they need outsiders to articulate their problems. Chief Kadashan's words show that they have done that quite well on their own for decades. His request articulated the inextricable indigenous links between culture, place, and economies of subsistence. What we have tried to show by deconstructing the discursive formations articulated in the *North Star* is that power itself can be actively and persistently resisted as indigenous peoples recognize themselves in these invidious evaluations. In chapter 2, we will see how southeast Alaska Natives formed organizations and produced a newspaper, the *Alaska Fisherman,* to contest this Western hegemony.

NOTES

1. The *North Star* was not the first missionary newspaper in Alaska. The *Glacier* was launched in 1885 at the Tlingit Training Academy in Fort Wrangell by Reverend S. Hall Young, one of Sheldon Jackson's first recruits to Alaska. The *Glacier* ceased publication in 1888.

2. Jackson was given this nickname by John Eaton, U.S. Commissioner of Education, in a letter on November 2, 1881 to President Chester A. Arthur (Sheldon Jackson Papers, Record Group 239, Presbyterian Church [U.S.A.] Department of History and Records Management Services, Philadelphia, hereafter SJP).

3. Despite appointments to various posts in Alaska, Jackson never actually lived there. At the time of this first appointment, he lived in Denver, and in 1883, he moved to Washington, D.C., to facilitate his lobbying efforts on behalf of Alaska. From the time of his first appointment, Jackson usually spent the summers in Alaska, assisting in the establishment of missions and taking groups of church or political leaders around the territory in order to drum up interest and support. Altogether, he made some twenty-six trips to Alaska (Stewart 1908, 466).

4. Clifford offers a trenchant critique of salvage ethnography for its assumption that the "other society is weak and 'needs' to be represented by an outsider" (1986, 112–13). Furthermore, the concern is not with the living culture and its future so much as it is with its past in an idealized essence or authenticity.

5. Jackson enjoyed public speaking. According to estimates, he delivered more than nine hundred addresses on Alaska between 1877 and 1883 (Hinckley 1965, 29).

6. As the dates show, the *North Star* had two deaths. Letters from editors Alonzo Austin and Alfred Docking around the time the newspaper first ceased publication provide evidence of financial problems as well as factionalism among the staff over whether the school ought to be responsible for a newspaper (see Austin letter to Jackson, November 28, 1892, and Docking letter to Jackson, April 17, 1893, SJP). Jackson's lengthy absences from Alaska and his preoccupation with establishing a reindeer industry in Arctic Alaska meant that he devoted less energy to the newspaper over time. The newspaper's final issue in April 1898 alludes to the fact that its demise was necessitated by the removal of one editor and the withdrawal of another. These

ambiguous statements suggest that factionalism was at the root of the problem once again.

7. Passengers included such notables as D. C. Gillman, president of Johns Hopkins University, and Nicholas Murray Butler, president of Columbia University (DeArmond 1987, 3).

8. While Jackson served as the newspaper's editorial figurehead, his coeditors, missionaries at the school in Sitka, handled the day-to-day operations. Kelly served in this capacity until 1891.

9. Given the high costs of maintaining missions in Alaska, Jackson realized that competition among missions would be prohibitively expensive. Accordingly, as early as 1880, he negotiated the spiritual apportionment of Alaska through a set of informal agreements with representatives of other Protestant denominations (Stewart 1908, 364–65; Hinckley 1966, 745).

10. The language here, with the explanatory parenthetical word, infantilizes the Native use of the term "Boston" as an adjective for "American," a practice that stemmed from contact with Yankee traders.

11. Reindeer are not indigenous to Alaska. About the time the child was taken to Sitka, Jackson was introducing Siberian reindeer to settlements along the northwestern coast of Alaska. A traditional Alaskan Eskimo may have dressed in a caribou parka, but not one of reindeer.

2   How Raven Gave Voice to a Talking Newspaper: The Case of the *Alaska Fisherman*

FROM TIME IMMEMORIAL—long before history's printed records—the Tlingit and Haida peoples fished the waters in what is present-day Alaska. The rivers, streams, bays, lakes, and open sea presented them with a bounty of fish, none more important than the salmon, and they developed a rich oral literature to account for these gifts. This chapter tells the story of how southeast Alaska Natives, with their long and proud oral traditions, turned to the print media to "reclaim" their cultural voices and to fight for their fishing rights. We begin with a few of the stories they told themselves about fish and people. While there is some variation in the respective mythologies of different southeast Alaska Native groups, the multidimensional Raven is the central player in many of the stories, for he was their creator, culture-hero, benefactor, and trickster whose ruses and magic reveal a contradictory and complex character (Beck 1979).

Kadashan,[1] whom we left at the end of the last chapter, believed that Raven-at-the-head of the Nass River (Nas-ca-ki-yel) was the principal deity and the creator of Raven (Yel), whom he made head man over the world. When Raven was young, all the world's people lived and fished in darkness along the mouth of the Nass River for eulachon, a saltwater fish prized for its oil. Because many fishermen congregated closely together in the dark to fish, they often made quite a noisy racket. To quiet them down, Raven threatened to bring daylight to them. They had heard of daylight and were fearful of it, but did not believe Raven's threat since daylight was said to be boxed and in the possession of Nas-ca-ki-yel. But Raven had persuaded Nas-ca-ki-yel to give him his box of daylight as a gift and when the noisy fishermen persisted, he unleashed daylight on them.

Next, Raven used a dirty trick to steal a huge mouthful of fresh water from Petrel's (Ganu'k) spring at Fort-far-out, which Petrel jealously guarded. Raven escaped up the smoke hole of Petrel's house and dropped small amounts of water from his beak here and there, creating the great rivers of the world—the Nass, Skeena, Stikine, Chilcat, and others. In order to populate the inland waterways with fish, Raven went far out to sea where he first acquired a spear from a monster by marrying the monster's daughter. He used the spear to pull himself and his canoe to a floating house where all the fish were kept. He opened the door, releasing some of the fish to go to the Stikine River, some to the Chilcat, and "some to go to the small creeks to provide the poor people [and] that is how fish came to be all over the world" (Swanton 1909, 94). Then Raven taught the people how to fish for halibut and salmon and how to make a canoe. Since he had been under the ocean, he knew all the sea animals and he taught the people that they were just like human beings. In fact, the Natives say that everything is like a human being with its own way of living and that is why fish die when they come out of the water, "because they have a 'way of living' of their own down there" (149).[2]

In these myths—passed on by Kadashan to ethnologist John Swanton in Wrangell in 1904—the cultural significance of nature was manifested in the moral, ethical, and entertaining lessons its creatures offered to the Tlingits. Tlingit oral literature commonly reiterated fundamental covenants between humans and animals and the interconnections between natural and spiritual life (Dauenhauer and Dauenhauer 1990, xxiii). But by the turn of the century, the invasion and domination of nature in southeast Alaska by Americans had rendered subsistence economies and their cultural underpinnings increasingly problematic. Fishing became rationalized and industrialized by the concentrated capital of cannery concerns, while culture was deracinated by the heavy religious and educational pressures of frontier Presbyterianism.

Most historical accounts of Alaska pay significant attention to the development of these fisheries, showing how outside capital, benefiting from federal laissez-faire policies, rapidly increased the volume of their resource extraction. While these narratives detail the problem of resource depletion due to over-fishing, they do so from the perspective of a free-market economy, casting subsistence fishing practices as antiquated (Gruening 1954; Drucker 1958, 1965; Hinckley 1970, 1972; Mitchell 1997). Historical and anthropological accounts of southeast Alaska Natives take for granted the "success" of Sheldon Jackson's assimilationist creed and give Presbyterianism high marks for its humanistic, albeit paternalistic, evangelism. These accounts generally agree that, in the space of two short decades, Jackson had successfully relegated Tlingit and Haida ways of life to museum cultures (Hinckley 1966, 1972; Corey 1987; Drucker 1958; Mitchell 1997). As Ted Hinckley puts it, by 1898, the magnificent seagoing canoes of the Tlingit "had been rocked by decades of stormy acculturation . . . [and] the fighting edge of the once proud Tlingit had been dulled, if not ruined" (1970, 265).[3] In short, southeast Alaska Natives were seen as the objects of forces over which they had no control and little understanding. They were said to be highly acculturated.

In this chapter, we will show how southeast Alaska Natives resisted some of these changes through organizational and communicative efforts that, over a number of decades, subtly and persistently gave political voice to their sense of political and economic injustice. While southeast Alaska Natives could not control the dominant culture, acculturation is too one-sided a term to account for the disruptive encounters between their cultures and the new colonizers. Mary Louise Pratt uses the term contact zone to refer to "social spaces where disparate cultures meet, clash, and grapple with each other, often in highly asymmetrical relations of domination and subordination" (1992, 4). While the contact zone is powerfully arrayed against indigenous peoples, Pratt argues that subjugated peoples do have some power to control what they absorb from the dominant culture and how they use what they absorb. She employs the term transculturation to describe how they engage in a process of inventing and selecting materials transmitted to them by a dominant culture (6). We focus our attention on the Alaska Native Brotherhood (ANB) and its primary communicative instrument, the *Alaska Fisherman* (*TAF*), a sixteen-page monthly published in Ketchikan and Petersburg for nearly a decade between 1923 and 1932. Both the ANB and the *TAF* were part of the Tlingit and Haida peoples' cultural strategy of transculturation in the contact zone.

Both the ANB and *TAF* give evidence of contradictory shifts and turns in their resistance as cultural persistence. As we will see, much of the combativeness of *TAF* can be attributed to its editor, William Paul, a Tlingit Indian who returned home in 1920 after many years of being educated and working in the contiguous forty-eight states. The ANB began as a Christian organization bent on eliminating traditional customs, but that focus soon shifted with the increase in membership of Tlingit elders. With their dignified sense of respect for their fellow beings,[4] the Tlingits were of a mixed mind

about how far to give way before the supposed superiority of Christian, capitalist civilization. Cultural tenacity was often a function of generational
conflict, with the older generation favoring traditional ways and the younger generation embracing innovation.

We can get a glimpse of this generational conflict over cultural continuity versus assimilation by looking at two representative Tlingit figures—Chief
Kadashan from the older generation and William Paul from the younger
generation. From the same home village called Wrangell by the Russians,
Kadashan and Paul had very different life experiences and very different ideas
about Tlingit culture, but in the final analysis, Paul's arguments in support
of Native fishing rights bridged the same cultural waters as Kadashan's impassioned pleas in 1898 to preserve the Tlingits' ancestral fishing grounds and
the rich cultural life that they made possible. A traditional Tlingit, Kadashan
was born before the United States "purchased" Alaska (Hinckley 1970, 270),
served as guide for naturalist John Muir's first trip to Alaska in 1879 (Turner
1985, 259–62), and was ethnologist Swanton's informant in 1904 for many of
the Tlingit myths we previously related (1909, 1). Muir's biographer notes how
Kadashan's subsistence-informed ethic of conservation was beyond the understanding of most 'Boston men' when he told Muir that the wise and powerful wolf did not kill all the deer because the "wolves knew better than to
kill them all and thus cut off their most important food supply" (Turner 1985,
261).

The more "modern" William L. Paul (Shgundi in Tlingit) was born in
1885, spent his first two years in Wrangell, and was raised and educated at the
Sitka Industrial Training School where his mother worked and taught. The
Presbyterian staff of the vocational school considered the Paul family a suc-
cessful model of assimilation, making them its poster family for the *North
Star,* with a lengthy feature story and photograph on the front page of its
November 1896 issue. William studied printing at the Carlisle Indian Indus-
trial School, business at Banks College in Philadelphia, and graduated from
Whitworth College in Tacoma, Washington, in 1909. He worked on insurance
claims for a banking concern in Oregon and earned a law degree through
LaSalle Extension University of Chicago (Paul 1971, 5). When he returned to
his mother's home in Wrangell in 1920, he fished in the ancestral waters at
Salmon Bay—not for subsistence purposes but to make money while he
prepared for the bar exam (Haycox 1994, 506). Three years later, Paul assumed
the editorship of *TAF* and used its pages for the better part of the next decade to battle for Native fishing rights.

If we see culture as embodying an unchanging set of beliefs and values—

an essentialism tied to a romantic view of the past—then Kadashan and Paul would indeed seem to belong to quite different worlds. On the one hand, while Native peoples have often been viewed through this singular and unchanging view of culture, it is of course a view of culture consonant with colonialism and a salvage anthropology in the service of an imperial power (see Eagleton 2000, 25–26). On the other hand, Pratt's concept of transculturation accounts for clever cultural strategies of negotiation and adaptation in much the same way that Valaskakis's concept of resistance as cultural persistence acknowledges that cultural transformations take many forms. Valaskakis claims that we can liken Indians' maneuvers through bureaucratic systems to the tricksters in Native narratives who survive bureaucratic entanglements by reterritorializing the discourse that eludes them (in Gilroy, Grossberg, and McRobbie 2000, 391). By understanding cultural survival on these everyday political grounds, we can see the cultural continuity between Kadashan's traditional oral petitions and Paul's published protests, and, by extension, we can begin to see and understand the linkages between their generational cohorts.

Let us return Paul to 1920 and the waters of Salmon Bay, explain what he found there, and set the parameters for how the rest of the chapter will unfold. The summer of 1920 was a revelation for Paul as he came to grips with the huge disparity between the powerful canneries' use of fish traps and the small, independent fishermen's use of seines (Paul 1986, 18). At the invitation of his brother Louis and the urging of traditional Tlingit Chief Shakes, William attended the annual meeting of the ANB. All historical accounts of this meeting agree that the Paul brothers changed what had been a thoroughly assimilationist, fraternal service organization into a grass-roots political force (Drucker 1958; Mitchell 1997; Champagne 1990; Dauenhauer and Dauenhauer 1990, 1994; Haycox 1994; Goldin 1996). Over the next few years, their transformation of the ANB challenged outsiders' control of the political economy of Alaska and altered the Tlingits' everyday conditions of existence.

One of the most important weapons in the formation of their oppositional discourse was the *Alaska Fisherman,* begun under William Paul's editorship in the spring of 1923 as the official voice of the ANB. In the second half of this chapter, we will see that, by virtue of Paul's position at the borders of the Tlingit and the White man's world, he was well-situated to take advantage of his vocational training, his college education, and his legal training to employ a White medium of communication, a Western style political process, and a legalistic combativeness to keep Kadashan's voice alive and to stabilize the Tlingit "canoe" on behalf of fish *and* people. While Stuart Hall explains how diasporic people—unable to go home again—speak from a position "in-between" different cultures, the term can also be applied with good effect to those who have been able to go home again. Hall tells us that "they are people who . . . have learned to negotiate and translate *between* cultures, and who, because they are irrevocably the product of several inter-locking histories and cultures, have learned to live with, and indeed to speak from, *difference*" (1995, 206). Paul clearly unsettled the ideological assump-tions of the political and economic elite in southeastern Alaska, and, occa-sionally upset his own people who were not always assured of his Tlingit identity.

Since southeast Alaska Natives rarely made sharp distinctions between nature, culture, politics, and economics, not surprisingly, Paul rarely articu-lated his arguments on behalf of regaining control of Alaska salmon fisher-ies from a cultural perspective. For a people whose survival was at stake, a cultural perspective would have been a foolish luxury. In fact, Paul rarely adopted an exclusively Nativist position, but his arguments always fore-grounded a collectivist ideology—for Alaskans, for Natives, for laborers, for resident fishermen, and for the little guys. *TAF*'s journalistic spotlight con-sistently illuminated the problem of the fish trap and its deleterious conse-quences for salmon and for indigenous ways of life. In short, William Paul and his fellow Tlingits struggled with a capitalist culture and its dominant, oligopolistic mode of production by trying to carve out a more distributively just way of fishing in keeping with valued aspects of their own culture's re-spect for nature and for community. In the end, they launched Alaska Na-tives on a quest for the resolution of aboriginal land claims—a quest that would take more than forty years.

The chapter then unfolds as follows. First, we provide some historical and ethnographic context on aboriginal fisheries in southeast Alaska. Second, we explore the political and economic circumstances that paved the way for the ascendancy of commercial fishing in Alaska. Third, we examine the devel-opment and evolution of the ANB in the context of two quite different Chris-tianizing impulses. Fourth, we look at how a Native-owned-and-operated medium of communication gave voice to the local, democratic concerns of the ANB and thus mounted a concerted challenge to the discursive terrain of Alaska's political economy.

While our interpretation of *TAF* in the fourth section of this chapter owes its conceptual grounding to Valaskakis, our emphases in the other three sec-tions have been shaped by relatively recent scholarship in history, ethnogra-phy, and cultural studies—all of which either soften the monolithic and univocal interpretations of corporate and missionary contact with southeast Alaska Natives or give theoretical reasons why such all-powerful influences need to be attenuated. Ideologically, historian Robert Berkhofer's pioneering work on Protestant missionary activities among Indians deflates the view of missionization as a powerful exogenous force unilaterally impinging upon passive recipient peoples (1978). Furthering this interpretive position, ethnohistorian Sergei Kan has uncovered previously untranslated Russian documents which show that, in the 1890s, many Tlingits turned from Presbyterianism to Russian Orthodoxy because the latter was more tolerant of Tlingit customs and allowed the use of the Tlingit language for instruction and prayer (1985, 208).[5] Kan contends that Tlingit persistence in retention of their traditional values, beliefs, and ceremonies was effected by indigenizing Christianity while the missionaries remained either unaware of these surviving customs or chose to look the other way (196, 213). Kan's concept of indigenization fits with Hall's notion of hybridization or syncretism whereby elements from different cultures are fused together to produce a new cultural meaning (193–96).

In their studies of Tlingit rhetoric, literature, and biography, Nora and Richard Dauenhauer (1987, 1990, 1994) emphasize continuities in Tlingit culture and heritage, while at the same time they document, during the time period in question, Native frustrations with attempts to maintain connections between land, culture, and subsistence practices. Richard Cooley (1963) offers a historical analysis of the politics of conservation in Alaska fisheries while Robert Price pays particular attention to the history of the aboriginal fisheries in the territory (1990). Finally, from a cultural studies perspective, Mary Louise Pratt tells us that in any historical analysis of dominating and resisting cultures, we need to pay close attention to certain experiences, meanings, and values that cannot be expressed or substantially verified in terms of the dominant culture (1992, 6). As she puts it, "transculturation is a phenomenon of the contact zone" (6).

The Cultural Materialism of Aboriginal Salmon Fisheries

While most indigenous struggles have historically turned on questions of land claims, in southeastern Alaska the major issue involved access to, and control over, the salmon fisheries. Nothing was more important to the Tlingit and Haida peoples than the salmon catch, for salmon served multiple purposes: it was their basic and preferred food, it played a significant role in their mythology and ceremonial activities, hence their cultural identities, and its abundant supply furnished them with the leisure time to develop rich and variegated cultures (Drucker 1965, 13; Dauenhauer and Dauenhauer 1994, xviii).

The ritualistic importance of salmon for Pacific Coast cultures was ceremoniously commemorated each summer when the first salmon was caught. In his important work on the politics of salmon conservation, Cooley argues that the indigenous peoples' attitude toward the salmon was one important factor that helped to ensure that their fishing practices would not deplete the salmon stock (1963, 19). In the "first salmon ceremony," Tlingit and Haida peoples engaged in ritualistic practices to ensure that a portion of the salmon would return to the spawning grounds each year. Cooley says that they believed that "all living things—animals, fish, birds, and men had a common origin and shared the world in a state of equality and mutual understanding. They believed that salmon were a race of supernatural beings who went about in human form feasting and dancing beneath the sea. When the time came for these annual runs, these 'salmon people' assumed the form of fish and ascended the stream to sacrifice themselves for the benefit of mankind. The salmon migration was considered to be a voluntary act and it was thought that if human beings were careful not to offend their benefactors, the spirit of each fish would return to the sea, resume its original life and humanlike form, and prepare for the trip the next season" (21–22).

Prior to the "sale" of Alaska to the United States, the salmon fisheries were largely under the control of the indigenous peoples. In southeastern Alaska, Russian fur traders were too preoccupied with intensive exploitation of the sea otter for fabulous profits in the international capitalist marketplace to bother much with tapping into other marine resources. During the first decades of the nineteenth century, salmon played such a small part in Russian economic development and everyday sustenance that the Russian-American Company established an agricultural outpost at Fort Ross in northern California just to feed its small Russian population. For more than three-quarters of the nineteenth century, then, the indigenous peoples in southeast Alaska were relatively undisturbed in their aboriginal fisheries.[6]

While the Tlingit and Haida peoples fished extensively and harvested a wide variety of sea life, salmon were the dominant species. Salmon are anadromous fish whose spawning runs are dictated by species and stream of birth. Because salmon have a sophisticated homing instinct that takes them back to spawn in the stream of their birth, fishermen need not exert extraordinary and dangerous open sea efforts to capture them. They merely need to set their nets or gear near the coastline where salmon move in schools toward their spawning beds. The key to a continuing healthy supply of salmon is allowing enough mature salmon to escape to the spawning beds to replenish the cycle (Cooley 1963, 7–9). There are five distinct species of Pacific salmon with different periods of maturation, referred to popularly as red or sockeye, king or chinook, silver or coho, the pink or humpback, and chum or dog. While the red or sockeye salmon is the first of the species to run, and is the most nutritious and most highly prized, the Tlingit fished for all five species and put up large quantities of silver, pink, and chum salmon for sustenance during the winter months (4–5).

During the aboriginal fishing period, the time Natives spent fishing could vary from just a few days to a few weeks from July through early fall. Kalervo Oberg highlights the centrality of the salmon subsistence season for the Tlingits when he notes that the Tlingit year began in July, for that is when the prized red salmon returned and was caught by the Natives for immediate consumption (1973, 65). July, however, was not the start of the subsistence cycle, for that was kicked off in March when halibut, cod, and eulachon fishing was begun and carried through the rest of the spring (65–69). The most important month of the year, though, at least from an economic standpoint, was August for it was then that the Tlingit would catch and dry their salmon for consumption during the winter. If villagers had to set up temporary fishing camps, this was the period when they did so, remaining at them until their boxes and baskets were full of dried salmon (71–72) Philip Drucker highlights the fruits of the aboriginal fishery and the cultural creativity it endowed: "In a comparatively few days, including the time it took him to ready his harpoons, nets, and traps, to repair the smokehouse, and to do his share in building the weir, a man could catch and his wife could prepare enough salmon to feed his family for several months, thus providing him with his leisure. . . . As a rule, leisure has been a concomitant of the invention or introduction of agriculture. The North Pacific Coast is unique among areas where man lived on the so-called 'hunting and gathering' level in that the inhabitants developed a rich culture, and this circumstance can be traced directly to the nature and abundance of the area's basic food source, the salmon" (1965, 13). Drucker's rich description recalls for us the contradictory impulses motivating Sheldon Jackson's salvage ethnography and puts the lie to the *North Star*'s touristic flourishes touting Tlingit and Haida craftsmanship and artistry while at the same time bemoaning the idle time that made them possible. Indeed, the disciplined vocational education at the Sitka Industrial Training School was meant to instill a commercial version of fishing on the Natives and to occupy their "idle" time.

As Cooley noted earlier, the richness of the aboriginal fishery was due, in part, to the indigenous peoples' philosophy of nature, but it also had to do with their well-worked-out sense of property. Kadashan's lament on White man's territorial encroachment referred to Native creeks and streams where they had fished since time immemorial. Their property rights were a function of their social organization. Socially and culturally, the Tlingit were organized into two matrilineal, exogamous moieties, the Raven and the Eagle, with about twenty-five clans each. These moieties and clans were distributed over numerous villages and fourteen territorial groupings or tribes (Champagne 1990, 57–60; Cooley 1963, 20). Tlingit property encompassed all of their subsistence practices including salmon streams, hunting grounds, berry patches, and sealing rocks (Oberg 1973, 55). These fishing sites were held in common by the clan and used by the kinship group for community purposes. The rights to the fishing sites were passed on by inheritance to the yitsati, the individual heading up an extended house group, or to the group itself. Fishing in a stream owned by another was not allowed except by invitation (Cooley 1963, 20). The location of Native settlements was usually dictated by ease of access to these salmon streams, and the very size of villages was dictated by the quantity and runs of various species of salmon (Oberg 1973, 56). It was common practice for extended house groups to set up temporary fishing camps during the height of the subsistence season.

Before the intrusion of commercial fishing, then, the Tlingit people engaged in a short but intensive period of fishing and spent the winter months in relative quiescence, feasting, making speeches, and telling stories. The success of the subsistence season was important for two reasons: first a housegroup's nutritional well-being depended on it and, second, surplus foods were distributed to different house-groups of the same clan during winter feasts, and this distribution was a way for a hosting house-group to accumulate power and prestige. Oberg emphasizes the second point, maintaining that this economy should be understood primarily as a means for the acquisition of honor. As he describes it, "[the great man] was not a successful fisherman or hunter, . . . [He] was eminent . . . because he had acquired honor through the distribution of goods derived from food" (1973, 103). Under this economic logic, for the Tlingit, wealth was not an end in itself, but what Duane Champagne calls a form of "'social capitalism,' that is, a rational and regulated system for gaining moral approbation, social prestige, and rank" (1990, 65).

Because of their spiritual relationship to nature, their well-developed property rights, and their small populations, Tlingit and Haida fishermen could use highly efficient fishing techniques and gear without jeopardizing the future of the fisheries. In 1880, the estimated Native population of the southeast region was around 7,500 (Petroff cited in Gruening, 1954; Rogers and Cooley 1963, 28). Estimates varied widely on the annual consumption of salmon per Tlingit—from a wildly inaccurate census estimate at 4,000 pounds of all species to a more plausible estimate of 500 pounds (Price 1990, 13). In qualifying the admittedly suspect census estimates, Price argues that the figures, in any event, show that federal authorities were aware of the importance of fish to southeast Alaska Natives at the moment when their importance was about to be endangered by commercial canners (1990, 12). Finally, it is important to note that while the salmon catch was the key to Tlingit nutrition, it would be a mistake to suggest that their diet was tasteless and monotonous. Oberg emphasizes the fact that the subsistence foods of the Tlingit were rich, varied, and artfully prepared. Indeed, while conducting ethnographic interviews in the early 1930s, Oberg's older Tlingit informants unanimously spoke with disgust for the White man's food and stressed the delicacy of their own (1973, 115).

The Conflict between Aboriginal and Commercial Fisheries

When the United States purchased Alaska from Russia and signed the Treaty of Cession in 1867, the industrial revolution was in its infancy. Grounded in laissez-faire principles and its "free market" environment, the industrial revolution meshed with a highly compatible social Darwinian philosophy that paved the way for powerful economic forces to claw their way to the top. Typically, in colonial situations, economic forces precede the establishment of a political infrastructure, facilitating unfettered resource exploitation. This was certainly the case in Alaska. With a vast territory, a sparse population, and few political stewards, Alaska presented a door opened wide for the invasion of capital interests. The 1867 Treaty of Cession was, of course, negotiated between Russia and the United States with the aboriginal population having virtually no say in the matter. The Treaty did provide that the "uncivilized tribes" would "be subject to such laws and regulations as the United States may, from time to time, adopt in regard to aboriginal tribes of that country" (McNickle 1973, 61).

In 1871 the federal government abandoned treaty-making policies previously marking its relations with Indian nations, replacing them with congressional acts. Thus, the determination of what laws and regulations would apply to Alaska's "uncivilized tribes" was up to Congress to decide. Early on, Alaska and her diverse indigenous peoples were thought to be part of Indian Country, but then an 1872 court case reversed that ruling. For the next twelve years there was a great deal of ambiguity regarding the political standing by which Alaska Natives were to be "allowed" to act. The 1880 census determined that Alaska's population was just 33,426 with all but 430 of them members of diverse Native groups (Rogers and Cooley 1963, 19). Lacking positive congressional recognition of their standing, the Native population was either left alone, or, as in the case of the southeast Alaska Native groups, subjected to the heavy hand of first the Army and then the Navy (Price 1999, 23–42). Without political or economic rights, Alaska Natives were easily manipulated by powerful corporations.

Finally, after seventeen years of relative political neglect, Congress passed an Organic Act in 1884, establishing civil government and providing some promise that Alaska Natives could regain control over their traditional resource base. It held "that the Indians or other persons in said district shall not be disturbed in the possession of any lands actually in their use or occupation or now claimed by them." At the same time, it gave "no indication that [Alaska] Natives might have prior rights by reason of aboriginal occupancy, or that 'others' might be in possession of lands to which the aboriginal title had not previously been extinguished" (McNickle 1973, 151–52). It reserved clarification of Native acquisition to land titles to future congressional legislation. That clarification would be a long time coming. The Organic Act also extended the 1872 Mining Act to Alaska whereby only citizens of the United States were authorized to stake mining claims. Since Alaska Natives lacked citizenship, their ability to control land, rivers, and other resources was severely circumscribed. In essence, Alaska Natives were in a classic colonial situation, ripe for exploitation by economic developers.

Mining and fishing interests were the first of these corporate invaders. Over the course of the next half-century, the salmon canning industry would establish its hegemony. As Ernest Gruening notes, salmon fisheries surpassed mining as Alaska's major industry, with the largest investment of capital, the biggest annual profits, the largest employer of labor, and the greatest single source of territorial revenue. Thus, the leaders of the corporate salmon canning industry became the dominant players in Alaska's political, economic, and social life (1954, 246). The Pacific salmon canning industry began in California in the 1860s around the Sacramento River. Entrepreneurs from the state of Maine started catching and canning salmon in California and soon expanded their operations into the Columbia River basin. Price dates the "golden age" of salmon canning on the Columbia River to the period between 1867 and 1884 when fortunes were made (1990, 49). With an abundance of salmon all up the Pacific Coast, it was inevitable that industrial expansion in the canned salmon industry would reach the shores of southeastern Alaska. In the spring of 1878, canneries were established at Klawock and Old Sitka (49). Given the distances between the cannery capitals of San Francisco and Seattle and southeast Alaska, the growth of canneries in Alaska was slow, with only the Klawock facility surviving the first few years. Because its pack was very low, Tlingit and Haida salmon fisheries were relatively undisturbed. The biggest effect on Native life was the employment of Tlingit laborers. In fact Tlingit resentment over the importation of Chinese labor threatened to disrupt operations at the Sitka cannery (49–52). But the biggest effect of early cannery employment was interference with subsistence fishing, and thus the onset of fundamental alterations in Tlingit economy and culture. Champagne calls the partial loss of traditional subsistence practices the semi-proletarianization of the Tlingit, with part of their livelihood earned in the subsistence economy and the rest earned by the sale of their labor power to the canning industry (68).

As more and more canneries were established in Alaska in the late 1880s, cannery owners sought to maximize their packs by filing squatters' claims to obtain exclusive right to streams—an option not open to Alaska Natives. Drucker argues that even if Alaskan officials had interpreted the law liberally and allowed Natives some claim to streams on the basis of use and occupancy, cannery claimants could point to Native abandonment of sites as subsistence salmon runs dictated their movement and thus their relinquishment of sites due to lack of continuous use and occupation (1965, 215–16; see also Dauenhauer and Dauenhauer 1994, 38–39). By 1889, twelve canneries were in operation in southeast Alaska and the whole competitive landscape had shifted dramatically in the space of a few short years. To maximize their packs, cannery owners began barricading streams. While indigenous fishermen had also employed barricades in the past, their sparing use under noncompetitive conditions had not proved problematic (Cooley 1963, 72–73). With intensifying commercial competition, the canneries' use of barricades together with usurpation of the best streams for their exclusive use led to a phenomenal increase in the cumulative pack in southeast Alaska from just 8,159 cases in 1878 to 136,760 cases in 1889, with each case containing forty-eight one-pound cans. Furthermore, most of the canned fish consisted of the highly prized red salmon (Price 1990, 52). When the catches from the waters of south-central and southwest Alaska were added to those of the southeast, the total Alaska salmon pack exceeded the combined pack of California, Washington, and Oregon canners by a wide margin, 719,196 cases to 477,659 cases (Gruening 1954, 247). By the late 1880s, these efficient fishing methods and their alarming "success" caused concern not only with southeast Alaska Natives, but also with federal officials in charge of overseeing fishing.

In the 1880s, the U.S. Fish Commission was the organization responsible for sorting out fishing disputes in federal waters. As an agency under Treasury Department aegis, the U.S. Fish Commission had a small staff and meager funding. Most of its activities avoided policing and regulation for the less controversial tasks of scientific investigation. Toward the end of the 1880s, the Fish Commission charged Dr. Tarleton Bean with studying salmon fisheries on the Sacramento and Columbia rivers and he concluded that they had been nearly destroyed, a fate he predicted for Alaska as well unless regulatory steps were undertaken (Gruening 1954, 245). To prevent fulfillment of Bean's prophecy, Congress passed legislation in 1889 "making it unlawful to erect dams, barricades, or other obstructions in any of the rivers of Alaska for the purpose of preventing or impeding the ascent of salmon to their spawning grounds" (Cooley 1963, 71–72).

There were two problems with this regulation. First, it made no distinction between subsistence fishermen and commercial operations and their contrasting approaches to access and control over fishing sites. Second, it lacked teeth since Congress failed to appropriate policing money for Treasury Department enforcement for the first three years. When money was finally appropriated, it covered salaries for an inspector and an assistant, but no money for transportation. Cannery and fishing gear inspection was thus a farce since these governmental inspectors usually traveled on cannery boats, thus negating the possibility of surprise visits (Cooley 1963, 73). Without special provisions to uphold the private property rights of Alaska Native groups, the fisheries were open to all comers as a common property resource. Thus, the so-called even playing field enabled powerful canners to establish their sites and to work out tacit agreements with their competition to keep others out. These "free market" practices marked the beginning of the decline of subsistence fishing with the big fishing enterprises essentially swallowing up the small fry. Drucker succinctly summarizes the situation at the end of the 1880s: "there was a plant on every river in southeast Alaska that supported a major salmon run. The Tlingit and Haida were forced to get the winter's supply of their basic food from the smaller streams with inferior runs or to ask permission of the cannery manager to fish the best streams when he had all the fish he could handle" (1965, 214). Forced to take action, the Tlingit held meetings in 1889 and hired a lawyer, who wrote a letter the next year to President Harrison on their behalf (Price 1990, 52–53).

Southeast Alaska Natives were thus marginalized in their own homelands, forced to earn wages from a few absentee cannery owners who had rationalized production and sales for an international marketplace. Outside capital—primarily from San Francisco and Seattle—had quickly turned Alaska fisheries into an oligopoly as a handful of firms had effected a nearly vertically integrated marketplace with control over supplies, transportation, production, and even much of the labor they brought north with them from the Pacific Northwest. The major canners not only disrupted centuries-old subsistence patterns, but they also spent much of their operational monies outside Alaska, a fact that continued to draw the attention and ire of resident Alaskans. One of the prime players in this concentrated marketplace was the Alaska Packers Association, a company that owed some of its organizational strength to its relationship to the old Alaska Commercial Company, an organization that had dominated the seal fur business in the 1860s and 1870s. In 1894, the Alaska Packers Association, a San Francisco-based corporation, effectively controlled about 90 percent of all canneries in Alaska and packed almost 72 percent of the total output (Cooley 1963, 28). Ten years later, its share of the marketplace had shrunk some, but it was still the biggest salmon packer with fourteen canneries in Alaska and three in Puget Sound, facilitated by twenty-four large sailing vessels and sixty steamers and launches (Gruening 1954, 252). So, at the dawn of the twentieth century, the competition for Alaska salmon had stabilized around a few major concerns whose continued economic vitality was spurred by the introduction of a new and very efficient form of fishing gear, the fish trap.

For Alaska Natives and a few White territorial leaders, the "Fish Trust"—as it came to be derisively called—and its fish traps became the omnipresent symbols of all that was wrong with Alaska fisheries for the next six decades. They would be the focal point of William Paul's relentless journalistic crusades through most of the 1920s and early 1930s. Why there was such antagonism toward the fish trap can be gleaned in part by Cooley's description of its structure, placement, and operation:

> The trap is a huge permanent installation of log piles and wire netting that extends out far from the shore about a half mile across the path the salmon travel as they wend their way toward the rivers and streams. Salmon follow

much the same travel routes from year to year, and the traps are located to take maximum advantage of this fact. As the salmon move along the shore they strike a barrier of netting which guide them into the trap. They pass through a series of V-shaped openings of webbing until they reach the pot from which they cannot find their way out. From the pot the salmon are allowed to pass through a small tunnel into the spiller where they can be brailed into a scow alongside. Traps may be either pile driven or floating, the latter being more common. They are nearly always removed each fall and reconstructed at the same site at the opening of the next season. Usually a single watchman is hired to live on each trap during the season to check on maintenance needs and to prevent the pilfering of fish. The annual costs of construction are high, but operating costs are small in relation to the efficiency of the traps. (Cooley 1963, 46–47)

Besides their efficient, around-the-clock operation, the placement and siting of fish traps were also highly proprietary because regulations kept other traps away for a distance of a mile and boats were prevented from approaching them within three hundred feet in any direction. In practice, the traps created exclusive fishing zones (Colt 2000, 9).

In addition to the weak regulatory regimes governing federal fishing policy in the 1890s, the canneries' installation of fish traps in the early part of the twentieth century helped to sediment their political and economic power and made them the joint powers-to-be in Alaska alongside the finance capitalism of the Morgan-Guggenheim transportation and mining combine.[7] Occasionally Alaska's governors flexed their weak muscles and took issue with this outside capital, but they were themselves political appointees, usually carpetbaggers, and thus they were most often either in league with these economic juggernauts or no match for their far-flung power.

The powerful cannery interests were also able to shape the conservation movement whenever its proposed resource management threatened their productive capacities. One of their greatest challenges came early in President Theodore Roosevelt's administration. Roosevelt ordered the U.S. Fish Commission to study the Alaska salmon fishery and to recommend regulatory steps needed for conservation. In 1904 its final report concluded that drastic measures were needed, including more power to the Treasury Secretary to restrict fishing, to close certain areas, and to consider limiting the number of canneries. More than anything else, though, the report urged the establishment of government hatcheries so that supplies could be replenished without curtailing production (Cooley 1963, 76–77). While the report was being written in 1903, ongoing bureaucratic reorganization soon replaced the

U.S. Fish Commission with a Bureau of Fisheries and agency operations were transferred out of the Treasury Department into the Department of Commerce and Labor. In 1906, the Bureau shaped a comprehensive Alaska fisheries conservation bill and engineered its introduction on to the floor of the House. The bill sought to extend the Secretary's control over all Alaska's waters, to limit the types of fishing gear, and to impose weekly closed periods. C. W. Dorr, counsel for the Alaska Packer's Association, objected to the bill's extension of the Secretary's power on the grounds that it was an unconstitutional delegation of law-making power to an executive agency. Dorr lambasted provisions to prohibit fishing off the mouths of rivers and streams, claiming that salmon were so abundant that they were destroying each other on the spawning grounds. The bill that eventually passed the House in 1906 was so watered down by the powerful cannery lobby that it bore little resemblance to the Bureau's original draft (Cooley 1963, 79–82).

Ultimately, the bureaucratic shuffling had little regulatory effect in Alaska for, as Cooley points out, there was a carryover of scientists from one organization to the next and their primary interest turned on artificial fish propagation rather than on policing and regulating fishing (1963, 77). Tellingly, one provision of the Bureau's original bill that escaped intact provided tax rebates for canneries that established and operated hatcheries (82). Clearly, fishery conservation in Alaska in the early twentieth century fits environmental historian Samuel Hays's conclusion about conservation in general in the United States as collaborative work on the part of leaders in science, technology, and government to bring about more efficient development of physical resources (1987, 13).

While the threat to maximization of the canners' fish catch was not realized in the 1906 congressional legislation, Congress did alter the balance of political power in Alaska by providing for the election of a nonvoting delegate to Congress (Gruening 1954, 139). Two years later, in 1908, Progressive Republican Judge James Wickersham was elected to this position. Wickersham provided stalwart opposition to both outside mining and fishing interests for the next twelve years—often in league with southeast Alaska Native positions (Gruening 1954, 143). But Wickersham was no match for distant imperial control and a political apparatus in the Department of Commerce and Labor that more often than not promoted the interests of its fishing clientele—the big cannery owners—rather than regulated them.

In particular, major canners found common ground with the artificial propagation interests of the Bureau of Fisheries. Their shared interest in hatcheries allowed the cannery industry to continually deny charges of over-fishing. On the consumer end, the canned salmon industry also received an inadvertent boost from muckraking exposés on the meat industry, especially the 1906 publication of Upton Sinclair's fictional account of hygienically unpalatable conditions in meat processing plants in *The Jungle,* and the debates leading up to the passage of the Pure Food and Drug Act. The industry's biggest promotional push, though, came from the Bureau of Fisheries' leaders who were persuaded by the industry early in 1914 "to undertake a worldwide advertising campaign to popularize canned salmon" and to distribute, at Bureau expense, one hundred thousand copies of a canned salmon bulletin to all major newspapers in the United States and in selected foreign countries (Cooley 1963, 89). The collaboration between Bureau and industry was made easier that same year when the office of the Alaska division of the Bureau of Fisheries moved from Washington, D.C., to Seattle and was housed in the same building as twenty major salmon packing concerns (89). In short, with regulators among their best friends, the canning industry developed at a phenomenal rate in Alaska from the beginning of the twentieth century through World War I, with the number of canneries growing to over eighty plants in the southeast alone and the territorial-wide salmon pack peaking at 6.5 million cases in 1918 due to wartime demand (35, 41). The fish trap fueled this dynamic growth with the number in operation rising from sixty in 1906 to well over six hundred in 1920 and with canneries accounting for 70 to 95 percent of the trap ownership (31, 48–49).

Throughout this period of phenomenal growth, the major canners continued to make light of protests against over-fishing, aimed, primarily, at the efficiency of the fish trap (Cooley 1963, 92–95). However, two developments in 1912 ensured the likelihood of a protracted battle between fish trap owners and their opponents. First, over cannery and mining opposition, Congress passed a Second Organic Act for Alaska, establishing an elected legislature with the governor and the judiciary remaining as federal appointees. To the delight of the cannery cartel, fish and game laws were kept under federal control, a provision at odds with practices in other U.S. territories (Gruening 1954, 151–53; Nichols 1924, 383–409). The act failed to address either the issue of citizenship for Alaska Natives or the resolution of their aboriginal land rights. The second development was the establishment of the Alaska Native Brotherhood (ANB), in part to address the lack of citizenship and the loss of Native control over fisheries.

Before turning our attention to the ANB and its collective voice of protest, the *Alaska Fisherman,* we need to put in place one final piece of the puzzle that permanently altered the way the fishing business was conducted in Alaska following World War I. Just after the war, demand for canned salmon decreased substantially, setting in motion a drastic decline in the industry over the next three seasons with the pack falling to about 2.5 million cases in 1921 (Cooley 1963, 35). The collapse of the market precipitated a new attitude toward "conservation" among the cannery owners, an attitude underwritten by their capitalist desire to rationalize the marketplace with governmental help on terms once anathema to them but now judged to be industry saving. Canners took the initiative in November 1919, proposing, to both territorial and federal officials, legislation assuring greater escapement of salmon to the spawning beds while at the same time maintaining their dominance of the market (103). With more cannery control of the fisheries looming, the ANB decided to politicize its association.

The Alaska Native Brotherhood: Germination, Growth, and Maturation

Philip Drucker's ethnographic fieldwork in southeast Alaska in 1953–54 established the standard interpretation of the development of the Alaska Native Brotherhood. He based his interpretation on a model of acculturation, emphasizing the heavy influence and success of Presbyterianism on Tlingit and Haida life. As we noted earlier, recent scholarship, though, has forced revisions in Drucker's analysis, assigning less determinism to the acculturationist thesis (Kamenskii 1985, Kan 1985; Champagne 1990; Dauenhauer and Dauenhauer 1987, 1990, 1994; Price 1990; Pratt 1992). While none of these revisionists doubts the influence of Presbyterianism, their studies do invest the Tlingits, in particular, with a sense of agency that subtly illuminates social and political strategies aimed at maintaining Tlingit cultural differences. In our analysis of the germination, growth, and maturation of the ANB, we will focus on stresses, strains, and contradictions in the everyday lives of Tlingits that highlight these differences as examples of resistance as cultural persistence.

One contradiction that puts the univocal interpretation of Presbyterianism in high relief was a Tlingit petition to the president of the United States in 1897. Signed by ten Tlingit leaders who were spokesmen for the Russian Orthodox Church in Alaska, their petition expressed opposition to the activities of the Presbyterian mission in southeast Alaska, to the sale of alcohol to the Tlingit, and to the interference of fish traps with their fishery (Price

1990, 59; Dauenhauer and Dauenhauer 1990, 136). By 1897, Presbyterian missions had been in Alaska for two decades so this antagonism seems strangely out of place. If Presbyterianism was such a profoundly powerful acculturative force, then how does one account for this petition?

In his translation of Russian Orthodox parish archives and analyses of the *Russian Orthodox American Messenger,* Sergei Kan's ethnohistory offers a compelling explanation (Kamenskii 1985, Kan 1985; see also Dauenhauer and Dauenhauer 1994, 81–83). He points to a significant decline in Native membership in the Sitka Presbyterian Church in the middle of the 1880s and a correspondingly significant rise in membership in the Russian Orthodox Church so that "by the early 1900s almost the entire Tlingit population of Sitka had converted, as had large segments of several smaller Tlingit communities" (Kan 1985, 199–201). Given the fact that Sitka was the heart of Presbyterian efforts in Alaska, this decline is surprising. Both churches pursued similar Christian missions, sought to eradicate the scourge of alcohol, and aimed to eliminate "pagan" cultural practices. The major difference that swung the tide, at least temporarily, toward Russian Orthodoxy was its greater tolerance for Tlingit customs and its use of the Tlingit language for instruction and translation of major prayers so that the Orthodox Church came to be seen as a "[N]ative church" (Kan 1985, 208). Kan also suggests that, for some Tlingits, Presbyterianism suffered because of a close identification of its missionaries in the 1890s with governmental authorities. Indeed, Governor John G. Brady, whom Kadashan and his fellow Tlingits had importuned on behalf of their subsistence rights in 1898, had spent at least a couple of years working for the Presbyterian mission in Alaska.[8] Brady's angry response to the poignant pleas of Kadashan and his fellow interlocutors was both coercive and disingenuous. He said that they could be put on an island and retain their customs with agents watching over them to keep them straight or they could be citizens of the United States, "obey White men's laws [and] have all the privileges that he has" (Dauenhauer and Dauenhauer 1990, 136). As a federal appointee over a geographical expanse lacking even territorial status, Brady's "promises" lacked the power of delivery and infringed on congressional prerogatives.

While many Tlingits resented this lack of governmental respect, they also took umbrage at the Presbyterians' practice of forced school attendance and their attacks on potlatches and other traditional Native beliefs and practices (Kamenskii 1985, 78). While Presbyterian disaffection was peaking, the Russian Orthodox ministers were organizing social societies, or brotherhoods.

Their popularity, Kan contends, was aided by conformity of Orthodox social and religious practices with indigenous notions of human and superhuman power. In the traditional Tlingit hierarchy, the house group and its leader—the yitsati—acquire prestige and power from both real and spiritual property, and this wealth invests the yitsati with the right and the obligation to wear and display clan crests, costumes, and ceremonial regalia representing their kinship groups, and to be a leader in all ceremonial events (Kan 1985, 206). Kan argues that these indigenous practices were carried over into brotherhood activities, strengthening the Tlingit voice in parish affairs and slowing the pace of Tlingit Americanization (215). In particular, Kan singles out Orthodox brotherhood societies' tolerance for memorial dinners and the Tlingit penchant for oratory at such events (201, 209). In short, Orthodox brotherhoods were common in southeast Alaska in the early twentieth century because their organizational structure contributed to traditional Tlingit leadership practices, especially testimonial speeches reinforcing the importance of Tlingit community and identity (Dauenhauer and Dauenhauer 1994, 78). In Pratt's terminology, the contact zone was being managed by the Tlingit to bring about a hybridized religion appropriate to their spiritual needs.

To counter the decline of Presbyterianism and the nearly decade-long persistence and popularity of Orthodox brotherhoods, Presbyterian lay missionary George Beck and Tillie Tamaree (formerly Tillie Paul, the mother of William and Louis Paul) founded the New Covenant Legion in 1905,[9] ostensibly as a temperance organization (Drucker 1958, 18; *Thlinget* 1908). In late 1908, the editor of the *Thlinget*, the Sitka Industrial School's successor to the *North Star*, announced that the purpose of the New Covenant Legion was "doing away with the old customs that were interfering materially with the growth of the church." While the New Covenant Legion was just one of a number of Protestant temperance and self-improvement societies, it is the one most often given credit for molding subsequent ANB leadership. Fred Paul, William Paul's son and Tillie Tamaree's grandson, notes that "Gramma . . . organize[d] her league of the New Covenant with her favorite students, Ralph Young, Peter Simpson, George Haldane, Frank Mercer" (Paul 1987, 43). Young, Simpson, and Mercer would later be among the thirteen founders of the Alaska Native Brotherhood (Dauenhauer and Dauenhauer 1994, 619–95).

Kan's research shows that Tlingits were themselves quite divided about the sociocultural changes swirling about them. The formation of the ANB mirrored this divisiveness, with the power of Presbyterianism and the dominance of English tempered somewhat by the Orthodox brotherhoods' cultural and linguistic sympathies for all things Tlingit (see Dauenhauer and Dauenhauer 1994, 74). The ANB grew out of an educational conference called by W. G. Beattie, district superintendent of federal Indian schools in southeast Alaska for the Bureau of Education. Beattie, a former superintendent of the Sitka Industrial Training School and editor of the *Thlinget,* envisioned this conference of educators and Sitka school graduates as a means to advance assimilation. The timing of the conference in early November of 1912 coincided with the first election of the Territorial legislature, a fact not lost on the Alaska Native educational conference participants who, of course, were not eligible to vote. Three days after the educational conference on election day, eleven Tlingit men, a Tlingit woman, and a Tsimshian man formed the ANB at the Tlingit Presbyterian Church in Juneau. While ten of the thirteen founders were strong Presbyterians, Eli Katanook and Paul Liberty were prominent leaders of the Russian Orthodox Church and Marie Moon Orsen had been raised as a Quaker. Liberty was a brilliant Tlingit orator and a member of the St. Gabriel Brotherhood while Katanook spoke three languages—Tlingit, English, and Russian (Dauenhauer and Dauenhauer 1994, 83–84, 635, 643, 655).

What the formation of the ANB indicated more than anything else was its founders' impatience with a system that promised the rewards of citizenship and economic success but that was slow on deliverance. This impatience was underscored by the ANB's fundamental purpose: the material, political, and social advancement of its people (Dauenhauer and Dauenhauer 1990, 28–29). Among the more youthful founders of the ANB, no policy was more important than the adoption of English as the group's official language. At that time, Native languages and cultures were still very strong, a fact that Beattie and many of the ANB founders believed was detrimental to assimilation and advancement (29).

However, the slow pace of organizational efforts, especially lagging ANB membership, raised questions about the wisdom of restricting eligibility to English speakers. Tlingit historian John Hope claims that the prohibition on speaking the Tlingit language at ANB meetings effectively discouraged many traditional clan leaders from attendance (quoted in Goldin 1996). Consequently, the ANB began to hedge its policies on language and customs. The ANB essentially went through two phases. In the first phase, from 1912 to 1920, it emphasized the exclusivity of English and the elimination of Tlingit customs. In the second phase, after 1920, the ANB leadership softened its position on Native customs, arguing against those that were considered harmful, such as witchcraft, and allowed ample time for the liberal translation of

English into Tlingit at annual ANB meetings (Drucker 1958, 41–42; Champagne 1990, 73). Some Native historians have suggested that Tlingit speech may have become a widespread practice at local camp meetings as early as 1918 as more and more villages added ANB chapters (Hope quoted in Goldin 1996). The ANB leadership realized that opening membership to traditional Tlingit-speaking clan leaders meant sociocultural prestige and increased financial security for the fledgling organization.

By 1918, ANB chapters numbered twelve with a cumulative membership in excess of two hundred (Goldin 1996; Drucker 1958, 20). Despite this growth, the ANB's first chairman, Peter Simpson, understood that what the organization needed more than anything else was a fiery leader. When William Paul learned of the plight of Alaska Native fishermen upon his return to the territory in 1920, he was persuaded by his brother, Louis, and a traditional Tlingit-speaking leader, Chief Shakes, to attend the annual Grand Camp meeting of the ANB in Wrangell. Louis was elected Grand President and William was elected Secretary (Drucker 1958, 35, 38; Mitchell 1997, 209). The Pauls convinced attendees of the need for aggressive political action.

Twice in the next two years, William Paul lobbied for the ANB's position against the canneries' use of fish traps. In 1921 he received Bureau of Education funding to testify before the House Marines Fisheries Committee about the canneries' usurpation of Tlingit/Haida traditional resources. In January 1922, Paul told the Subcommittee on Fisheries and Fish Hatcheries that a drastic reduction in the salmon catch was serious, but that the possibility of a closed fishery would mean poverty for Indian fishermen. Paul's congressional appearances established the ANB as a political force to be reckoned with on both subsistence and commercial fishing issues (Price 1990, 92; Mitchell 1997, 211–12; Haycox in Dauenhauer and Dauenhauer 1994, 509). To keep local ANB camps apprised of Paul's congressional lobbying and of decisions of the Grand Camp's executive committee in the months between its annual meetings, the *Alaska Fisherman* (*TAF*) was established in 1923 as the official organ of the ANB with financial support drawn primarily from annual assessments of each of the local camps (Drucker 1958, 26).

The Alaska Fisherman: *The Lesson of the Raven on the Power of Native Voices*

As we have seen, the historical formation of the ANB was accomplished by an interesting mix of Tlingit cultural persistence amidst Presbyterian Americanization. Often these everyday practices of cultural continuity were carried out quietly in order not to detract from the Tlingits' apparent "civilizing" adaptations. Indicative of these quiet, yet important, changes was the October 1922 amendment of the ANB constitution doing away with the provision restricting membership to English-speaking Natives (Dauenhauer and Dauenhauer 1994, 92). Yet, *TAF*'s editorial page continued to publish the ANB platform, including its patriotic call for "one nation, one language, one flag," until May of 1924. Since the adoption of English was seen as a civilizing move, it is reasonable to account for this lag as a strategic move by southeast Alaska Natives to secure economic gains through the acquisition of citizenship. By 1915 some Alaska Natives had begun testing an act passed by the Territorial legislature that offered citizenship for Indians who met a number of conditions, including having lived "separate and apart from any tribe" and having "adopted the habits of civilized life" (Gruening 1954, 363; Mitchell 1997, 212). When President Coolidge signed legislation establishing citizenship for all Indians in the middle of 1924, there was no longer any strategic necessity for parading one's so-called civilized habits.

For traditional Tlingits, the establishment of a newspaper was itself a concession to the changing political and economic circumstances in southeast Alaska. As members of an oral tradition who prized oratory, Tlingit elders had developed a strong suspicion of, and antipathy for, print literacy, because of inaccuracies and derogatory characterizations of Tlingit culture in a wide variety of printed materials (Dauenhauer and Dauenhauer 1990, x–xi). On the other hand, the younger generation, educated in Indian boarding schools, had developed at least a grudging admiration for the power of "the talking paper" of the White man (see Adams 1995, 22).

As a longtime boarding school student, well acquainted with the urban dailies in Philadelphia and later with those of San Francisco, William Paul understood the power of the press. In an article drawing upon Tlingit oral tradition—"A Thlinget Legend: How and Why the Cormorant Lost His Tongue," Paul articulated his philosophy of the press:

> Raven the Creator and Benefactor of mankind was walking along the beach with his servant Cormorant (but called Yuk by the Natives) . . . and [they] decided to go fishing.
>
> . . . Yuk being a real fisherman caught all the halibut and Raven caught nothing. As they were returning, Raven figured a way to hide his disgrace from the townspeople, so he said to Yuk: "My partner, what is on your tongue? Stick out your tongue so that I can look at it." . . . Raven now seized Yuk's tongue and pulled it out. Then Raven said, "Let me hear you talk." Yuk tried

to talk and was only able to say "Wah-h-h." Raven then said, "That is fine.
You talk much better now than you used to," and Yuk believed it. . . .

When they came to town, Raven appropriated all the halibut, taking his
time, lifting the halibut out in full view of the crowd who had gathered to
watch such a successful fisherman. . . . [Yuk] called to the people that the
halibut was his but nobody could understand him . . .

Paul then added his gloss on the Raven narrative: "And thus it has ever been.
The means of speech or the control of the press has meant that the servant
who has indeed caught the halibut has been cheated. The person or group
of people without the power of telling what they have done can be robbed"
(*TAF* April 1926, 6).

There are a number of typical and consistent lessons Tlingit and Haida
peoples traditionally drew from stories of Raven's greed, especially when it
was satisfied by thievery. One of them was that Raven would tire of his theft
and that sooner or later, the objects of his greed or gluttony would be shared
(see Bringhurst cited in Martin 1999, 60). Most of the time, when a Tlingit
person was behaving in a greedy or foolish manner, or if he lied to gain some
advantage, then he would be reminded of his selfishness, stupidity, or lying
indirectly through one of the Raven stories. The stories that cast Raven in a
bad light were meant either to aid in the wrong-doer's development or as
Kadashan told Swanton, they were told by older people to their children so
they would not be greedy and selfish, but honest (Swanton 1909, 92; Beck 1978,
53). Given what Paul consistently said about the mainstream press and its
greedy promotion of the interests of privilege, it is safe to say that he wanted
his readers to be wary of the lies it propagated. With the political and economic borders of Alaska defined and dictated by absentee owners and absentee politicians, Tlingit political and economic consciousness required that
the "little fellows" steal back their voices and reclaim their fish. His articulation of press freedom in this trickster narrative affirmed the necessary linkage between the material and symbolic dimensions of justice.

Recognition of this common linkage recalls Marx and Engel's famous
dictum in *The German Ideology* where they write that "the class which has
the means of material production at its disposal, has control at the same time
over the means of mental production, so that thereby, generally speaking, the
ideas of those who lack the means of mental production are subject to it"
(1976, 74). In an early issue of *TAF*, Paul wrote that the mission of the paper
was to tell the other stories, those that don't get told by the kept press (May
1923, 2). In this same issue, he ran a self-promotional advertisement that

described *TAF* as, "A paper for the common folk treating subjects of labor and fishing and taxes without fear or favor, depending for its life on support from the 'Little Fellow'" (May 1923, 16). While *TAF*'s "little fellows" were not exclusively southeast Alaska Natives, they were Paul's most important imagined community of readers. His characteristic mode of address was populist, pitting the working classes against the privileged. He seemed to relish the appropriation of the White man's journalism in order to hold it to its vaunted standards or to force it to tell the truth lest it appear foolish in its lies.

On both his news and editorial pages, Paul's strident language articulated the politics of class conflict, and his muckraking style foregrounded, with obvious ideological significance, which political actors he held responsible for Alaska's political and economic problems. With tongue firmly in cheek in an early article on the Alaska legislative scene entitled "Mirrors of Juneau," Paul asks why other newspapers with their abler writers and observers have not taken their estimation of the legislators and their work in Juneau. Then, with word choices reminiscent of the best of the leftist political lexicon, Paul skewered his opponents with caustic tones and deprecatory forms of address that would become commonplace in *TAF* in the coming years. In reference to the appointed governor, Paul wrote that he surrounds himself with "a coterie of hand-picked advisers who fawn upon him . . . and whose attitudes are not in sympathy with the people as against the hosts of privilege." One Territorial legislator was described as "aid[ing] the fishing trust," while another was assailed for voting "for the corporations and against the people." A representative from south-central Alaska was said to have a legislative record of "supine obedience to the predatory interests . . . delivering his voting prerogative over to the corporation lobbyists." The most experienced man in the Alaska House, Paul wrote, was "a sly, sleek, foxy man of 'interests' who feigns support of progressive measures but knows where to put the knife." Finally, in a piece of biting doggerel, a legislator from copper country was hailed as "com[ing] from fair Cordova, in the land of Guggenheim. If you ask him what brought him over, he'll say, in roundelay, he came to serve the fish trust, on Territorial pay" (*TAF* May 1923, 2–5).

Paul's spirited editorial challenges to the political, economic, and journalistic establishment in southeast Alaska inevitably drew equally enthusiastic ripostes, especially from the editors of the *Daily Alaska Empire* (Juneau) and the *Ketchikan Chronicle*. In their opposition to his leadership in forging the Indian vote into a cohesive bloc, to his vigorous opposition to the fish trap, to his election campaigning, and to his battles against literacy bills, they resorted to ad hominem attacks, calling Paul a "Dangerous Man," a "radical," a "Bolshevik," a "Boss," a "Menace," a "self-appointed dictator," and a "destroyer of business" (*TAF* February 1924, 7; *TAF* August 1924, 5; *TAF* September 1932, 1; Haycox 1987, 8, 11). While Paul clearly disliked the political and economic stands of those who so labeled him, he often reprinted their charges as foils to present his own ideas.

In response to a charge that he was "Promoting Bolshevism," Paul replied that "the causes of Bolshevism are not where the so-called 'better class' thinks they are. They are not in the laboring classes, or in the 'radical' class. The causes are to be found in the high places of the land, among governors, judges, commercial clubs, [and] 'leading citizens'" (*TAF* February 1924, 3). Obviously Paul was no Bolshevik, probably not even a socialist. He explained that his brand of progressive populism was honed in his youthful working days when he first came in contact with a "rough European class of workers" and saw corporations "grind out the profits from the blood of men and women." In his insurance work, he saw how employers treated their injured employees. Nevertheless, Paul said he "remained an idealist," believing that "the trouble with the world is not money, big corporations, or even the system of individualism; but rather that it is the 'love of money'" (*TAF* March 1924, 6). In a statement of principles announcing his campaign for the Territorial legislature in February 1924, Paul wrote, "on account of my present views, Cannerymen, Trapmen, Capitalists, and their dependents call me a 'Dangerous Man,' a 'Radical,' a 'Boss.' My so-called radicalism is nothing more than the application of the 'golden rule' to the practical affairs of government" (*TAF* February 1924, 7).

For Paul and the ANB, *TAF* was a major vehicle in the pursuit of three goals: (1) abolition of the fish trap and establishment of Alaskan control over the fisheries, (2) the acquisition of civil liberties for Alaska Natives, and (3) home rule for the Territory of Alaska. Nothing was more important to the ANB and to *TAF* than abolition of fish traps and Alaskan control over the fisheries. This importance was underscored by the graphic symbolism of a free-floating salmon on the front page of nearly half of the issues of *TAF* during its nearly decade-long run (see figure 3). By the 1920s Alaska Native fishermen were part of the commercial fishing economy, but most of them also continued to practice subsistence fishing on a scaled-down level. Therefore, when Paul offered arguments in *TAF* for protection of the fisheries from cannery over-fishing, he seldom differentiated between cash and subsistence economies. However, when these arguments were derived from ANB resolutions, then they almost always began from the perspective of aboriginal fisheries. Paul pragmatically framed his arguments in terms of fish *and* people

THE

Alaska Fisherman

VOL. 4   NO. 10   SEPTEMBER, 1927   20c. PER COPY

Figure 3. Tlingit, Haida, and Tsimshian Indians have often been described as the "salmon people," evidenced here by the symbolic importance attached to salmon by a typical front page of the *Alaska Fisherman,* the official organ of the Alaska Native Brotherhood until its demise in 1932.

[his emphasis] and, again, in doing so, he did not make distinctions between White fishermen and Indian fishermen. Instead, he articulated his position in terms of resident fishermen, although it should be noted that southeast Alaska was home to a lot more resident Indian fishermen than resident White fishermen. Paul believed that the fight for democracy in Alaska depended on the Natives for, as he puts it, "no one suffers more from the rule of foreigners than they do" (*TAF* November/December 1928, 1). However, his campaign on behalf of resident fishermen was not simply a convenient and covert argument for Alaska Natives. He genuinely believed that if the fish trap were outlawed—as was the case in British Columbia—and if only resident fishermen were licensed to fish—as was the case in Washington, California, and Oregon, then not only would the permanent population increase, but the income of the fishing population would treble (*TAF* February 1924, 15; *TAF* December 1927, 3).

One of the first issues of *TAF* posed the fishing problem succinctly in the context of a statement by a Territorial House member from Wrangell on a bill to abolish the fish trap. In the article, the House member said that "real observers, not the kind that travel about on cannery boats or fine gas propelled cruisers of the Bureau of Fisheries, or that sit in swivel chairs at Washington 4,000 miles away, know that the fish trap is the root of all evil" (May 1923, 7). That summer, President Harding and Secretary of Commerce Herbert Hoover visited Alaska, providing an opportunity for Paul to interview Hoover and explore, as his headline later put it: "What Did Hoover Learn?"

In order to understand the question and the thrust of Paul's article, Hoover's fishing policy needs explanation. In our discussion of the conflict between aboriginal and commercial fisheries earlier in the chapter, we noted that declining salmon packs in the postwar period led cannerymen, finally, to admit that over-fishing was a problem. In order to save the industry, they called upon both the territorial and federal governments to cooperate in the institution of measures to curtail the catch. The Bureau of Fisheries agreed that conservation of the salmon resource could not be rationally approached without taking into consideration basic economic motivations (Cooley 1963, 106–8).

For the Bureau of Fisheries, the question of whose basic economic motivations were at stake was not at issue. By strategically raising the question of conservation when they did, the big canning concerns positioned themselves to set the parameters for the new fishing regimes. By the time Hoover called a conference in Seattle in 1921 to act on the Bureau of Fisheries' recommendations to restrict fishing, the leading canneries had already met and agreed to a plan to put parts of the Alaska salmon fishery in reservations with a system of licensed control over the number of canneries and over the gear they could employ. Cannery owners were banking on the possibility that, under their plan, their fish traps might acquire the status of property rights (Cooley 1963, 109). While no action was taken at the Seattle conference, Hoover knew that the salmon packers would back a plan to create fishery reserves. Thus, at Hoover's request, President Harding created, by executive order, two fishery reserves in Alaska in 1922—the Alaska Peninsula Fishery Reserve in February and the Southwestern Alaska Fishery Reservation in November, the first such reserves to be created in the United States. While the canned salmon industry was elated, most Alaskans were outraged. Alaska congressional delegate and friend of Alaska Natives, Dan Sutherland best articulated this opposition: "The sole purpose in the minds of those who originated the proposition [for the establishment of fish reserves] was the granting of a monopoly to the red salmon trust. The proposition was conceived and engineered to completion by the Fish Trust, and now the Department of Commerce hypocritically pretends that it was projected in the interests of conservation. . . . Congress has refused to act in the past . . . and while Congress holds aloof, the Fish Trust secures full control of our natural food supply upon which the people of the Territory depend more than upon any other resource for a livelihood" (Cooley 1963, 112). While the President had the authority, under the General Withdrawal Act of 1910, to set aside lands/waters under the public domain for public purposes, Delegate Sutherland was nevertheless incensed that reserves were created without any notice "to the people most vitally concerned—the coastal people of Alaska" (112).

Given this context, Paul answered his headline asking what Hoover had learned by saying it was clear that "he came committed to the reserve system and the trap system and therefore he learned nothing but what he wished to learn." In his class-based analysis, Paul opined that, "Mr. Hoover is what he has been from the first, a special interest man whose friends are among the packers not because he is bad or corrupt but because he belongs to their class; he thinks as they do, he likes them. He cannot understand us, the little fellow who had never been able to earn more than a couple of thousand dollars a year. He understands money, millions of it, power, plenty of it" (*TAF* January 1924, 10).

Since the major canneries and Hoover had a working agreement on reserves in 1921, Paul's analysis was accurate, but his own response was fraught with contradictions. Despite his collective labor-oriented approach to commercial fishing and his communal orientation to subsistence fishing, Paul's single-minded determination to abolish the fish trap left him with a simple-minded, individualistic solution within a free market system.[10] Paul told Hoover that the problem of the Indian "could be solved in two ways . . . : in keeping with the traditional American way of reserving everything for the Indian, and the other way being to solve it for the benefit of all citizens." Paul opted for the latter by arguing for the elimination of traps. In the ensuing exchange, Paul's response indicated his belief that a return to an open, common fishery absent the fish trap could serve the interests of conservation and fishermen by the use of more inefficient gear. Hoover said that if the trap were abolished, then "the canneries would not be able to get up their packs," to which Paul replied, "We do not want the canneries to pack all the fish they are planning to pack. They are planning to pack more fish than there are fish in the water . . . the canneryman is never satisfied, but wants to pack the last fish that swims" (*TAF* January 1924, 9). At this particular juncture, neither Paul nor the ANB seriously envisioned turning the whole matter of reserves upside down and using them as a way to secure their aboriginal land and fishing rights. By the end of the decade, the ANB would embrace land claims and begin to equivocate on the question of reserves, but in 1924, Paul's dismissal of reservations was firmly in keeping with his education at the Carlisle Indian Industrial School where Lieutenant Pratt had strongly opposed reservations. ANB policy also opposed reservations and favored a free market approach to fisheries. Indeed, reservations established at Hydaburg in 1912 and at Klawock in 1914 were revoked in 1926 because of ANB opposition to them (Price 1990, 164, 170–71).

While Paul worked assiduously on behalf of ANB goals and devoted long hours to producing *TAF*, the temporal rhythms of his news practices were more befitting the practices of an oral tradition and the cycles of the subsistence season than they were the timely products of a commercial news organization. News stories and ANB resolutions were often repeated years after their first publication to drive home an ideological point. Commerce Secretary Hoover's visit to Alaska at the start of the salmon run in 1923 provides a good example of Paul's leisurely news pace and his didactic news style. While the visit began on July 7, 1923, when Paul's readers were busy fishing, his interview appeared in the January 1924 issue. By then, Congress was poised to alter Hoover's reserve system, renewing discussions and hearings on a series of competing bills first introduced in 1923 on how to manage and conserve Alaska fisheries. Delegate Sutherland's bill proposed giving Hoover wide powers to regulate fishing in Alaska, but without reserves and fish traps

(Cooley 1963, 115). His bill drew support from the ANB and three major West Coast labor unions but was opposed by Bureau of Fisheries Chair Henry O'Malley and Commerce Secretary Herbert Hoover. Representative Wallace White of Maine introduced a compromise bill, vesting significant power in the Secretary of Commerce, denying grants to exclusive rights of fishery, and retaining fish traps. Again, Delegate Sutherland attached an amendment to White's bill essentially outlawing fish traps. In the ensuing hearings on the amendment, cannery friend and California representative Free charged that if Sutherland's amendment were passed, the fishery would be in the hands of a few Indians in Alaska (119–21). While the House passed Sutherland's amendment, Washington's Senator Wesley Jones eviscerated key sections of the House bill, including the trap provision. Jones's version of the White bill became law on June 6, 1924 (122–24).

While the White bill was considered an important piece of conservation legislation, Alaska Natives only reluctantly supported it because of its elimination of fish reserves. Because it failed to give the secretary power to control traps, they saw it as a plan that locked into place the power of the canneries. In an article headlined, "Conservation for Traps," Paul maintained that the burden of conservation was placed on the little guy, the small seine fishermen and that this "'hooverized' conservation is no conservation at all" (*TAF* July 1924, 13). In a signed editorial in his capacity as secretary of the ANB, William Paul's brother, Louis, also contested the idea that the White bill was really a conservation measure, reminding readers that the Bureau of Fisheries and the Fish Trust had only lately come to recognize the need for conservation: "It is well to remember that the Indians first declared the danger of the coming destruction of the fisheries as early as 1902 and the territorial legislature made investigation in 1913 where [*sic*] the effort to enact legislation was blocked by the Bureau of Fisheries and other agents of the Fish Barons. It is well to remember that when resident fishermen were declaring the need for protection of our fisheries the Bureau of Fisheries declared the industry to be in just as healthy a condition as during the previous twenty years" (*TAF* July 1924, 5).

Over the next few years, the Paul brothers increasingly emphasized two points in *TAF*: that conservation was not some kind of rarefied scientific management problem, but that it was always about fish *and* people, and that conservation had begun with the aboriginal fisheries of the Indians.[11] In a March 1925 editorial, Paul defended himself from attacks in a Seattle newspaper called the *Alaska Weekly* for his advocacy of the abolishment of the trap, arguing that, "The true fishery problem is very comprehensive. The cannerymen claim that the entire problem is conservation of fish. This is not true. We Alaskans say that it is the conservation of fish AND of bona fide residents of Alaska, for under the present system our resident Alaskans are becoming as badly depleted as the salmon." He knew that the Indian population was not going anywhere, but that an increase in the white population was dependent upon the availability of a resource by which they could make a living. As we will see, his population equation was also tied to getting home rule for Alaskans, a political condition dependent upon a greater population base. He followed his conservation editorial three pages later with an article "About Protecting the Ancient Rights of Indians." In it, he rhetorically asked, "of what use did the Indians make of the fisheries before the coming of the white man?" "The Indians," he wrote, "had the right to catch all the fish they required for food for themselves and their always too numerous dogs. That is all. Let us put it another way: the Indians had the right of subsisting off the country. This they did by killing all they needed of fish and game" (*TAF* March 1925, 7).

Similar subsistence claims were regular features of ANB resolutions at annual Grand Camp meetings held each fall at the conclusion of the commercial and subsistence fishing seasons. The *Alaska Fisherman* featured this annual event, reprinting its resolutions in full. Fishery resolutions always contained detailed plans to address the problem and did so with preambles establishing participants' credentials as experts. In one such resolution to abolish traps, the ANB "maintains that there is no body of people in Alaska more competent to speak on the subject of fisheries than the Natives of Alaska, of whom we are the representatives" (*TAF* December 1926, 2). And, again, at the November 1927 Grand Camp, under the "problem of fish AND population ... the Alasaka [*sic*] Native Brotherhood calls attention to the fact that neither Henry O' Malley nor any other officer of the Bureau of Fisheries ever consults the expert resident fishermen of Alaska, that the [N]ative fishermen of Alaska are among the most expert and have the most abiding love for the future of this country" (*TAF* December 1927. 3).

The protests of the ANB and *TAF* against traps continued to fall on deaf ears. In April of 1931, William Paul turned the editorship over to his brother Louis. While Louis's editorship of *TAF* up until its death in September of 1932 was consistent with his brother's approach to the salmon fishery problem, his maiden issue was noteworthy for its equivocation on the questions of reservations *for* Native fishermen. As Louis cautiously writes, "theoretically, we are opposed to the creation of reserves. But this pre-supposed that the chance to make a livelihood would be equalized. In view of the practical difficulties, we are not so firm in our opposition to reserves for the Indians of Alaska . . . a reserve does two things, it saves the animals from extermination. It also saves the [N]ative people from starvation" (*TAF* April 1931, 1). Louis followed up this equivocation with a reprint of a subsistence-based argument from the 1925 Grand Camp of the ANB entitled, "An Appeal to Congress for Justice to the Native People of Southern Alaska."

Meanwhile, two other stories dominated the pages of *TAF*—the related issues of civil liberties for Alaska Natives and home rule for Alaskans. Even before President Coolidge signed legislation granting Indians citizenship in 1924, some Alaska Natives had been casting ballots in Territorial elections. In the January 1924 issue of *TAF*, Paul recounted for his readers an important voting rights case he had litigated on behalf of a traditional Tlingit, Charley Jones—then Chief Shakes—and his mother, Tillie Paul Tamaree.[12] Jones, an elderly Tlingit educated in the traditional ways and thus unable to read or write, had been challenged at the voting booth on November 7, 1922, by election officials at Wrangell who claimed he was not a citizen. Tillie Paul Tamaree was indicted for perjury for claiming that he was a citizen. Paul won acquittals, but the question of voting rights, even after the granting of Indian citizenship, was not yet settled because Territorial legislators and members of Congress sought to impose literacy tests on potential voters.

In an article headlined, "Literacy Test for the Voters," Paul asked his readers to ponder whether proposed literacy legislation was really about intellectual fitness. He again parsed the issue on class terms, arguing that "the true purpose was to cut down the votes of the class of people who today vote with the laboring man because he is a laboring man. With the Indian fisherman out of the lists, the [W]hite fisherman would have to stem the [cannery] tide alone" (*TAF* May 1923, 10). He added that "the rich masters" could then elect their own delegate to Congress instead of Dan Sutherland, whom the ANB and *TAF* supported. The battle, Paul maintained, was the laboring classes against the monopolistic owners of the means of production and transportation. As he writes, "The big mines and the big canneries worked together for this bill because they consider Dan Sutherland the enemy: the mines because Sutherland is fighting for fair freight rates from the steamship companies owned by the mines; and the canneries because Sutherland is against their trap system and in favor of the small resident fisherman" (*TAF* May 1923, 10).

Despite Paul's claim that Sutherland was the primary target of outside cannery and mining interests, he knew he was their primary enemy in the arena of territorial politics (Haycox 1987, 1). They took aim at his increasing political power by throwing their weight behind a literacy bill introduced in the territorial legislature in 1923. In his capacities as an ANB officer and as its attorney and publicist, Paul frequently visited Indian villages, advised the Natives of their rights, and instructed them on how they ought to vote to further their rights. Since many Tlingit elders were unable to read, Paul prepared sample ballots and cardboard templates that would match up with the appropriate candidates (3; see also *TAF* May 1924, 15).

While the 1923 literacy bill narrowly failed, it became a focal point of the next two legislatures (Haycox 1987, 3–4). Paul led the opposition. In an excerpt from a *Seward Gateway* article entitled "For Literacy Test," he showed how the Native vote was being treated in the mainstream press as an object of fear. The writer claimed that "the object of the bill is to shut out the half-civilized Indian who has not sufficient intelligence to know for whom he is voting. It is a good bill and should be indorsed [*sic*] . . . by every citizen who believes his or her vote to be worth more to the government than an Indian's" (quoted in *TAF* January 1924, 6). On the editorial page of the same issue, Paul opined that "the primal purpose of a literacy law was to place power with election judges, selected by the gang [cannerymen, mining men, and their attorneys], to prevent unlettered men from exercising the franchise in opposition to the gang. The gang is never opposed to illiterates except when the gang cannot control" (*TAF* January 1924, 5).

In February 1924, Paul announced his candidacy for the Republican nomination for a House seat in the Territorial legislature. From this point forward, the battle for a literacy law was a thinly veiled effort to stop Paul by disenfranchising the voters he could deliver (Haycox 1987, 1). After Paul won the May primary, the political discourse in the mainstream press—primarily John Troy's the *Daily Alaska Empire*—became more and more inflected by racist rhetoric. Paul felt very uncomfortable being drawn into arguments articulating race consciousness. Nevertheless, continuing racist volleys from the *Daily Alaska Empire* forced Paul to confront the race issue. In response to his rhetorical question, asking, "when did the race problem begin?" Paul wrote: "It began with the advent of the Wilson Democrats. These office holders were southern born Democrats who brought with them certain notions of their superiority over every other person whose skin is not white. Men like John Troy who frequently violates the constitution of our country . . . but who is unmolested because he belongs to and serves the gang who feed at the public crib, men like these are in control of the press. They feed what race prejudice there is, they nourish it because it serves their purpose" (*TAF* June 1924, 6). To combat this racism, Paul demonstrated his political acumen by forging the newly enfranchised Indians into a solid voting bloc. The so-called canoe vote carried Paul to an election victory. In recounting this election, Paul's biographer maintains that the "[W]hite political leadership went berserk over this. Here's an Indian moving in, playing by [W]hite rules, playing a [W]hite political game, and being in control" (Haycox quoted in Goldin, 1996).

In a postelection editorial, Paul threw down the gauntlet to establishment press and politicians, vowing that "the fight has just begun":

> ... The original principles of the Alaska Native Brotherhood were to prepare its members to exercise their privileges as citizens and to do it intelligently without prejudice and without distinction as to race....
>
> ... In deciding on which side the vote of this organization should be placed two factors ... were considered. First: the moral issue. Second: the economic issue. In deciding the first issue we found that there was a political ring composed of the attorneys of the large cannery and mine corporations who operated by and with the Juneau *Empire* and who controlled the Democratic or Republican Federal Brigade for their common purpose, and that at all times these attorneys were enlarging the profits of foreign corporations at the expense of resident Alaskans ...
>
> ... On the economic question, the personal experience of the Brotherhood required the abolishment of the fish trap in order that resident fishermen and small business men of this Territory might secure enough money to remain in the country. It is no secret that the Alaska Native Brotherhood is in politics and it is there to stay, with the avowed purpose of driving from public positions of power those interests which are contaminating the public mind ... not the least of these influences is John W. Troy ... who daily poisons the public mind by stirring up race prejudice. (*TAF* December 1924, 4)

In April 1925, the Territorial legislature passed a literacy bill, but not before Paul's amendment exempted previous voters, thus solidifying his political base (Haycox 1987, 10; Mitchell 1997, 218–20). The day after the bill's passage, Troy published an editorial arguing that a "[W]hite man's party is necessary," to which Paul replied that such a party would miss all the important issues because Troy's leadership was only good for creating discord and race hatred (Haycox 1997, 10; *TAF* June/July 1925, 4). In November 1926, Paul would ride the canoe vote to a very easy reelection. Three months later, Congress passed a literacy bill with the same exemptions as the Alaska bill, primarily due to some vigorous on-the-scene lobbying from Paul (Mitchell 1997, 220).

With the passage of literacy legislation at the Territorial level, Paul took his "fight" to Alaska's absentee government—the Federal Brigade—as he called them. Paul had long been appalled by absentee economic and political domination of Alaska and the consequent need for Alaskans to assert control over their political economy. As he saw it, the best means to accomplish control was to abolish the fish trap and elect three officials to a Board of Control—a Controller, a Secretary, and a Treasurer (*TAF* April 1926, 4). Paul introduced a Controller bill in the 1927 legislature and won House passage but it died in Senate chambers on a 4-4 vote (Mitchell 1997, 220–21).

While Paul failed to win a third term in the legislature in 1928 after some late charges in the mainstream press accusing him of Indian betrayal, he continued to use *TAF* to call for some measure of home rule.[13] The crowning moment—what some consider a turning point in Alaska Native history—came at the 1929 ANB convention in Haines when Grand Camp President William Paul and Alaska Congressional Delegate James Wickersham convinced attendees to fight for their land. Calling for a show of hands, Paul won a unanimous vote to initiate steps to sue the U.S. government for taking land and fish from the Tlingits and Haidas[14] (Dauenhauer and Dauenhauer 1994, 97).

The *Alaska Fisherman* ceased publication in September 1932, because of apparent financial problems. Reminiscing before the Grand Camp meeting at Kake in 1937, the paper's last editor, Louis Paul, recounted the paper's troubled financial circumstances: "Think back to the days William published *TAF* and was authorized to collect $100 from each ANB camp. I have the exact amount the Wrangell camp paid and the amount they owed. . . . It will surprise you but every camp owes on that account. And the last two years of its existence, William paid $100 per month to keep it going—this from his own personal earnings" (Mitchell 1997, 412). In his interviews with many ANB members in the 1950s, Drucker found that they "took considerable pride in the journal and say that they would have liked to have [had] it continued" (1958, 27).

Conclusion

If we were to take the perspective of much contemporary cultural studies and postcolonial scholarship in which cultural interpretations seem to trump politics and economics, then it would be easy to conclude that the Alaska Native Brotherhood, the *Alaska Fisherman* and William Paul sold out their culture to Presbyterian missionaries and cannery dollars. However, before drawing such a conclusion, we would be wise to heed Terry Eagleton's recent warning not to inflate the importance of culture when a people's civil rights are at stake, for in these emancipatory struggles, culture almost always takes a backseat to politics (2000, 122–23). We have tried to show that Tlingit and Haida Indians' resistance to the loss of hunting and fishing rights was both a political and economic matter with cultural overtones. William Paul made politics a practical imperative for the ANB, and *TAF* was an enormously important part of their efforts to win their civil rights, to contest their economic rights, and to reclaim the capacity to tell their own cultural stories. To his credit, Paul understood that the battles of his peoples required a class-consciousness. Furthermore, he knew that when the dominant class enlisted racial arguments to support its hegemony, then everything was up for grabs, including cultural questions. His frequent refrain that the question was always about fish *and* people showed his understanding of the linkage between the material and symbolic dimensions of justice.

As a lawyer and a publicist with a penchant for an aggressive, confrontational style, William Paul often rankled the older generation of Tlingit leaders whose cultural predispositions favored mutual respect and reciprocity. Indeed, some of them rightly questioned his cultural identity. Tlingit historian John Hope expressed such skepticism about Paul: "I heard William Paul speak to the delegates [at an ANB Grand Camp meeting] one time, and, in Tlingit, I could hear the remarks of the older people saying he thinks like a [W]hite man but I would add that he was right on the political and economic issues" (quoted in Goldin 1996). In explaining his notion of those who speak from the "in-between" of different cultures, Stuart Hall says that they always unsettle the assumptions of one culture from the perspective of another (1995, 206). Given Paul's educational background and the identity-transforming goals of the institutions he attended, it would be surprising if he had not exhibited multiple cultural identities. Perhaps William Paul had a bit of the Raven in him, a trickster who stirred up the communicative and political order so that Tlingits could participate in both. When he became the editor of the *Alaska Fisherman*, he may have spoken with a White voice, but as he became reintegrated into the Tlingit cultural milieu, he began to find his Indian voice. By showing the way in the Native land claims movement, Paul and his fellow Tlingits were exhibiting resistance as cultural persistence.

In 1962, William Paul gave a lecture on Native land rights to a Mount Edgecumbe high school class in Sitka. The speech piqued the interest of Charles Edwardsen Jr., an Inupiat and a student from Point Barrow. Four years later, Edwardsen (better known as Etok, see Gallagher 1974), Guy Okakok, and Samuel Simmons wrote a letter to Paul asking him to assist their

Native association in "securing our aboriginal rights and title to said land" on the northern slope of the Brooks Range. Paul quickly signed on and registered a formal protest with the Bureau of Land Management (Paul 1986, 141–42). For the first time, Alaska Natives from the farthest northern settlement to the tip of the southeastern archipelago were joined in a battle for aboriginal land rights. Now, it was oil rather than salmon that was the material force behind the Native land claims movement and a new communicative vehicle was needed to bridge the information gap over these twelve hundred miles. That communicative vehicle was the *Tundra Times*, the subject of chapter 3.

NOTES

1. The spellings for the chief's name vary in the historical literature. Hinckley (1970, 267) uses Kah-du-shan. John Muir's biographer, Frederick Turner (1985, 259), calls him Kadachan. Ethnologist John Swanton (1909, 1) credits Katishan for being the informant for many of his Tlingit stories. Nora and Richard Dauenhauer (1990, 134–35) note that his Tlingit name in modern spelling is Kaadashaan.

2. In a wonderful book entitled *Trickster Makes This World*, Lewis Hyde draws on another Raven story told around Sitka in which Raven's trick on Petrel is scatological. In this version, Raven spends the night at Petrel's, and before the morning arrives but while Petrel is sound asleep, Raven "goes outside, takes some dog shit, and smears it on Petrel's buttocks. As the sun rises, Raven cries out, 'Wake up, wake up, my brother, you've shat all over your clothes.' Petrel runs from the lodge to clean himself, whereupon Raven takes the cover from Petrel's spring and begins to drink. As he flies away, water falls from his beak and turns into the great rivers of Alaska and all the little salmon creeks" (1998, 189). Hyde argues that Raven exhibits a shameless preoccupation with "dirt" in order to make a world, not a perfect heavenly world, but a "world of constant need, work, limitation, and death" (27). In a further explanation of trickster's attraction to dirt, Hyde draws on Mary Douglas's two definitions of dirt: as matter out of place and as something so anomalous that it is an abomination (176, 189). The significance of keeping the dirt out—of silencing the shame—is the creation of an order that structures the world. In this sense, tricksters violate the line between the clean and the dirty in order to transform the world.

3. The title of Hinckley's article, "The Canoe Rocks—We Do Not Know What Will Become of Us," is a play off of the third ceremonial speech of Kadashan's contingent of six Tlingit speakers. The Speaker, Chief Koogh-see from Hoonah, is cited by Nora and Richard Dauenhauer (1990, 134–35) as the only one who used figures of speech. The canoe was a metaphor for the Tlingit culture and its subsistence practices, now both of them in doubt. Wendell Oswalt tells us that "the most prominent item manufactured by [Tlingit] men for subsistence activities was the canoe used for fishing and coastal voyages" (1966, 304).

4. In their study of Tlingit oratory, Nora and Richard Dauenhauer emphasize how traditional Tlingit speeches stress the importance of community and the value of

respect, the concept that Tlingit elders cite as most important to an understanding of their culture (1990, xxiii, xxix).

5. Unlike the Presbyterian insistence on English-only for education and religious services, Russian Orthodox priests and educators pursued a bilingual policy. Indeed, the Tlingit language was first rendered in written form for scholarly and community use by Bishop Ioann Veniaminov, who also produced translations in Aleut and Central Yupik (Dauenhauer and Dauenhauer 1987, 39; Krauss 1980, 15–16).

6. While he is not historically specific about the time period in question (the 1800s), economist Steve Colt argues that the Russians may have caused some Alaska Natives some distress over their salmon fishing (2000, 4).

7. Led by Chief Nicolai, an Ahtna Indian legally disqualified from filing mining claims, White prospectors "discovered" three rich copper fields in 1899–1900 in the shadow of the Wrangell Mountains in what is now the Copper River valley. Stephen Birch, a New York City–based mining engineer, organized the Alaska Copper Company and bought the richest of these claims. He realized the prohibitive costs of developing this very pure copper in remote and rugged terrain so he prevailed upon the Guggenheim family, owners of a trust that controlled the country's smelting industry, to organize the Alaska Syndicate. With finance capital from John Pierpont Morgan, the group was formed in 1906. Morgan's bank had financed other interests in Alaska, specifically a holding company, the Northwest Steamship Company and the Pacific Packing and Navigation Company, operators of both salmon canning and transportation companies (Allen 1985; Mitchell 1997, 164–65).

8. Ten years before, in 1888, Brady had been involved in a dispute with Sitka Tlingits over land upon which he wanted to lay a road and construct a sawmill. Nora and Richard Dauenhauer argue that contemporary documents indicate that "Brady personally seized Tlingit land and directed the building of a road through the center of Tlingit burial grounds" (1990, 136). Ted C. Hinckley, Brady's biographer, is less harsh in his assessment, although he does argue that Brady probably unduly overstepped his power as a judge at the time and that Brady did not deny that "two sheds housing cremated bodies did remain on the 'ground'" which he intended to fence (1982, 118).

9. There is some confusion surrounding the date and place of origin of the New Covenant Legion. Donald Mitchell (1997, 194) suggests that it was founded in 1905 at the Sitka Indian village. Drucker does not give an originating date but places it at the Sitka Presbyterian Mission and notes that Tillie Paul was now Tillie Tamaree. Ricketts (in Dauenhauer and Dauenhauer 1994, 493) cites an article in the *North Star* that dates the New Covenant Legion to 1896 and credits the name to Dr. Wilbur, who was associated with the Sitka Industrial Training School. Since Tillie Paul moved from Sitka to Wrangell in 1903 and married William Tamaree in 1905, it seems likely that the organization was begun in 1905, although it may have also had an earlier incarnation. Even though Tillie Paul spent the rest of her life in Wrangell, it is likely that the weekly meetings of the organization were held in Sitka.

While most of Tillie Paul's work on behalf of Presbyterianism was thoroughly assimilationist, she was an important Tlingit leader in her own right. As a fixture at the Sitka Industrial Training School from 1887 to 1903, Tillie (Kah-tli-yudt) often "sympathized with the cultural pain of her students torn between two worlds" and orally translated many of the Tlingit legends for them into English while injecting her own Christian lessons at the end (Goldin 1996). Given what we now know of cultural contestation, many of the students who delighted in hearing Tillie tell these stories may have appropriated these myths as part of their own social and cultural capital. But this was surely not her intent, for, as her biographer puts it, "despite her work of translating into Tlingit, and working on Tlingit grammar analysis, she held herself and her boys [William and Louis] to the ideals set by the missionaries, one of which was that they were not allowed to talk Tlingit" (Ricketts in Dauenhauer and Dauenhauer 1994, 490).

10. William Paul was the recording and financial secretary of the Fishermen's Protective Association in southeast Alaska for a number of years. It was organized by seine fishermen in 1924 (*TAF* May 1926, 5). The purse seine is a large net maneuvered by two boats around a large school of fish like an upside-down purse. A drawstring on the bottom of the net closes off any escape routes for the encircled fish. This mobile fishing gear became more efficient after 1910 when gasoline-powered special purpose purse seiners were launched (Colt 2000, 6).

In fairness to William Paul and to the ANB, their solution to the fishery problem was not elimination of the fish trap and nothing else. In calling for the elimination of the fish trap, they were following a precedent set by British Columbia, which prohibited such devices in its waters. ANB resolutions regarding Alaska fisheries were adopted at every annual Grand Camp and always included a number of conservation-minded provisions. The 1925 convention is a good indicator of some of these plans: after calling for the elimination of the fish trap, the ANB called for thirty-six-hour closings each week to allow for salmon escapement, a prohibitively high tax on nonresident fishermen following the regulations of Washington and Oregon, the prohibition of the use of herring as fertilizer, and, as long as traps were still allowed, it resolved that no trap should be allowed to hold any fish for more than an hour after any closed period (*TAF* April 1926, 7).

11. Alaska Natives had long been calling for conservation and that point was driven home again and again in *TAF*. Perhaps their earliest published calls for conservation appeared in the very first issue of the *Thlinget,* the Sitka Industrial School's successor to the *North Star*. In an August 1908 editorial, the editor inveighed against the fish trap and described its deleterious effects on the Native people. In its January 1909 issue, the editorial—"Natives' View of Fish Traps"—reported the demands of a mass meeting of Sitka Natives whose petition to the Secretary of Commerce and Labor said: "The white man has been given our land and forests. We are not permitted to own land outside of our own crowded villages. Now the government has allowed fish traps to be used near the mouths of salmon streams to take our salmon. In doing this it is taking away our means of making a living. Not only this, but in a few years the traps will destroy the fishing business entirely." While the Natives were protesting the use of all fish traps, their ire was particularly directed at J. R. Heckman's patenting of the mobile fish trap in 1907, a technological improvement on the fixed trap.

12. In an unpublished manuscript, William Paul's son, Fred, provides the following account of his grandmother's assistance to Charley Jones. He writes:

One day in 1922, Gramma ran into an old friend, Charley Jones, who was looking downcast.

"Kah-da-nay-eek," she asked him in Tlingit. "What is the matter?"

"I've just come from the voting place," he replied, "and they won't let me vote."

"Come with me," she said. "We're going right back there to talk with them."

Her old friend . . . born around 1875 . . . could neither read nor write. He was a natural leader, chairman of the Wrangell Federation, and caught up in the Indian movement's determination to become first-class citizens of the United States of America.

. . . Gramma was not intimidated. Dad had instructed members of the Alaska Native Brotherhood and Sisterhood in the rules of legal procedure, and she demanded Charley's right to challenge their decision. He then swore that he was a citizen, and he voted. (Paul 1986, 26)

13. The weekend before the November vote, the *Ketchikan Chronicle* and the *Daily Alaska Empire* ran banner headlines accusing Paul of betraying his Indian followers by taking money from canners. According to Mitchell, Paul was the victim of a political vendetta by Senator Forest J. Hunt, but Paul did admit to taking money under the shaky rationalization that his private legal practice and his political philosophy were separate matters. Despite this weak defense, Paul never wavered in his public opposition to fish traps (*Daily Alaska Empire* November 2, 1928, 1, 8; Mitchell 1997, 220–23).

14. Tlingit elders and historians give William Paul and Peter Simpson credit for the decision to fight for their land and fish, a decision they trace to Simpson's advice to Paul in 1925 that they ought to fight for what was theirs. Paul researched the legal theory of aboriginal title and found Supreme Court legitimacy for the claim in the 1823 case of *Johnson v. M'Intosh* (Paul 1986; Goldin 1996; Dauenhauer and Dauenhauer 1990, 30; 1994, 97). Mitchell gives credit for the land claims suit to Wickersham (1997, 228–31).

On June 19, 1935, President Roosevelt signed the Tlingit and Haida Jurisdictional Act of 1935 allowing the Tlingit and Haida Indians to bring suit in the U.S. Court of Claims. Finally, on October 7, 1959, the court ruled that the Tlingit and Haida Indians were original owners of southeast Alaska. In 1968 they were awarded $7.5 million for lands withdrawn for the Tongass National Forest and Glacier Bay National Monument (Dauenhauer and Dauenhauer 1994, 97–98).

3   Voices of Subsistence in the
Technocratic Wilderness: Alaska Natives
and the *Tundra Times*

THE PURPOSE of this chapter is to examine three critical challenges to the cultural integrity of Alaska Natives in the late 1950s and early 1960s as pivotal episodes in the process of Native resistance to cultural dominance. In particular, we historically situate the fragility of Alaska Native cultures in the face of political, economic, and scientific interests expressed in the mainstream Alaskan press while we foreground the resiliency of indigenous peoples and their cultures as they articulate their resistance in their alternative press. As we have seen thus far, the vulnerability of Alaska Native cultures to foreign penetration and distant federal control was partly rooted in the geographical isolation and ethnic fragmentation of the people. Seven major ethnic groups, each with its own distinct languages, customs, traditions, and physical characteristics, are widely scattered throughout Alaska's 586,000 square miles. The first mass medium to effectively span the distances and bridge the differences that had historically separated Aleuts, Yup'ik and Inupiat Eskimos, and Athabascan, Tlingit, Haida, and Tsimshian Indians was a pan-Native newspaper, the *Tundra Times*. This chapter charts the events leading up to its establishment as an instrument for the definition of common indigenous problems and analyzes its central role in forging a relatively unified indigenous struggle for aboriginal land claims.

In earlier chapters, we documented threats to the physical and cultural well being of Alaska Natives, including the barbarousness of Russian fur traders in the eighteenth century, the paternalistic mentality of Christian missionaries in the nineteenth century, and the rapacious and oligopolistic fishing practices of canneries based in the contiguous forty-eight states in the twentieth century. While these practices followed a familiar model of repression of indigenous peoples elsewhere, the ongoing story of Alaska Native resistance as cultural persistence remains, too often, untold. As Thomas Berger poignantly notes, "the struggle of Native peoples takes place far from the consciousness of most Americans on rural reservations glimpsed from the highways, or, in Alaska, in villages on the edges of the Arctic Ocean, where few White Americans have been—off camera, so to speak" (1985, 156). Native and non-Native contact throughout Alaska's history has usually been punctuated by the latter's exploitation of a singular resource until their extractive processes exhausted the resource's capital returns. In its late territorial years and its early years as a state, Alaska's political and economic leaders were constantly engaged in a quest that would solve the problem of over-dependency on one resource and that would, at the same time, bring more permanent settlers to the region able to secure year-round employment. Two of the three challenges we will examine fall under this quest for a more diversified capitalist political economy. These challenges threatened to bring relatively autonomous indigenous people into contact with scientists and economic developers whose plans would have radically reconfigured traditional Native lands and adversely affected their subsistence economies and cultures.

First, the U.S. Atomic Energy Commission (AEC) planned an experiment (Project Chariot) in excavation and cratering, ostensibly to create a harbor on the northwest coast of Alaska by exploding six atomic bombs equal to 2.4 million tons of TNT, or 120 times the tonnage dropped on Hiroshima (James and Daley 1984, 44; O'Neill 1994, 41). Project Chariot would have forced the relocation of some Inupiat villagers and would have threatened the subsistence practices of many others. Second, from 1959 to 1967, the state's business leaders, its political establishment, and some members of its scientific community advanced a plan to create the world's largest hydroelectric facility at Rampart Canyon in Alaska's northern interior. Rampart Dam would have created a reservoir larger than Lake Erie, would have caused the relocation of seven Native villages and two thousand Athabascan Indians, and would have disturbed the subsistence practices of many other villagers who depended on the land for moose, bear, furbearing animals, wildfowl and fish in the Yukon River and its tributaries. Third, during the transitional period from territorial government to statehood, Alaska Natives' subsistence practices were again threatened when federal responsibilities for game and fish management intensified, severely affecting longstanding Inupiat Eskimo hunting practices. Specifically, the U.S. Fish and Wildlife Service sought to conserve natural resources and enforce treaty obligations by applying rules to Native subsistence hunters that reflected the relationship of White sports hunters to nature: agents began to enforce a previously overlooked seasonal ban on the hunting of migratory birds.

Before turning to the nuclear and hydroelectric engineering projects, the enforcement of game regulatory regimes, and the multifaceted resistance they engendered, we will situate their genesis in the context of Alaska's emergence as an important geopolitical player during World War II and its continued prominence during the cold war period. Given its proximity to Japan, Alaska assumed geopolitical importance during the war. It received billions of dollars in federal expenditures for the establishment of defensive perimeters. The wartime boom also brought an influx of military personnel, many of whom elected to stay after their tours of duty were up. After the war, with Russia's border visible only a few miles away, Alaska's strategic value intensified as the volume of cold war rhetoric escalated. By definition, the cold war was an ideological battle with the press willingly playing its part in heralding technological feats as evidence of American freedom and the superiority of the capitalist system. Given Alaska's strategic location, many of its territorial leaders and some of its more prominent newspaper publishers believed that the political moment to mount a concerted campaign for statehood had finally arrived. In the 1950s, Project Chariot was articulated in the mainstream press as a fitting prelude to statehood, while the plan for Rampart Dam was touted as the economic linchpin of industrial modernization and stability in the immediate aftermath of statehood. Both of them were fundamentally grounded in a clash of cultures that found economic articulation in the hegemony of a postwar capitalist order that sought to reconfigure nature and Alaska Native cultures.

To understand these megaprojects and their infringement on indigenous lives, it is important to recall how mass communication scholarship conceived of the place of the press during this cold war period. Both journalists and media researchers were prone, as Hanno Hardt tells us, "to exhibit a political bias that disregarded the autonomy of cultures and political systems, particularly outside Western models of society" (1998, 143). The ideological rhetoric in Alaska fit within the research model of modernization applied to developing countries, highlighting connections between economic and political decisions as they relate to the cultural institutions of society. In his trenchant critique of such studies, Hardt says that they concentrated on the effects of economic and social change absent a historical context or a culture-specific explanation of such development (144).

In numerous domestic studies of the effects of mass communication on readers and audiences, researchers also adhered to ahistorical paradigms. While they described communication as a social process, their positivistic analyses were nevertheless cast from the standpoint of the intentioning self and the passive recipient. Under this simplistic individualistic model, power and influence were explained as a direct consequence of behavioral influence on decision making (Hall 1982, 59). News and public opinion were understood in terms of a structural-functional model. From this perspective, mass-mediated messages were situated in terms of readjustments to an objective normative order of society. Thus, news was not implicated in structures of power and authority so much as it was seen as blandly reflecting a fairly balanced field of more or less numerous and relatively equal interests. Indeed, in the aftermath of World War II, the normative order of society was firmly ensconced in pluralism as the model of the modern industrial social order. Stuart Hall argues that this essentially American model was so strong that it had a global reach and represented a moment of profound theoretical and political closure. However, as Hall also notes, the presumed "integral and organic consensus did leave certain empirically identifiable groups beyond the pale" (62). Certainly Alaska Natives were among these groups, now, reluctantly thrust into an atomic age. Furthermore, as original inhabitants of the land, Alaska Native groups could not be merely "explained away" as subcultural groups or as deviants who had not yet "made it" in individualistic America. Because the economic order was assumed to be just and fair, its assumptions went unquestioned and challenges to its order made little headway in mainstream news and public opinion formation.

A central argument of this chapter, then, is that, in the years prior to, and just after, the passage of the 1958 statehood act, the mainstream urban press in Alaska served as cheerleaders and agents for a technocratic hegemony. In their boosterism, they tapped into ideological arguments that had strong resonance in American history and that continued to represent the country and the state of Alaska monoculturally, thus rendering indigenous cultures invisible. In light of these conditions, our theoretical analysis of resistance as cultural persistence turns on the critical paradigm in media studies, in particular what Hall calls the rediscovery of the ideological dimension (1982). It is a rediscovery in the sense of its indebtedness to Antonio Gramsci's concept of hegemony. By now, critical communication scholars are well acquainted with the sophistication of Gramsci's explanation from hegemony—how consent is won in modern industrial democracies. His account allows for an understanding of "democratic" social change through restricted kinds of subjectivity. Therefore, we are using the term "hegemony" in the Gramscian sense of effecting a tenuous equilibrium between civil society and political society whereby balance is effected primarily by leadership or direction based on "consent" and, only secondarily, by domination based on coercion in the broadest sense (Gramsci 1971, 12–13, 52–53). For Gramsci, this distinction sorts out problems of culture from those of political power and enables us to see how a cultural institution such as the press can present information—seemingly on its own—to marshal "the objective facts" for the "incontestable forces of progress." Using Hall's articulation and refinement of Gramsci's work, we will show how, in Alaska, a hegemonic process at first succeeded in threatening indigenous cultural and economic ways of life, but then was "forced" to shift as Natives asserted a measure of control over the definitions threatening their cultures and their very lives.

This process was played out in the Alaskan press whenever issues of development offered promises of economic payoff through the quick fixes of scientific, technological, and military expertise. Dissent was managed by appealing to the vaunted technical and scientific knowledge of certified experts. Under the cold war challenges of Sputnik, "missile gaps," and a military-infused space race, cold war rhetoric was not to be taken lightly. This was nowhere truer than in Alaska where the percentage of the population's involvement with the military was the highest in the nation. Scientific claims found easy and ready acceptance under professional journalistic rules of objectivity and impartiality and the privileged position accorded scientists in the journalistic hierarchy of source credibility. In this historical climate, legitimated sources had relatively free rein in a state with such a small population. They could articulate economically shaky schemes as accepted dogma with little threat of challenge to their interpretations. Indeed, in rural Alaska where most Natives lived, even the most conventional forms of exchange and argumentation were difficult in the communications environment of the 1950s and 1960s. There was no access to television signals, little telephone service, and highly unreliable communication via high frequency radio. For the most part, communication and transportation were synonymous, for communication between villages depended on transportation by bush plane, by snowmobiles, and by boats.

Alaska's 1960 census—its first as a state—documented a population of 226,167, of whom about 40,000 were counted among the seven Alaska Native groups. More than 85 percent of Alaska Natives lived in rural areas and many of them were actively engaged in subsistence activities. In fact, most of Alaska's population was classified as rural. Of its total population only 38 percent—85,767 residents—lived in five urban areas with populations in excess of 2,500. By 1962 each of these five cities had daily newspapers. The two largest cities, Anchorage and Fairbanks, comprised 85 percent of the state's urban population. The other three cities with dailies were all in southeast Alaska—Juneau, Ketchikan, and Sitka. In the post–World War II era, the two most influential newspapers were the *Fairbanks Daily News-Miner* and the *Anchorage Daily Times,* having supplanted the once dominant *Alaska Daily Empire* published in the capital city of Juneau. Both of these newspapers had relatively long histories by Alaska standards. The *News-Miner* was established in 1903 while the *Anchorage Daily Times,* the state's largest newspaper in 1962, had begun publication in 1915. Both papers were financially successful and both were strong supporters of the statehood movement in the 1950s. Robert Atwood, publisher of the *Anchorage Daily Times,* was a two-time president of the state chamber of commerce in the 1940s and was chairman of the Alaskan Statehood Committee from 1949 to 1959. Atwood was one of the early promoters of both Project Chariot and Rampart Dam. C. W. Snedden took over as publisher of the *Fairbanks Daily News-Miner* in 1950 from Cap Lathrop and carried on a six-year campaign for statehood. Like Atwood, he too was involved in the upper echelons of the state's chamber of commerce. Snedden's paper became a strong editorial voice for Project Chariot. In 1963, Snedden served as the first president of Yukon Power for America (YPA), a private promotional group formed to win state and congressional support for Rampart Dam (Alaska Blue Book 1963, 33–34, 48).

Project Chariot and the Mainstream Press in Alaska

The story of Project Chariot began in 1954, when Congress authorized the Plowshare Program, a plan to seek peaceful uses for atomic energy by extending the AEC's control over atomic weaponry to the realm of domestic experimentation. In its enabling legislation (*Atomic Energy Act of 1954,* 42 U.S. C. section 2011), Congress declared that atomic energy should be developed "to promote world peace, improve the general welfare, increase the standard of living and strengthen free competition in private enterprise." Even before this act, the cold war climate had nourished the AEC's autonomy, heightened its ethos of scientific legitimation, and insulated it from accountability. This autonomy, legitimation, and insulation was born of necessity with the World War II Manhattan Project, but it was furthered by the Atomic Energy Act of 1946, which declared an entire body of knowledge secret (Demac 1990, 93).

In his history of the Manhattan Project's atomic scientists, Robert Jungk captures the extension and expansion of this scientific ethos well: "The atomic scientists had become important people. That was their first discovery when they returned from their laboratories to the world at large. 'Before the war we were supposed to be completely ignorant of the world and inexperienced in its ways. But now we were regarded as the ultimate authorities on all possible subjects from nylon stockings to the best form of international organization,' one of them remarked with mildly ironic self detachment" (1958, 236). National security concerns thus resulted in the growth in power of governmental technocrats. Because the subject of atomic/nuclear energy is complex and technical, a seemingly natural trend developed: "to leave complex problems to the experts, the Atomic Energy Commission, and the President's scientific advisors" (Kreith and Wrenn 1976, 4).

While the cold war atmosphere insulated the AEC's decision making from public scrutiny, it was equally beneficial to the growth of Alaska's economy and population. Until the postwar period, Alaska's efforts toward political recognition had gone unrewarded, in part because of the territory's small population. As the nation's first line of defense against the Japanese, Alaska's military population had mushroomed during the war. During the 1950s, a second military building boom brought millions of dollars worth of projects to Alaska for air defense and warning installations for the North American continent, the Distant Early Warning System or DEW Line. Alaska's population in 1955 was estimated at 209,000, one-quarter of which was connected with the military (Alaska Territorial Resource Development Board 1955, 2).

The announcement of Project Chariot preceded congressional passage of statehood on June 30, 1958, by three weeks. The *Anchorage Daily Times* and the *Fairbanks Daily News-Miner* ran the same Associated Press (AP) story on June 9, datelined Washington, D.C., announcing AEC plans to use atomic blasts to dig a harbor between Cape Seppings and Cape Thompson north of the Arctic Circle in northwest Alaska. Underground and surface atomic explosions had been a priority of the Plowshare Program from its inception. Edward Teller, the father of the hydrogen bomb and the moving force behind Project Chariot, has recounted how the 1956 Egyptian blockade of the Suez Canal precipitated a meeting of scientists at the Lawrence Radiation Laboratory to discuss the possibility of cutting another canal through friendly territory with nuclear explosives. Whether Project Chariot was a direct outcome of those talks is unclear, but it was on the drawing board just a few months later (see Teller, Talley, Higgins, and Johnson 1968).

One thing was clear: even though Alaska was a remote area with a small population, the experiment would have to be "sold" to the resident population. In early explanations of the value of Project Chariot to Alaskans, the AEC's selling point was the creation of a harbor. According to the AEC, the harbor would facilitate the development of potentially lucrative mining and fishing industries by providing nearby transportation facilities. No mention was made of the transportation difficulties posed by ice for more than half the year in the waters above the Arctic Circle. During the AEC's process of site selection, no commission member had actually visited Alaska. The initial AP story ended with a statement of support from Alaska territorial delegate Bob Bartlett (soon-to-be Senator) who described the proposal as "inspiring and dramatic and useful." Bartlett added that AEC officials had assured him that "the most careful studies will be made to preclude the possibility of danger to anyone or anything."

Articulated by elite scientific and political sources, the news story framed a narrative of general economic promise with a politically legitimated salute to the aura of technology, thus reiterating a salient theme in Alaska's historic economic cycles of boom and bust. In their informed account of the nature of media discourse on nuclear power, sociologists William Gamson and Andre Modigliani refer to the news media's employment of what they call a progress package whereby issues of nuclear power tend to be framed in terms of the nation's commitment to technological development and economic growth (1989, 2). While Project Chariot was not about the nuclear power industry, its news coverage in Alaska was framed in terms of this "progress package." In the context of Alaska's economic past, the AP story and other early press accounts of the project masked particular interests by asserting the apparent general interest in jobs and the requisite populational stability those jobs would guarantee for the new state. Ruling bureaucrats and mainstream journalists, Hall maintains, share such background assumptions— that no major political and economic discrepancies exist and that all disagreements can be solved through legitimate institutional means. However, the most salient aspect of this complex story is that the purported consensus is itself the social product of a structured relationship between the media and the dominant bureaucracies. As Hall puts it, "the structured relationship . . . permits the institutional definers to establish the initial definition or *primary interpretation* of the topic in question" (1978, 56). Alaska Natives were not only far from these institutional definers in a purely geographical sense, but also, even more important, vast cultural chasms separated them from Alaska's symbolic and material movers and shakers.

Editorially, the *Anchorage Daily Times* lauded Alaska's steps into both the missile age and the nuclear age. With perverse optimism, the paper maintained, on June 14, 1958, that the missile defense systems confirm the argument that "military construction will remain Alaska's main industry from now until the next war." To use Hall's term, the paper seemed to go beyond the editorial "we" to "tak[e] the public voice" (1978, 63). As we noted previously, both newspapers had been staunch supporters of statehood and tended to greet events promising jobs and economic progress with uncritical applause. Alaska Natives had been much more equivocal about statehood since the act specified the state's right to take 103 million acres of land to ensure it an economic base while the Natives continued to struggle to resolve their aboriginal land rights—still on hold ninety-one years after the Treaty of Cession with Russia had been signed (McBeath and Morehouse 1994, 79).

Just a few weeks after the Project Chariot announcement, the *Fairbanks Daily News-Miner*'s enthusiastic endorsement of the project set the tone for its ensuing coverage. In an editorial on July 24, 1958, the paper proselytized: "We think the holding of a huge nuclear blast in Alaska would be a fitting overture to the new era which is opening for our state." The newspaper's editorial writer was George Sundborg, soon to be Senator Gruening's administrative assistant and chief promoter of Rampart Dam (O'Neill 1994, 37). The battle for the control of Alaskan hearts and minds was on.

To that end, Edward Teller, director of the Lawrence Radiation Laboratory, which was then under AEC contract, led a contingent of scientists and AEC officials to the state in July 1958 to drum up the needed support in Alaska's urban centers. The movers and shakers in these audiences were assured that two-thirds of the $5 million earmarked for the project would land in Alaska (Brooks and Foote 1962, 64). Teller's sales effort not only resonated with the accredited status accorded scientific authorities in 1950s America, but it also allowed the AEC to define the project on grounds of economic legitimation, practically guaranteeing that Alaska's booster press would frame the story on his terms. As Hall notes, there is a [big] "difference between those accredited witnesses and spokesmen who [have] had a privileged access, as of right, to the world of public discourse and whose statements carried the representativeness and authority which permitted them to establish the primary framework or terms of an argument; as contrasted with those who [have] had to struggle to gain access to the world of public discourse at all; whose 'definitions' were always more partial, fragmentary, and delegitimated" (1982, 81).

Those people who would be most affected by the proposed blast were left out of the public relations equation—to paraphrase Berger, they were out of sight and out of mind. Thus, Point Hope Inupiat Eskimos learned of survey-ors in the Ogotoruk Creek area in the summer of 1958 only because of chance encounters by subsistence hunting parties. Point Hope Village Council Pres-ident Daniel Lisbourne and his nephew, Peniluke Omnik, stumbled upon AEC tents and investigators when they were caribou hunting near the mouth of Ogotoruk Creek in August of 1958 (Morgan 1988, 164; O'Neill, 1994, 29–30). According to Don Charles Foote, a human geographer under indepen-dent contract to the AEC's Project Chariot, the first details of the plan were briefly presented to Point Hope residents by a Kotzebue missionary in April of 1959. As Foote notes, "The concept of Project Chariot held by Point Hope residents in Autumn 1959 was a mixture of hearsay derived from numerous mainstream newspaper reports of informal lectures delivered by AEC offi-cials throughout Alaska during the preceding year" (Foote 1961). A team of scientists did visit the Inupiat villages of Kivalina and Point Hope in Septem-ber 1959. However, their purpose was to interview hunters about the use of marine mammals and caribou, not to provide information to the villagers (Arctic Health Research Center 1959).

Obviously without adequate information and explanation, Inupiat Es-kimos could hardly mount an effective protest let alone make their voices heard in public arenas. But even while the Inupiat were relatively silent, the enthusiastic response of the Alaskan press did not meet with unequivocal support. One reason for public equivocation over Project Chariot was the shaky factual ground on which the AEC built its public relations case. Two independent reports produced for the AEC in 1958 indicated that the pro-posed harbor would be ice-locked for nine months each year and that ex-tensive mineral deposits could not be tapped for twenty-five years (Brooks and Foote 1962, 64).

Logistical problems as well as wavering public opinion forced the AEC back to the drawing board. However, it returned with renewed vigor and a scaled-down program in January 1959. Instead of a harbor excavation project, the blast was to be an experiment to test the theory that nuclear explosives buried at specified depths "will produce a crater and, at the same time, trap a significant amount of the total radioactivity below ground" (*ACS News Bulletin* March 1961). The size of the blast was also reduced to one-fifth of its original tonnage.

A new public relations campaign in early 1959 complemented these sci-entific changes. Scientists toured the state, warning the public that the suc-cess of Project Chariot hinged on legislative approval and chamber of com-

merce backing. Again, the aim here was to enlist widespread support in order to pass off particular interests as the general interest. These public relations tours genuinely allowed the media coverage to remain "impartial" while
still carrying out the AEC's ideological work as source attributions remained
confined to a tight circle of supportive legislators and Project Chariot promoters. As Hall writes, "the 'impartiality' of the media thus requires the
mediation of the state [the legislature]—that set of processes through which
particular interests become generalized, and, having secured the consent of
'the nation' [in this case, the state's governing apparatus], carry the stamp
of legitimacy" (1982, 87).

In response to the AEC public relations efforts, newspaper publishers and
editors began urging their readers to write positive letters on the project's
behalf to their chambers of commerce (Brooks and Foote 1962, 65). By March,
both the Fairbanks Chamber of Commerce and the Alaskan legislature had
lent their endorsements. And yet, the public discourse concerning Project
Chariot was still enmeshed in a relatively complex field of competing interests. One competing definition of the situation that vied for hegemonic control was the Sierra Club's environmentally conscious public opposition announced in March of 1959 (Atomic Energy Commission, Project Chariot
Collection). Another dissenting voice came from Alaska U.S. Senator Bob
Bartlett, who expressed misgivings during the AEC's volte-face from economic to scientific motives. In fact, economic and scientific incentives often beck-
oned in tandem, or at least tottered on an uneasy ethical tightrope, as governmental grants and contracts for environmental studies were awarded. But
a number of principled scientists who stood to profit personally and profes-
sionally from a successful Project Chariot began to cast a jaundiced eye. Al-
bert W. Johnson, a University of Alaska botanist who would later conduct
studies in conjunction with the project, expressed concern, in a letter to the
Fairbanks Daily News-Miner on January 13, 1959, over what he perceived to
be heavily biased representations of the AEC position. Johnson cautioned that
"glowing accounts of future financial benefit to Alaskans seem to provide
sufficient justification for everyone to jump on the atomic bandwagon."
Later, Don Foote, the outspoken human geographer who had befriended
Point Hope residents, would not have his AEC contract renewed, and University of Alaska-Fairbanks biologists William Pruitt and Leslie Viereck would
be given terminal contracts from the university for their critical remarks of
the AEC's environmental statements.[1]

Meanwhile, as the Project Chariot story moved into the summer of 1959,
the press began to couple its litany of multiplying economic benefits with a

minimization of threats associated with atomic blasts. Using a figure that would be revised downward later in the summer, Teller was quoted in the *Fairbanks Daily News-Miner,* saying that the amount of radiation leakage would be as little as 20 percent, perhaps much less (June 30, 1959). To the technically unsophisticated reader, 20 percent might have seemed a low figure, but even by nuclear venting standards at the time, this was a significant amount of radioactive fallout. In a story in the *Anchorage Daily Times* on June 26, Teller was asked to comment on a Russian accusation that Chariot was really a weapons test. He answered that "very serious considerations [would be given] to shooting at such a time when the wind is blowing inland so that what little radiation there is will land on the snow and ice." While these remarks seemed calculated to ease cold war tensions at best, and perhaps flippant when considered in the context of villagers' lives, Teller was quite serious, for the AEC was interested in tracing the movement of the fallout and that was best accomplished on land (O'Neill 1994, 154–64). Eighteen months after Teller's answer, the AEC's Committee on Environmental Studies issued a report in which it noted that in fall, winter, and spring, Point Hope Natives depend on snow and ice for drinking water both at home and during subsistence hunting excursions (AEC Environmental Studies 1960).

Despite the AEC's acknowledgment that a harbor was no longer in its plans, the Alaskan press continued to report the Chariot story as if nothing had changed. Both the *Fairbanks Daily News-Miner* and the *Anchorage Daily Times* lavished acclaim on the project and on AEC scientists. In their unwavering praise for these experts, they dismissed the questions of ordinary citizens as unreasonable and unwarranted, further closing off the public sphere from legitimate dissent.

Early in March of 1960 a small contingent of AEC officials, including its chief public relations officer, visited Point Hope in an attempt to allay villagers' fears. This visit was prompted by pointed requests from Senator Bartlett and a few Alaska legislators. For the first time, Point Hope villagers were able to ask their own questions. Posing questions in both Inupiaq and English, the villagers sought firm confirmation or denial of the hearsay that had drifted their way (Brooks and Foote 1962, 67).[2] Don Foote's report, issued a little over a year after the meeting, indicates that the answers the officials gave were what we would generously call public relations spin today, but perhaps a more apt characterization would be outright duplicity. For instance, they said "that the fish in and around the Pacific Proving Grounds were not made radioactive by nuclear weapons tests and did not show anything that was considered of any danger to anyone if the fish were utilized; that the effects of nuclear weapons testing never injured any people anywhere; that once the severely exposed Japanese people recovered from radiation sickness, after the World War II atomic bombs, there were no after effects; that the residents of Point Hope would not feel any seismic shock at all from Project Chariot" (Foote 1961, 9). A nuclear accident in the Pacific in 1954 had been widely covered by the popular press, including *Life* magazine (O'Neill 1994, 137). During a nuclear detonation conducted by the United States, a sudden wind shift had caused nuclear ash to maim and burn the crew of a Japanese fishing vessel (Lukacs 1966, 152). Despite the Commission's artifice, its visit to Point Hope fooled no one. The Point Hope Village Council wasted no time in rejecting Project Chariot. On behalf of the village's 290 citizens, council members sent a letter of protest to President Kennedy, expressing their stern objections to the proposed blast and its potential destruction of their hunting and fishing areas (see figures 4, 5, and 6).

After the March meeting, the AEC clearly realized that its problems were not just technical but political as well. The "attitudinal problem" of villag-

Figure 4. Daniel Lisbourne's team of Point Hope Inupiat Eskimos land a bowhead whale in May 1961. Lisbourne was Point Hope Village Council President when his people learned about the dangers of Project Chariot to their traditional subsistence whaling practices. (Don Foote Collection, Box 56, University of Alaska Fairbanks, Archives)

Figure 5. Alan Rock's team of Point Hope Inupiat Eskimos butcher a bowhead
whale in May 1961. While brothers Howard and Alan Rock were united in their
opposition to Project Chariot, their personal relationship was more equivocal.
(Don Foote Collection, Box 56, University of Alaska Fairbanks, Archives)

ers was discussed in an environmental report on marine biological observations conducted in April 1960: "Of some concern to us was the village antagonism against the Atomic Energy Commission as representing to them a
poorly understood activity at Cape Thompson, their traditional trailing and
hunting grounds. This attitude of the villagers was reflected in their poor
cooperation in our initial attempt to buy specimens of [caribou] skulls for
age and sex ratio studies" (Arctic Health Research Center 1960, 11–12).

As the summer heated up, the press intensified its coverage, lavishing
kudos on those Project Chariot supporters with prestigious professional la-
bels and hurling brickbats at a growing group of opponents. Ad hominem
arguments abounded as the press fine-tuned its well-ingrained booster mentality. On August 15, 1960, *Jessen's Weekly,* Fairbanks's number two newspaper, admitted some unidentified criticism of the program but quickly added that it had come from misinformed people and that only the AEC's
environmental studies committee could make the final evaluation. This same
story nicely framed the quotations of an "eminent scientist"—John Wolfe,
the environmental committee's chief—who gave his assurances that the det-

Figure 6. Fallout from Project Chariot would have threatened the safety of such traditional ice-fishing practices as those exemplified by this Inupiat Eskimo in northwestern Alaska. (Accession number UA70-25-8N, Vertical File, University of Alaska Fairbanks, Archives)

onations would be no threat to human or animal life, now or in the future. Symbolically thumbing its nose at the opposition, the newspaper's editor, Albro Gregory, an outspoken and self-described Alaskan booster, added, "And he should know." Editorial comments such as this one bear out Hall's contention that, in the mainstream press, the "expert" is an "accredited source" whose calling—the disinterested pursuit of knowledge—is sufficient rationale to certify the "objectivity" of his or her statements (1978, 58). Unfortunately, the AEC's longstanding compartmentalization of knowledge, together with its unprecedented practices of secrecy, put the lie to the scientific tradition of the disinterested pursuit of knowledge in the Project Chariot case. In furthering the power of expertise to lay claim to the definition of the situation, *Jessen's Weekly* resorted to trivialization and comedy in order to buttress its certitude. It quoted Wolfe, saying that a rock might hit a caribou in the head, and it cited another scientist who declared that it was silly to talk about whales being killed. *Jessen's Weekly* directed one more salvo at skeptics, quoting Dr. William R. Wood, new president of the University of Alaska-Fairbanks and a witness to many tests in Nevada, who disarmingly said, "If the United States Government decides that the project is a safe one, there is no reason for concern" (August 15, 1960).

Nationally, the *New York Times* ran a similar news story growing out of the same press conference from which Gregory had generated his copy. The *Times's* reporter, Lawrence Davies, framed the story with assurances from the AEC that this was a medically and environmentally safe project. Davies added that "the Arctic was chosen for its nearly primeval conditions, where the Eskimo does little to disturb the balance of nature and where the human population is sparse." Despite widespread opposition from Point Hope villagers, the *Times* offered readers a "balanced" account, including an acknowledgment that the vice president of the Village Council was on the AEC payroll. Finally, Davies concluded his story with a quote from an AEC radiation biologist who doubted that "'a single fish or other sea organism [would] be killed by radiation'" (*New York Times* August 17, 1960).

Despite these assurances, the shaky ground on which Project Chariot stood shifted some more with the aforementioned defections from its contractual ranks. On December 29, 1960, Leslie Viereck, a recently hired University of Alaska biologist and Project Chariot contract employee, removed himself from the staff, writing in the *Alaska Conservation Society News Bulletin:* "At the time [I took the position as botanist with Project Chariot], I felt the study would be purely biological in nature and would in no way become involved in the politics of the AEC. Subsequent events have shown that this is not to be the case, and the situation has now reached the point where I can no longer maintain my personal and scientific integrity and work for the AEC projects" (March 1961). Viereck had undoubtedly misjudged Teller's already legendary reputation as one who was willing to flex his own political muscle to move forward one of his pet scientific endeavors. Viereck's employment at the University of Alaska had been funded in part through AEC grant money so this principled move precipitated his dismissal from the University (O'Neill 1994, 179–83). Viereck was soon joined by William Pruitt and Don Foote, two other environmentally oriented scientists with AEC contracts. Pruitt was fired by the University of Alaska on January 22, 1962, while Foote's contract with the AEC was not renewed when it ran out on May 31, 1961. All were members of the Alaska Conservation Society, an organization started in Fairbanks in 1960 (see O'Neill 1994, 190–205).

By 1961 a rising chorus of national opposition was audible. The *National*

Wildlife News, a monthly conservation publication, devoted its February editorial to the potential hazards of Project Chariot. The Sierra Club Bulletin reprinted the entire March Chariot-related issue of the *Alaska Conservation Society News Bulletin* in its May issue. And in its Sunday, June 4 edition, the *New York Times* reported the devastating caveats of the Committee for Nuclear Information (CNI), a St. Louis organization led by Barry Commoner, who would later be one of the leaders of the environmental movement. The CNI was composed of scientists and lay people and founded in 1958 to promote public understanding and knowledge of nuclear problems. Summarizing and interpolating mostly previously unpublished studies by University of Alaska biologists and botanists, CNI established that tundra lichens obtain their mineral nourishment from dust carried by rain, snow, and winds, thus making them particularly susceptible to radioactive fallout. Caribou, in turn, feed heavily on lichens, and the Inupiat Eskimos on caribou, completing a food chain that could produce a high concentration of strontium-90 in Inupiat Eskimos' bones. Although the *New York Times* lead framed the story in cautionary terms, it nevertheless was quite clear about the food chain evidence provided by the CNI's synthesis of University of Alaska researchers' studies and it labeled the findings "unexpected difficulties" for the AEC's plans (June 4, 1961, 63).

While AEC press releases still tried to work their legerdemain, the nuclear cards were on the table. Politicized reports were exposed, and even the laudatory incantations of the Alaskan press were subsiding. Most notably, the *Fairbanks Daily New-Miner,* under the byline of Thomas Snapp, began a four-part series on Project Chariot in August 1961, reversing that paper's more than three-year-long congratulatory coverage of the proposed project. Snapp had scrutinized the *News-Miner's* files on Project Chariot and found stories noticeably lacking in the views of Alaska Natives and in the strong reservations voiced against the project by University of Alaska professors. Snapp's exposés were written with material supplied by the Alaska Conservation Society and with letters and interviews from the Point Hope people. Snapp noted that when the second article appeared, a representative of a firm selling supplies to the AEC flew to Fairbanks and tried to get the series stopped (Snapp 1962). While Snapp's disclosures were far from scoops, they nevertheless served to establish his credibility among Inupiat Eskimos.

Eider Ducks and the Migratory Bird Treaty Act

Meanwhile, another subsistence-oriented conflict was set in motion by a regulatory decision of the federal government in one of Point Hope's sister whaling communities, the farthest northern community in the country, Point Barrow. The dispute erupted in May 1961, when U.S. Fish and Wildlife Service agent Harry Pinkham arrested Barrow Natives Tom Pikok and John Nusunginya, a state representative, for taking eider ducks out of season. The arrests were based on a 1916 Migratory Bird Treaty Act with Canada and Mexico, restricting the season on certain migratory birds to the period between September 1 and March 1. An Alaska Game Law enacted in 1925 had given Natives the right to hunt ducks for subsistence purposes and had affirmed that these rights were within the provisions of the Migratory Bird Treaty Act. However, the 1925 law was fraught with ambiguity, apparently guaranteeing Alaska Natives the rights to take ducks only if there were no alternatives available and food needs were critical. To ameliorate this ambiguity, Congress softened the rigidity of the previous interpretation by inserting a clause saying that Natives had the right to take ducks for subsistence purposes when "other sufficient food is not available." Further complications arose in 1944 when the newly created U.S. Fish and Wildlife Service instituted a regulation banning subsistence harvests (Ross 2000, 32).

Prior to these arrests, however, federal wildlife agents had exercised considerable tolerance for Native subsistence practices, recognizing the differences between sport hunters and Native subsistence hunters. Inupiat Eskimo hunters were always careful to avoid taking eider ducks that were about to nest, thus complying with the spirit of the conservation laws. In essence, the enforcement of this ban meant that Alaska Native subsistence hunters were allowed to hunt the ducks only at a time when they had already migrated to southern climes.

Within a day or so of the arrests, 138 Inupiat Eskimos delivered eider ducks to game wardens staying at the Top of the World Hotel and signed statements admitting their civil disobedience. The evidence filled nine sacks and totaled 600 pounds (*Indian Affairs,* "The Challenge of Alaska," July 1961). The conflict turned on aboriginal hunting rights and the restricted diet that a subsistence economy sometimes imposes upon its practitioners in the sensitive environment of the Arctic north. Each year, the long, harsh winter depleted Inupiat Eskimo food caches, so the return of the ducks in the spring represented an opportunity to replenish the larder with a welcome break from the monotony of winter staples. Because eider ducks fly low to the ground, they had been a prized quarry for centuries, well before the use of guns.

Not only did the law defy centuries-old practices, its enforcement also overlooked the fact that the culturally and geographically isolated Inupiat Eskimos had few opportunities to learn about the changes in enforcement practices. Their frustration was poignantly illustrated by Point Barrow Eskimo Guy Okakok's letter appealing for aid to LaVerne Madigan, executive director of the Association on American Indian Affairs (AAIA): "We just had a meeting yesterday in school, right after evening service. We discuss about our ducks, eider ducks and Pacific. We did not know that we can't shoot ducks when they come through our shore. Anyway, please come so I can let you know everything. It's a long story. One native up at inland along the river bank was taken prisoner. Warden took all the geese he shot. Our country here don't compare to their countries southside. I mean the climate. Oh, I wish I'd tell you everything" (*Indian Affairs*, "US Treaty Threatens Native Hunting Pattern," July 1961). The sentiments expressed by Okakok were widely shared in a state where many resident non-Natives placed a high premium on individual rights and where historical resentment against "outside" governmental interference remained strong. Important political leaders quickly voiced their support for the Natives' position and appealed to the secretary of the interior, Stewart Udall, for a positive resolution to the conflict. Typical of such political remonstrances was Congressman Ralph J. Rivers's written plea to Udall: "Continuance of such tolerance for so many years also took into account that Eskimo hunters are so few in number as to do no appreciable harm to the migratory bird resource . . . although such birds have been killed by the tens of thousands each year by licensed hunters in Canada, the United States, and Mexico" (*Indian Affairs* July 1961). Governor William Egan was also frequently quoted in the mainstream press, venting his outrage at federal agents for enforcing this law and harming Native aboriginal rights. While it is not clear why federal agents began flexing their regulatory muscle, the impetus to do so probably arose from a dispute between new state agents and federal agents over whose policing powers were to prevail.

To counter this violation of their aboriginal rights, Point Barrow Natives followed the lead of their Point Hope cousins by sending a petition of grievance with three hundred signatures to President Kennedy (*Anchorage Daily Times* May 31, 1961). Inupiat Eskimo culture—once defended by remoteness—was suddenly trapped between the Scylla of antisubsistence and the Charybdis of nuclear bombs. While Inupiat Eskimos found themselves thrust into the atomic age and confronted by alien regulatory regimes, they were not about to let their independence of spirit slip away. In this farthest northern community in the United States, resistance as cultural persistence was about to begin.

The Kennedy administration was unmoved by the Inupiat Eskimos' appeals, apparently hamstrung by international treaty obligations. In a news conference in Seattle in early June, Interior Secretary Stewart Udall said, "'It is hard to see how we can wink at law violations,' and if the Eskimos are 'to get special consideration, it must be done by law'" (*Anchorage Daily Times* June 10, 1961). However, in response to the pleas for assistance from Point Hope's Frankson and Point Barrow's Okakok, the AAIA sent Madigan and Henry Forbes, chairman of its Committee on Alaska, to meet with the Natives. One of the attendees of the meeting in Point Hope was Howard Rock (Sikvoan Weyahok).

Rock had just returned to Point Hope from Seattle where, except for a stint in the Army Air Corps during World War II, he had spent the better part of the past two decades. Although he had family in Point Hope and the financial means to visit them, this was Rock's first visit to his family since 1948 when his brother angrily called him a tanik, an epithet for a White man, for having deserted his family (Daley and O'Neill 1993, 264). While in Seattle, Rock had taken art classes at the University of Washington and supported himself by selling drawings, paintings, and scrimshaw. But he had tired of the cookie-cutter aspect of his artwork and spent much of his time drinking. When he returned to Point Hope in 1961, Rock was depressed over his dependence on alcohol. He intended to make peace with his family and then walk out to the sea as an honorable way to die (Morgan 1988, 158). However, he found that his Native villagers were in a collective state of despair over Project Chariot.

Point Hope was a close-knit Inupiat community and many of the villagers who attended the meeting with Madigan and Forbes had not embraced Rock's return. Sharing his brother's views, they considered him an outsider and chided him for having forgotten much of his Native language. Rock's lengthy absence had severed the intimate connections indigenous peoples make between culture, place, and identity—those shared meanings so important to the social cohesiveness of indigenous communities. They too questioned whether he was a tanik or an Inupiat. Rock was, as William Paul had been before him, a man "in-between" cultures. Years later, to paraphrase Stuart Hall (1995, 206), Rock's ability to inhabit more than one identity and to have more than one home would stand him in good stead as he would use these identities to help Alaska Natives negotiate a pan-Native land movement through the *Tundra Times*. But, for now, Rock just listened. He was careful to speak only when the opportunity presented itself. He suggested that there was strength in numbers and therefore the Point Hope villagers should develop some means of communication—tape recordings or a newsletter—to inform other villages about the imminent dangers from the AEC plans. Even though Rock had kept a low profile at the meeting, Forbes and Madigan had been impressed by him. Because of his proficiency in English, Point Hope villagers asked him to write a letter to Interior Secretary Udall, requesting revocation of the Bureau of Land Management's withdrawal of 1,600 square miles of land for AEC use in Project Chariot (Daley and O'Neill 1993, 267).

As a result of the Point Hope meeting and other village meetings conducted by Madigan and Forbes, the AAIA decided to sponsor a conference on Native rights in Barrow in fall 1961. To ensure wide representation and participation, Okakok and Madigan spent a month in late summer flying from village to village lining up delegates. At a preconference planning session, village leaders formally extended invitations to Assistant Interior Secretary John Carver and Indian Commissioner Philleo Nash, both of whom accepted.

Inupiat Paitot and the Tundra Times

The Inupiat Paitot, as their meeting was called, convened on November 17, 1961. The name Inupiat Paitot refers to the People's heritage, that is, their aboriginal rights to inherit the land and minerals of their ancestors and the right to hunt and fish without restriction. While the Inupiat Eskimos had a long tradition of intervillage meetings for trade and celebration, this historic occasion marked their first large political gathering. In a moving policy statement, Inupiat Eskimos from many villages recognized their common predicament:

> People have thought that we did not have problems because we did not say something. But when we came together, we found that we Inupiat all share the same problems. Our problems are two kinds: Aboriginal land and hunting rights. Economic and social development.
>
> The rights of us Inupiat have never been explained truthfully and properly to us, which we Inupiat were entitled to understand. We were told that if the government reserved our aboriginal land for us, we could not be citizens of the United States—could not vote—would be tied on reservation like a dog—could not have businesses come on our land or sell products of our land.
>
> That was a lie told to us Inupiat to take away our aboriginal land and mineral rights. Talking at this meeting, about what we were told about aboriginal rights and reservations, we found that each one of our villages were told

the same lies. But we never knew that, because we never had a chance to talk
to each other. (Inupiat Paitot November 17, 1961)

The amazing consistency in stories told by fellow villagers suggested that they
had been the targets of a systematic propaganda campaign dating back to the
1930s. With statehood a fait accompli and still no congressional resolution
of their land and hunting rights, two hundred Native attendees from twenty
villages resolved that a united voice was needed to counter propaganda and
to facilitate communication.

In addition to the AAIA's LaVerne Madigan, three other non-Native persons attended the conference: the aforementioned Carver and Nash, and
Thomas Snapp, the *Fairbanks Daily News-Miner* reporter who had covered
the eider duck controversy in the spring, and Project Chariot in August, from
a Native and environmental perspective. Snapp said that he was sent to cover the conference at the insistence of attorney Ted Stevens who visited the
News-Miner offices one week before the conference and prevailed upon his
friend—publisher Snedden—to send a reporter to Barrow. Stevens, a solic-
itor in the Interior Department during the Eisenhower administration, had
been doing pro bono work on land claims for Athabascan Indians in the
state's interior (Snapp 1962).

While he was at the conference, Snapp roomed with Rock, whom he had
met earlier that fall in Fairbanks. Using his less than stellar command of Inupiaq, the Inupiat language, Rock did his best to translate the conference
proceedings into English for Snapp. In a 1983 interview, Snapp told us that
he kept hearing his name and Rock's but he had no idea what was being said.
Snapp was amazed to learn that he and Rock were being appointed to explore the establishment of a newspaper to cover Eskimo issues. As a reporter for an established newspaper that included the northern half of Alaska in
its beat, Snapp knew what a gargantuan task it would be to cover issues per-
taining to a landmass greater than the size of Texas. Nevertheless, in March
1962, Rock, Madigan, and Snapp met in Fairbanks to name the paper, to figure
out how to finance it, and to set a date for its start. They decided to publish
a weekly paper called the *Inupiat Okatut,* meaning "The Eskimos Speak," and
set May 1962 as the date of its inaugural issue. They planned to feature a story on Project Chariot (Snapp 1962, 1983).

However, even before their March meeting, Rock had been thinking that
the newspaper's mission had to embrace land claims for all the indigenous
groups in the state, not just the Inupiat Eskimos. Rock, Snapp, and a few

others sympathetic to Native rights had formed a Native Rights Association headquartered in Fairbanks, and they began laying the groundwork for a conference of Athabascan Indians, who were widely scattered in villages in Alaska's huge interior. Madigan urged them to orient the proposed newspaper to Athabascans as well. Planning for this conference delayed the publication's debut (Snapp 1962).

Rock, Snapp, and Alfred Ketzler, an Athabascan from Tanana—a village situated at the confluence of the Yukon and Tanana rivers—worked tirelessly to raise the funds to bring delegates to a meeting of Athabascan leaders, the first such meeting since the Tanana Chiefs Conference of 1915.[3] Originally the conference was to have been held in early June to coincide with the revival of the Nuch-lo-woh-ya, an Athabascan cultural festival that had been dormant for forty years. However, an Interior Department task force on Native affairs requested that the meeting be moved back three weeks so that agency officials scheduled to be in the state at that time could interview the participants. Thus, the conference was convened for June 24 at Tanana, the traditional meeting ground of the Athabascans.

The name chosen by the Athabascans for their organization, Dena Nena Henash, appropriately articulated their central concern, for it means "The Land Speaks." Like the Inupiat Paitot conferees, the Athabascan chiefs found that they shared common problems. Most important among these was loss of territory as the state moved forward in its selection of land pursuant to the 103 million acres it had been granted by the statehood act. A representative example of their concern was the remarks of Chief Frank of Minto:

> The displaced people of Nenana went to Minto and settled about 1918. They built a good village. Then statehood came and the new State has made a map of our village. Now a man can only own land where his house is. The State is taking land right at Minto. If they take the land, our village will have to move. We do not want to move.
>
> White men are all over the land we held by right. For 15 miles around our village, we hunt rats [muskrats] and moose. Everywhere you turn you are bumping into a [W]hite man. White men's dredges at Ester are even ruining our fishing lake. Now I heard this summer they are going to build a road into our hunting area. We cannot live when the highway gets to that lake. Without our hunting land, our village is finished. (Dena Nena Henash Chiefs' Conference June 24–26, 1962, 1–2)

In their recommendations, the Athabascans joined the Inupiat in requesting that the Interior Department withdraw from the public domain tracts of land around all Native villages, pending reservations or some other settlement of Native land claims.

In addition to helping plan this conference, Snapp also covered it for the *Fairbanks Daily News-Miner,* but to his dismay, the story he drafted—focusing on the land claims issue—and the story that appeared in print varied greatly. But even more dismaying to Snapp and to the conference delegates was a *News-Miner* editorial entitled, "Reservations? No!" The editorial writer, having taken the job just two weeks earlier from his prior employment at a California newspaper, opined that Indians were being spoon-fed by outsiders—the AAIA in league with the Interior Department—into foisting reservations on the Natives (Snapp 1962). Misrepresentations such as these further drove home the urgent need for a newspaper to address critical issues from an indigenous perspective and to contest the work of the mainstream press and Alaska's congressional delegation and state leaders who were equivocal, at best, about Natives' aboriginal rights to the land. At Ketzler's urging, Rock, Snapp, and a few others discussed a new name for the future newspaper. Sandy Jensen, a member of the Native Rights Association and Snapp and Rock's secretary, suggested the *Tundra Times,* since the tundra is the basic ground cover of Alaska (Morgan 1988, 197).

With the Athabascan conference behind them, Rock and Snapp refocused their attention on getting the *Tundra Times* up and running. The major stumbling block was money. Coverage of the vast expanse of "the bush" would be expensive and local printing costs were high. While printing costs could have been lowered by farming them out to plants elsewhere, say, to printing companies in the Pacific Northwest, Madigan was sensitive to potential charges of outside interference that might accompany such a cost-cutting move. Unable to come up with a sound financial plan to combine traditional advertising and subscription revenues to make the paper a viable venture, Rock and Snapp asked Madigan for the names of AAIA's five wealthiest contributors. After some hesitation because of ethical qualms, Madigan supplied them with a list of names that included Henry Forbes, a descendant of Ralph Waldo Emerson and a medical school classmate of Alaska's junior senator Ernest Gruening. As chair of AAIA's Alaska Committee, Forbes was already conversant with Alaska Native issues and acquainted with Howard Rock. In the summer of 1962, Rock and Snapp each sent lengthy letters to Forbes, outlining in painstaking detail why a Native newspaper was necessary and detailing the financial assistance such a venture would require. Moved by the passion of their requests and the apparent urgency of the situation, Forbes decided to support the newspaper with a grant of $35,000, contingent on

Howard Rock's editorship and Snapp's assistance (James and Daley 1984, 55; Daley and O'Neill 1993, 268). While Rock agreed to set aside his artist's palette and serve as the fledgling newspaper's editor, he lacked journalistic experience. He persuaded Snapp—the increasingly frustrated *Fairbanks Daily News-Miner* reporter—to heed Forbes's conditions and become his assistant editor and chief mentor. On October 1, 1962, the first copies of the *Tundra Times* hit the streets of Fairbanks and five thousand copies were soon winging their way to all corners of the state (Snapp 1962, 1983).

Dispensing with their initial plans to restrict coverage to Eskimo issues in Alaska's far north, Rock and Snapp's front page gave ample evidence of their intentions to unite all Alaska Native groups into a common public. In the upper corners of page one, the *Tundra Times* addressed its audience in two languages: Dena Nena Henash—"The Land Speaks"—(Athabascan) and Inupiat Paitot—"People's Heritage"—(Inupiat Eskimo). Soon, the Tlingit phrase, Ut kah neek—"Informing and Reporting"—and the Aleut phrase, Unanguq Tunuktauq—"The Aleuts Speak"—were added to the other two. In his first editorial (October 1, 1962), Rock spoke of the longstanding need for a Native publication and outlined two main objectives: "First: It will be the medium to air the views of the [N]ative organizations. It will reflect their policies and purposes as they work for the betterment of the [N]ative peoples of Alaska. It will also reflect their aims . . . their hopes. It will strive to aid them in their struggle for just determination and settlement of their enormous problems. Second: It will strive to keep informed on matters of interest to all [N]atives of Alaska, whether they be Eskimos of the Arctic, the Athabascans of the Interior and other Indians and Aleuts of the Aleutian Islands."

Native conferences in fall 1961 and summer 1962 had underscored the need for a focal point of expression, and Rock's editorial sought to keep this momentum alive by appealing to these infant organizations and by promising them the knowledge vital to social and political decision making. Two contributing editors added to Rock's clarion call for Native unity in the inaugural issue. Martha Teeluck, an Eskimo who would serve as secretary for the second Inupiat conference, entreated Indians, Eskimos, and Aleuts to unite, maintaining that "we cannot hope to solve our problems unless we know what they are, and [adding that] the main purpose of our paper is to inform each other." Similarly, Alfred Ketzler, past chairman of the Tanana Chiefs Conference, argued that Eskimos and Athabascans needed to stand together. He maintained that because communication was one of their biggest handicaps, the *Tundra Times* would go a long way toward ameliorating problems (*Tundra Times* October 1, 1962, 3–4).

While Rock and Snapp had long agreed to feature Project Chariot in their maiden issue, international political circumstances in 1961 and increasing opposition to the project in the national media in 1962 all but killed the nuclear cratering experiment before the *Tundra Times* was launched in October. First, in August 1961, the Soviet Union violated the informal moratorium on above-ground nuclear testing, observed since 1958 by the Soviet Union, Great Britain, and the United States. With this Soviet violation, the United States also resumed above-ground testing. In his book on Project Chariot, Dan O'Neill suggests that these new tests may have provided answers to questions that Chariot was designed to answer (1994, 249). Then, in April 1962, Paul Brooks and Joseph Foote's article on "The Disturbing Story of Project Chariot" appeared in *Harper's*. Finally on May 13, *New York Times* science writer Lawrence E. Davies framed his Project Chariot narrative with the educated guesses of scientists close to the Cape Thompson field studies that the project "may well be dead, killed by adverse publicity about its effects on Alaskan Eskimos and their hunting grounds." O'Neill argues that the May 13 article might have been an AEC trial balloon, floated to save face after having spent $3 million on the project (1994, 249–52). In any event, on August 24, 1962, the AEC announced that Project Chariot was being shelved (O'Neill 1994, 253–54). A number of scientists have concluded that Project Chariot died as a result of its backers' inability to engineer a public relations campaign credible enough to quell Native expressions of concern (see Johnson 1970, 15).

With Project Chariot apparently out of the picture, Rock and Snapp's first two issues of the *Tundra Times* highlighted the second Inupiat Paitot conference to be held in Kotzebue later in the month. Rock did author a long, two-part retrospective on Project Chariot in the back pages of issues two and three in order to set the record straight. But the paper's early news and editorial thrusts were aimed at land rights and the absurdity of enforcing game laws enacted for temperate zones where the taking of game was for sport rather than for food. Snapp recounted the year-and-a-half-long eider duck controversy in the first issue of 1963, pegging the story to a Canadian judge's affirmative aboriginal decision in a similar case. Snapp's story concluded with an announcement that Fish and Wildlife Commissioner Clarence Pautzke and Secretary Udall were quietly giving sanction to Eskimos to take ducks and geese for food whenever they were available.[4] Udall's tolerance was in keeping with his respect for "the land wisdom of the Indians," the title of the first chapter in his 1963 conservation book entitled *The Quiet Crisis*. He ended that first chapter with this observation: "It is ironical that today the conservation movement finds itself turning back to ancient Indian land ideas, to the Indian understanding that we are not outside of nature, but of it. From this wisdom we can learn how to conserve the best parts of our continent" (1963, 12).

Laying the Ideological Groundwork for Rampart Dam

With Project Chariot apparently no longer a serious threat to Inupiat Eskimos in northwestern Alaska, the struggle for aboriginal land and subsistence rights shifted to the state's interior. Here Udall's question of whose wisdom would prevail in conserving natural resources would meet its greatest test. That test turned on whether to go ahead with the greatest geographical engineering project of all time, a dam on the Yukon River near the village of Rampart that would require a land withdrawal of almost 9 million acres in an area two hundred miles long and between forty and ninety miles wide. The dam was slated to create a reservoir with a greater surface area than Lake Erie (Coates 1991, 135).

However, Rampart Dam's principal supporter—Senator Ernest Gruening—knew that the biggest engineering project was the public itself, not just in Alaska, but across the country. Gruening was a progressive politician whose political skills were honed before his participation in President Franklin Roosevelt's New Deal. A former newspaperman, Gruening had stints as either editor or assistant editor of the *Boston Herald,* the *Boston Journal,* the *Boston Traveler,* the *Portland Evening News* (Maine), and the *New York Post.* Twice, he had served as editor of the liberal opinion magazine, the *Nation,* first under Oswald Garrison Villard just after World War I and then under Freda Kirchwey in 1933 (Johnson 1998, 2–4, 13–16, 109–10). A Gruening biographer described him as a "transparently ambitious publicity director" who had a "simplistic view of both the malleability and power of public opinion" (53–56).

Another central aspect of Gruening's belief system was a deep-seated antagonism to monopolies, and nowhere was this antagonism manifested more strongly than in his antipathy to the predatory power of consolidated private power utilities. In 1929, Gruening waged a tough battle as editor of the *Portland Evening News* against power magnate Samuel Insull's Central Maine Power (CMP). Gruening campaigned against CMP's plan to sell hydroelectric power across state lines because he feared that this would lead to a rate hike for Maine's citizens. While advertisers put the squeeze on Gruening's paper, his side prevailed in a statewide referendum and established his national credentials as an advocate for the people's economic rights on the question of energy regulation. He was particularly appalled by the private utility company's use of its financial strength to shape public opinion. Prior to this campaign, Gruening had frequently expressed apprehension about consolidations and mergers in journalism and the threats they posed to public opinion and democracy (Johnson 1998, 75–82). As we will see, Rampart Dam would have sold electricity outside the borders of Alaska, and its public relations vehicle, YPA, used tax dollars to try to sell the plan to the American people.

Another major component of Gruening's political philosophy was anti-imperialism. He carried the torch of self-determination proudly in his editorial work and, with leading progressives of the day, revived the old Anti-Imperialist League in 1924, serving as its secretary. His anti-imperialism found practical applications in his interests in Latin America, particularly in Mexico and Haiti, and the American possession of Puerto Rico. In Mexico, he favored agrarian reform, believing that giving peasants title to land would have implications far beyond economics, laying the foundations for an informed citizenry (Johnson 1998, 65). His expertise in inter-American affairs won him a presidential appointment in 1934 to head up a new Division of Territories and Island Possessions (DTIP), including Alaska, Hawaii, Puerto Rico, and the Virgin Islands (114). Gruening devoted the vast majority of his time to Puerto Rico. There, he soon clashed with local officials, unable to forge compromises in the complex machinations among multiparty leaders. Gruening was also often at odds with Washington's appointed governor in Puerto Rico and Secretary of the Interior Harold Ickes. After numerous confrontations with the latter, Gruening was forced to tender his resignation in 1937. Roosevelt had not been happy with Gruening's work for the DTIP and so in 1939, when John Troy, the owner and former editor of Juneau's *Alaska Daily Empire* and now governor of Alaska, resigned because of bad health, Roosevelt appointed Gruening to the position, described as "the Siberia of the Interior Department" (153–54). As we will show in his advocacy of Rampart Dam, Gruening's principled avowal of indigenous self-determination in Latin America would be completely subordinated in Alaska to his wholly assimilationist and individualist positions.

When the United States entered World War II, Gruening's powers to direct affairs in Alaska were limited because of the strategic significance accorded the territory by the military. He also quickly antagonized legislative lobbyists for outside economic interests, particularly the salmon canners. He advocated taxing the rich and the absentee interests and soon became an advocate of statehood. Both his taxation and statehood proposals drew the wrath of the territory's newspapers with the exception of Robert Atwood's *Anchorage Daily Times*. Most of the newspapers in the territory favored low taxes and were not ready to support statehood because of the territory's small White population. Perhaps Gruening's strongest opponent was wealthy industrialist Cap Lathrop, owner of the *Fairbanks Daily News-Miner*, who did not mince words when he said he opposed Gruening's tax programs because they would harm his own business interests and profits. On the other hand, Atwood and his wife Evangeline were strong proponents of statehood and praised Gruening's efforts to take on absentee industrialists (Johnson 1998, 157, 163). To buttress his own political fortunes and to foster the people's right to know, Gruening advocated the establishment of more territorial newspapers so that Alaskans would not be dependent on the subsidized press. One of those creations was *Jessen's Weekly* in Fairbanks, a pro-Gruening paper with about half the circulation of Lathrop's *News-Miner* (158, 171). By the late 1940s, Gruening was primarily interested in advancing his two major goals: statehood and the development of the territory's "outstanding underdeveloped resource," hydroelectric power.

Before we turn our attention to Gruening's advocacy of the Rampart Dam project, let us put his stance on aboriginal rights in context. As we intimated earlier, Gruening's passion for civil rights and self-determination was clearly articulated in his anti-imperialist work in inter-American affairs, and this passion was carried over into his civil rights agenda in Alaska. When he arrived in Alaska in 1939, he was shocked at the overt discrimination against Eskimos and Indians displayed by signs in shop windows denying them service (Johnson 1998, 162). To counter these practices, Gruening sponsored and secured antidiscrimination legislation in 1945 (Gruening 1954, 377). However, his opposition to Interior Secretary Ickes's advocacy of reservations in Alaska, a progressive extension of the Indian Reorganization Act of 1934 to Alaska in 1936, renewed the enmity between the two that went back to Gruening's work in Puerto Rico. In his history of Alaska published in 1954, Gruening makes it abundantly clear that Secretary Ickes stood in the way of orderly democratic progress and the growth of harmonious racial relationships in Alaska. With a tone of deep skepticism, he added that Natives "had been led to believe that they had valid claims to extensive land or to compensation for it" (381). As we will see in the mainstream press's coverage of the Rampart Dam issue, aboriginal rights were rarely accorded much attention. In part, this lack of attention was a direct result of the ability of Rampart supporters to control the news frames that commanded accounts of the Rampart issue. Gruening and his chief aide George Sundborg were able to name the primary story lines better than anyone else.

Yet, it was precisely Gruening's blindness to other cultures in Alaska—a sensitivity that he had articulated well in Latin America—that contributed to the ultimate defeat of plans for Rampart Dam and to Gruening's electoral failure in his Senate reelection bid in 1968. Hall's work on Gramsci's relevance for the study of race and ethnicity puts cultural and economic racism in theoretical focus and helps us to understand the apparent contradictions in Gruening's political philosophy. He tells us that "popular beliefs, the culture of a people . . . are not arenas of struggle which can be left to look after themselves. They are themselves 'material forces'"(1986, 21). In another work, Hall makes a distinction between overt and inferential racism. He writes that, "By inferential racism I mean those apparently naturalized representations of events and situations relating to race, whether 'factual' or 'fictional,' which have racist premises and propositions inscribed in them as sets of unquestioned assumptions. These enable racist statements to be formulated without ever bringing into awareness the racist predicates on which the statements are based" (1981, 36). Clearly, Gruening was not an overt racist, but his liberal assumptions of market capitalism, possessive individualism, and individual equality of treatment, together with his Lockean liberal assumption of the moral imperative of physically "improving" the land, steered him to advocate practices that would have destroyed indigenous cultures in much the same way that Sheldon Jackson's missionary zeal and salvage anthropology had threatened Tlingit and Haida cultures in southeast Alaska three generations earlier. Even more important, his assumptions made him blind and deaf to genuine indigenous opposition and led him to conclude that Alaska Natives were the dupes of outside interests and "fanatical" conservationists. Much of the Athabascans' opposition to Rampart Dam was facilitated by the reportorial and editorial work of the *Tundra Times*. It countered the mainstream press's narrative of economic growth with its own narrative framing of aboriginal rights in the form of what we have called resistance as cultural persistence. Let us set the stage for an understanding of indigenous rights in the Rampart controversy by briefly looking at Athabascan beliefs and their subsistence practices.

Athabascan Cultural Beliefs: The Bedrock of Ideological Resistance to Rampart Dam

To bring this clash of cultures into bold analytical relief—accenting the contrasting ways in which the mainstream press and the alternative press would come to cover the Rampart Dam project—we need to explore the cultural beliefs of the Athabascan peoples of the Yukon Flats whose homes would have been flooded by Rampart Dam. It is these beliefs that were made invisible by the assumptions of Rampart supporters like Gruening but that were given headline billing by the *Tundra Times*. In the section that follows, we rely heavily on the nearly year-long ethnographic work of Richard Nelson, eloquently articulated in his book, *Make Prayers to the Raven* (1983).[5]

In the vast expanse of the northern interior of Alaska, the Athabascan peoples have long lived in villages and camps along the Yukon River and its tributaries where more than 36,000 lakes, ponds, and sloughs provide a rich habitat for wildlife and wildfowl (Brooks 1965, 56). Athabascans occupy and use large tracts of land where their daily life centers as much away from their settlements as in them. Here, they cut and haul wood from the forests. They take hunting and trapping excursions, and they set up fishing and hunting camps where they cut and dry fish and meat, and skin furbearing animals for clothing and cash (Nelson 1983, 6). Nelson found that the traditional ideology of Athabascan life was premised on the assumption that the natural and supernatural worlds were inseparable, each intrinsically a part of the other (226). Their cultural lives and identities were intimately bound up with the animals with which they believed they shared a communality of being, a spiritually bound moral unity (76). Nelson's Athabascan teachers explained their perceptions of nature on two interconnected levels: first, there is empirical knowledge requiring a deep, objective understanding of the environment, and second, there is a spiritual realm that includes an elaborate system of supernatural concepts for explaining and manipulating that environment (15).

Both the empirical knowledge necessary for their survival and the spiritual connections that ensure the continuity of their intimacy with the land are passed on by Athabascan storytellers in their rich oral history that constitutes what they call the "Distant Time." Distant Time narratives were related after the late fall subsistence season when the days were short and the conversations and visitations were long (Nelson 1983, 6–18). The Athabascans believed that—in the Distant Time—animals had human form and spoke human languages and while the lines between the human and animals have long since been made sharper, there are still residues of human qualities and personality traits in north-woods creatures. These Distant Time stories provided the Athabascans with their understanding of nature, and they "serve[d] as a medium for instructing young people in the traditional code" as well as offering a behavioral guide for everyone (16–18).

So, nature for Athabascans was not something to be taken lightly. It elicited a fondness and appreciation for the land that is difficult for Westerners to understand. Nelson explains that no part of the physical terrain is more important for Athabascans' consciousness than the water and the habitats it creates. Their whole orientation to geography is dictated by their direction and distance from major rivers, and, on the Yukon River, their most important resource is the salmon (Nelson 1983, 36, 66). They also take great joy in the first flight of migratory birds, an event, Nelson tells us, which is probably unsurpassed for them in sheer enthusiasm and pleasure (78). While ducks and geese are a secondary nutritional resource for them, they are nevertheless rich and delicious eating and invested with spirits that must be respected to avoid alienation (89–90).

It is very important to remember, then, that for Athabascans, hunting, fishing, and trapping involve a complex interplay between the empirical world and the spiritual world, for successful subsistence practices are as much a consequence of respect for the land and its creatures as they are a matter of knowledge and skill. Nelson gives a poignant example of White man's arrogance to nature, one that, in retrospect, has relevance for our understanding of the Rampart Dam project. His Athabascan teachers told him how one spring, when the Yukon was jammed with ice, outsiders from a nearby military base sent airplanes to bomb the river in an attempt to dislodge the ice jams. The Athabascans regarded this violent effort to overwhelm nature as extremely disrespectful for, as they understood it, "nature [was] to be petitioned and pacified, not forcibly conquered, because nature [held the] ultimate power" (Nelson 1983, 240). Finally, one other point bears mention in the context of the Rampart proposal, and that has to do with the Athabascans' views on sport fishermen and hunters intruding on what they consider to be their territory. They cite three points, which they believe give them a special subsistence priority. "First, their entire culture, their lifeway and world view, is founded on harvesting from nature and sustaining the intimacy with the environment that this entails. Second, they feel a strong attachment to their homeland and a favored right to its use and protection . . . and third, the land's resources are the basis of their economy and livelihood" (219–20).

Floating Rampart Dam in the Public's Imagination: The Ideological Construction in the Mainstream Press

As we explore the public discourses articulated by Rampart Dam proponents and opponents, we will need to keep these Athabascan beliefs and values in mind. While Gruening expressed strong enthusiasm for hydroelectric projects in the territory early in his governorship, the study of the potential uses of waterpower for hydroelectricity in Alaska did not begin until Congress passed the Flood Control Acts of 1948 and 1950. The Department of the Interior's Bureau of Reclamation identified over two hundred possible sites (Coates 1991, 134; Ross 2000, 121). Then, in 1954, the Army Corps of Engineers narrowed its list to nine sites on the Yukon River. In particular, the engineers favored building a dam at Rampart Canyon at the terminus of a one-hundred-mile gorge (Coates 1991, 134; Ross 2000, 121).

By then, though, Republican Dwight D. Eisenhower had captured the White House and Gruening was no longer in the governor's chair. Nevertheless, Gruening was far from finished with Alaskan politics. Alaska was granted statehood in 1958 and Gruening was elected to the U.S. Senate. Upon his election, Gruening strategically chose George Sundborg as his administrative assistant. Given Gruening's political interests, Sundborg was an excellent choice. He was well attuned to Alaskan political circumstances, having been a past editorial writer for the Juneau *Daily Alaska Empire.* Furthermore, he was an expert in hydroelectric power, having played an important role in the building of Washington State's Grand Coulee Dam as an industrial consultant for its developers, the Bonneville Power Administration (Coates 1991, 137; Johnson 1998, 163). In the early 1950s, Sundborg had written a book on the construction of Grand Coulee Dam, calling it an "'epic struggle' between man and nature" with the inevitable bending of nature to man's indomitable will (Coates 1991, 137).

To advance his hydroelectric agenda in Alaska, Gruening secured an appointment to the Senate Public Works and Interior Committee. From there, he sponsored a resolution on April 14, 1959, requesting that the Board of Engineers for Rivers and Harbors of the U.S. Army Corps of Engineers conduct a feasibility study on the Rampart Canyon site, funded with a $49,000 appropriation (Naske and Hunt 1978, 3). Later that year, Gruening and Maine senator Edmund Muskie spent a month touring large hydroelectric facilities in Siberia. Impressed by this tour, Gruening ingeniously leavened his progressive credentials periodically with cold war rhetoric to goad Rampart skeptics about the need to surpass the Soviets' hydroelectric prowess with Rampart Dam (Coates 1991, 138; Johnson 1998, 211).

In 1960, Gruening's preconvention endorsement of John Kennedy for the Democratic nomination for the presidency was repaid with a campaign swing through Alaska. Kennedy told receptive audiences that "if Alaska still belonged to the Russians, Rampart Canyon would be underway today." With grandiose campaign rhetoric, Kennedy said, "I see a land of over one million people. I see a giant electric grid stretching from Juneau to Anchorage and beyond, I see the greatest dam in the free world at Rampart Canyon producing twice the power of TVA to light homes and mills and cities and farms all over Alaska" (Coates 1991, 138). While the Alaskan mainstream press would soon jump on the Rampart bandwagon, not everyone favored the dam.

Two early opponents were Floyd Dominy, commissioner of the Bureau of Reclamation and usually a leading dam proponent, and the U.S. Fish and Wildlife Service. Dominy supported a much smaller dam at Devil's Canyon on the Susitna River because he did not believe the market existed to absorb the tremendous output of power that Rampart would produce (a generating capacity of five million kilowatts or nearly thirty-three billion kilowatts annually). The U.S. Fish and Wildlife Service supported Devil's Canyon Dam too, because it would inundate only a little more that 68,000 acres instead of Rampart's almost 7 million acres (Coates 1991, 139–40; Naske and Hunt 1978, 7). In a September 14, 1960, *Fairbanks Daily News-Miner* article, Alaska's senior senator, E. L. (Bob) Bartlett, attacked Dominy's "limited present market" argument as "do nothing partisan politics" in keeping with the Eisenhower administration's history of opposition to other great dams in the West.

Not surprisingly, given its historical record on dam construction projects, the U.S. Army Corps of Engineers ardently supported the Rampart Dam proposal. Its personnel frequently touted its possibilities at chamber of commerce luncheons around the state. In a March 16, 1960, news article, the *Fairbanks Daily News-Miner* detailed a half-dozen points favorable to Rampart's construction in remarks made to the Fairbanks Chamber of Commerce by Harold L. Moats, an assistant to the chief engineering division of the Corps of Engineers for the Alaska district. Moats emphasized the size of the dam, the generation of low-cost energy to Fairbanks residents and to private industrial groups expressing interest in the project, and the positive responses he had received from state and federal agencies that would be affected by it. With Alaska's three-member congressional delegation firmly behind Rampart, Congress passed the 1960 Rivers and Harbors Act authorizing $2 million for a four-year feasibility study, including the project's potential impact on fish and wildlife (Coates 1991, 136). Then, in early 1961, the Alaska congressional delegation appointed a Rampart Economic Advisory Board (REAB) composed of eight prominent members to assess an economic report to be commissioned by the Army Corps of Engineers. In April 1961, the Corps hired an internationally renowned firm, the New York–based Development and Resources Corporation (DRC) to conduct the economic study of the marketability of Rampart's huge generating potential. The DRC's chairman was David Lilienthal, former chairman of the AEC and a former administrator of the Tennessee Valley Authority (Naske and Hunt 1978, 8; Coates 1991, 136). Gruening and Lilienthal were good friends. When he was head of the DTIP in the 1930s, Gruening had held frequent dinner parties in Washington, and Lilienthal had been one of his favorite guests. Upon Gruening's election to the Senate, Lilienthal had "rejoiced at the return of Gruening, 'one of the Tennessee Valley' people to Washington" (Johnson 1998, 120, 204). Gruening and Lilienthal had long shared the New Deal vision of government spending to stimulate economic development.

Meanwhile, early in May, the Fairbanks-based Alaska Conservation Society's *News Bulletin* editor, Robert Weeden, wrote a lengthy analytical piece on Rampart Dam, asking how much land Alaskans were willing to dedicate to the storage of water for the production of electricity and at what sacrifice (*ACS News Bulletin* May 1961, 2). Weeden offered estimates of resource losses attributable to a Rampart Dam construction. Based on past and present studies, he anticipated the loss of nearly 700,000 salmon taken annually, over 300,000 nesting waterfowl, and more than 50,000 fur-bearing animals (6). He suggested that giant dams are products of speculative minds rationalized on three premises: "that their construction will provide work, that their tremendous surpluses will attract industry, and that their presence will bring admiration" (3).

Unwittingly lending credence to Weeden's premises, the REAB, together with Senator Gruening, Representative Ralph Rivers, DRC president Stanley Clapp, and Gruening's chief Rampart aide George Sundborg, embarked on a tour of the Rampart site in late May, flown in by helicopters to the otherwise inaccessible dam site. In a four-page public relations piece entitled "Wings over the Yukon," Gus Norwood explained that the Army engineers had flown in 220,000 pounds of gear to drill through the five-foot-thick ice in March and April and had established that the area had a solid granite rock foundation necessary for the dam's safe construction (see figure 7). Norwood's report, distributed courtesy of the Rampart Action Committee, included five photographs and one detailed chart of preliminary data on the Rampart project and ended with Gruening's projection that when we look back at this visit, "this year may prove to have been the time when America's largest hydroelectric project will have been launched" (Norwood 1961).

Despite Gruening's rosy prediction, all was not well on the political front. Shortly after the appointment of Stewart Udall as Kennedy's Secretary of the

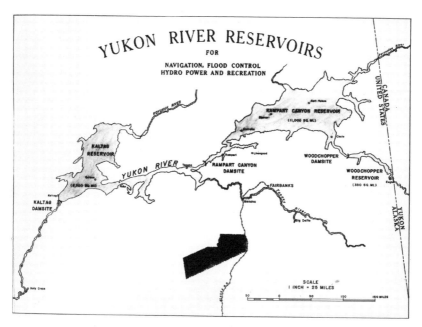

Figure 7. This map highlights the nearly 11,000 square mile reservoir that the Rampart Dam project would have created and shows some of the villages whose homelands would have been inundated, including Rampart, Stevens Village, Beaver, Fort Yukon, and Circle. (Box 537, Folder 51, Ernest Gruening Collection, University of Alaska Fairbanks, Archives)

Interior, Gruening traveled to Tucson to lobby him on Rampart Dam, but matters quickly soured when it became obvious to Gruening that Udall had severe reservations about constructing dams in environmentally sensitive areas (Johnson 1998, 214). Then, less than a month after his visit to the Rampart site, on June 28, 1961, Gruening, Senator Bartlett, and Congressman Rivers gathered in Udall's office for a meeting that had been postponed a number of times for one reason or another. Bartlett describes the meeting in terms that suggest that matters had, if anything, worsened between Gruening and Udall: "Since Ernest has been approaching the boiling point in connection with the Interior Department, I was quite content to have him be the spokesman for the delegation. . . . Ernest opened with a very savage attack. He said that the New Frontier had not come to the [Interior] Department at least in its relations with Alaska" and it was clear "that the conservationists have a hold on Udall . . . [he] is of them and with them" (Bartlett June 18, 1961 Memorandum).

Gruening's characteristic response when encountering resistance to a favorite issue was to launch a vigorous public relations campaign (Johnson 1998, 214). In a September 27, 1961, entry in the *Congressional Record* disingenuously entitled, "Alaska Has Shared in New Frontier Progress," Gruening wrote:

> The importance of constructing Rampart Dam on the Yukon River is essential to planning for economic development in Alaska. The Alaska congressional delegation has consistently worked to bring this project and its importance to national attention and also to obtain action which will make it a reality.
>
> This year the Kennedy administration recommended an increase of $200,000 over the $100,000 recommended by the outgoing Eisenhower administration in the budget estimate for continuing engineering and economic studies of Rampart. The fact that this magnificent dam has caught the attention and imagination of Congress as well as the administration, was demonstrated by the fact that the appropriation that was voted for this undertaking was even larger than the budget estimate. The Senate voted an appropriation of $400,000 for Rampart, an amount that was cut to $350,000 for the 1962 fiscal year in a conference between the House and the Senate Appropriations Committee.

While Gruening's public admiration for Kennedy's New Frontier programs and their applicability to Alaska clashed with his private fulminations against Udall, these contradictions did not slow down his public relations machine. In the winter of 1961–62, Gruening's Rampart aide, George Sundborg, had been working on a design for a Rampart Canyon Dam display for the Alaska section of the Century 21 exhibit in Seattle for the summer of 1962. The U.S. Army Corps's person responsible for the display, Colonel Christian Hanburger, wrote to Gruening in February that Sundborg's idea of placing a model of a well-known monument such as the Space Needle next to a model of Rampart Dam would be a good way to convey the sheer magnitude of the structure to fair attendees (Gruening 1962).

In addition to the unanimous support that Rampart enjoyed from Alaska's congressional delegation, state legislators and urban mayors were all but united behind the project and its enticing promises of economic prosperity, jobs, and cheap power. The lone holdout was state representative Jay Hammond, who wrote a guest editorial in the November 10, 1961, edition of the *Anchorage Daily Times,* lamenting the fact that a hotly contested debate over Rampart in Congress had received little publicity in Alaska. Calling Rampart a "sacred cow," Hammond was the first Alaskan official to publicly question the adverse consequences of the dam on Athabascan villages along the upper and lower Yukon River. Furthermore, he pointed out how ironic it was that state officials, who had expressed outrage over federal enforcement of the treaty that prohibited Eskimos from taking ducks, now had little or nothing to say about the hundreds of thousands of ducks whose habitats would be destroyed in one of the greatest waterfowl nesting grounds in the world if Rampart were to be built.

Hammond's lone cry of concern for Athabascan lives and Athabascan subsistence practices was drowned in the euphoria of a favorable marketing report from the DRC in April of 1962. According to it, market trends would follow supply, echoing, as one historical retrospective puts it, "the old theme of Alaska boosters: let the government supply the necessary stimulation and development would follow" (Naske and Hunt 1978, 13). The REAB, established to evaluate the economic study, gave it a hearty endorsement, noting that the report's authors estimated the creation of nearly twenty thousand jobs, exclusive of workers hired for the dam's construction (Coates 1991, 136). In keeping with its economic boosterism, the mainstream Alaskan press greeted this report with open arms. An editorial in *Jessen's Weekly,* a long-time Gruening supporter, typified the enthusiasm recorded by the DRC's "green light." The Fairbanks paper called it "one of the most significant documents ever written concerning Alaska." The report, *Jessen's Weekly* said, "states that the construction phase alone will exceed the fabulous boom years of Alaska military construction."

Jessen's Weekly failed to place this report in the context of a significant compromise that had been negotiated the previous month between Department of the Interior and the U.S. Army Corps of Engineers. As an agency under the Interior Department, the Bureau of Reclamation and the Corps had long engaged in duplicative and wasteful turf battles over dam projects. Under the negotiated agreement, limited to Alaskan rivers and to the Columbia and Missouri rivers, the Bureau of Reclamation was to carry out all feasibility studies, to operate projects, and to market power. The Corps would be restricted to matters of design, engineering, and construction. The upshot of the agreement was that the DRC's report—commissioned by the U.S. Army Corps of Engineers—would lose significance to those that would in the future be carried out by the Interior Department (Naske and Hunt 1978, 12; Coates 1991, 141). *Jessen's Weekly* was not alone in this neglect, for Rampart proponents would continue to cite the DRC report favorably for the next few years.

However, in January 1963, the U.S. Fish and Wildlife Service issued a devastating preliminary assessment of potential wildlife and waterfowl destruction in the proposed inundation area. This was the first substantial setback for Rampart proponents, precipitating another Gruening public relations offensive against a growing national chorus of opposition to Rampart from conservationists (Naske and Hunt 1978, 14). But the really devastating opposition would come from within the state as the previously silent Athabascan population in the Yukon Flats area of interior Alaska began to organize in defense of their land and their subsistence rights. At least initially, Gruening may have underestimated the threat to Rampart Dam posed by Athabascan dissent. However, Gruening had been at the Tanana Chiefs Conference meeting in June of 1962 and their organizational efforts in areas that would have been affected by Rampart could not have been lost on him.

In any event, Gruening visited six Yukon Flats villages in late July 1963 to inform villagers of how they would be affected by the dam project. The transcripts of these meetings speak volumes about the ideological chasm existing between Rampart proponents and inquisitive villagers and provide damning evidence about the bureaucratic procedures underpinning such village meetings. Speaking to Athabascans at Stevens Village on July 27, 1963, Gruening said that relocation for people in the reservoir area would be a "very fortunate thing for all these communities" because they will have places of "their own choosing" and "better community facilities." Gruening's litany of benefits included government-built houses with running hot and cold water and electric heat, lots of employment, a highway and railroad link to Fairbanks, a tourist industry, and a commercial fishery. Gruening concluded his prepared remarks, saying that "this community will be lifted from its, more or less, subsistence economy—why everybody will be pretty busy" (Gruening 1963).

Early in the ensuing question-and-answer period, Gruening said that he had no doubt that Rampart Dam—the "largest project in the Free World"—would be built, "the only question is 'when.'" Given Gruening's certitude, most of the questions here, and at a meeting in Rampart later that same day, turned on the dam's potential consequences for fish, animals, and birds. Villagers' questions revealed their apprehension, and Gruening's answers raised even more questions. One of the questioners wanted to know about the dam's effects on the salmon run. Gruening replied that "no one knows for sure [but] there is no problem of getting the salmon up over the dam, it can be done." Anticipating a question about wildfowl, Gruening added, "we hope that there will be no destruction of any of the fish and wildlife . . . for instance, if the nesting ground will be flooded . . . there will be additional duck nesting ground built all around the edge of the lake." Another villager asked what would happen to black bears and brown bears. Gruening noted that they would be a problem initially. They would have to be evacuated and the best way to do this would be to "keep disturbing them enough so that they will voluntarily move up." In Sundborg's weekly newsletter to Gruening's constituents, Gruening and Sundborg maintained that Natives could be employed as "patrols to drive game ahead of the rising waters" and as "beaters to keep ducks from nesting immediately ahead of rising waters" (Sundborg 1963, 2). Their response naively flew in the face of Athabascan practices geared to placating the black bear, which they regarded as "near the apex of power among spirits of the natural world" (Nelson 1983, 173). In his Athabascan ethnography, Nelson had noticed that even the tone of people's voices became lower and softer when they talked about black bears (184).

In the session at Rampart, villagers' questions repeated the concerns articulated earlier at Stevens Village. One questioner complained that he didn't like having the "land flooded all the way up" and wondered whether the rats [muskrat] wouldn't [*sic*] have anything to eat. Unable to guarantee a continued habitat for the muskrat, Gruening shifted the topic, asking, "wouldn't you rather have a nice home, the biggest man-made lake in the world, lots of tourists, recreation, a big fishery, and a situation in which everybody is going to be much better off?" The next questioner seemed unconvinced, asking about the fate of the salmon. Gruening replied that the fish would be taken up on elevators just the way we have seen them do it in Russia. He kept returning to his favored theme: the new homes the Natives would get, reminding them of the running water and assuring them that they would be gaining so much more than they lost. He then abruptly ended the meeting, apologizing that he and Sundborg were late for an appointment in Fairbanks (Gruening 1963). Gruening's newsletter to constituents about these meetings belies his own transcript of the question-and-answer sessions. In the newsletter, Gruening and Sundborg characterized villagers as being enthusiastic supporters of the Rampart project. The newsletter noted that while almost no concern was expressed about the dam's effect on fish resources, Gruening had assured them that elevators would lift the salmon so they could provide upstream residents with food. He added that there was "almost no outright opposition to the dam," although "two very old Indians said they did not like the dam proposal," mainly because of their fears about what would happen to the animals (Sundborg 1963, 2).

While Gruening may have felt secure about Native "support" for the dam proposal, his uneasy relationship with conservationists was deteriorating rapidly. On July 10, 1963, most of the state's press picked up an AP story that framed what a member of the National Wilderness Society called disturbing facts about the proposed Rampart Dam project (*Anchorage Daily Times* July 10, 1963). Then, in the August issue of *Field and Stream* magazine, Richard Starnes wrote that if Rampart were to go on line, it would be "one of the greatest disasters to wildlife conservation ever wrought by the hand of man" (August 1963, 12). He noted the long "romance" between the Corps of Engineers and Congress for pork barrel dam projects and maintained that Alaska's total population "could use only a tiny fraction of Rampart's electricity" (64–65). Alaska's mainstream press spent much of the summer running editorial responses to counter these conservationists' charges. The *Fairbanks Daily News-Miner*'s editorial riposte on August 15, entitled "Vaulting to Conclusions," typified these responses. The editorial writer charged *Field and Stream*'s Starnes with hasty and questionable conclusions, given the fact that many studies were ongoing. In particular, the writer questioned Starnes's contentions about wildlife disasters and limited marketability for Rampart power. Without any attempt to identify the carrying capacities of alternative marshlands, the writer simply asserted that they were there and faulted Starnes for failing to acknowledge the facts. In bold print, the editorial writer asked how a magazine with a Madison Avenue vantage point can know what the ducks will do. As to the marketability question, the writer pointed to the favorable conclusions of the DRC report, noting that *Field and Stream* is understandably biased toward duck hunters along the Pacific flyway while we conclude that the Rampart project would be good for Alaska and it would benefit the entire nation (August 15, 1964, 4).

Unplugging Rampart Dam: Counterhegemonic Arguments in the Tundra Times

Stressing the inseparability of people and nature, the *Tundra Times* launched a counterhegemonic argument against the proposed dam in a front-page editorial on April 15, 1963. Urging considerable caution before making a decision on Rampart, Rock challenged the positive economic rhetoric trumpeted by the proposed dam's supporters and chided the Bureau of Land Management's impending land withdrawal hearings because they were called without sufficient notice to Natives. In his editorial, he sought to shift the terms of the public discourse, writing that,

Very little has been printed on the adverse effects to human and wildlife resources, to the people and the animals in the proposed area to be flooded. . . .
Many [N]atives have expressed opposition to the project . . . in light of the
facts available at this time. Many of the [N]ative villages that would be affected have had for a great number of years [N]ative land claims pending with
the federal government. These villages insist that the claims be settled before
they are asked to uproot their homes to make way for progress.

The *Tundra Times* urges all [N]ative villages affected to send in any objections they may have to the project at once and urges the government to
extend the time limit so that all villages may have the opportunity to do so.
It is without doubt the desire of both the [N]ative and non-[N]ative people
of Alaska that hearings on the withdrawal be held in Alaska, not just Washington, D.C.

Rock's editorial conjoining concern for people *and* wildlife recalls the similar argument advanced in the last chapter by William Paul in the *Alaska Fisherman* on behalf of fish *and* people. A month later, in another front-page
editorial, Rock continued to develop the theme of people and wildlife threatened by the dam project. He noted the mainstream press's preoccupation
with the proposed dam's potential for job creation and its virtual neglect of
the subsistence perspective of "the [N]ative people involved whose economy and life would be upset should the project be approved" (May 20, 1963).

At the second annual Tanana Chiefs Conference in June, 1963, Athabascan concerns about aboriginal land claims became ever more insistent and
unified. Under a banner headline entitled "Native Groups Unite," *Tundra
Times*'s reporter Tom Snapp framed his story around the plan by the Dena
Nena Henash (the Athabascan organization in Alaska's interior) to affiliate
with the Alaska Native Brotherhood and the Inupiat Paitot Eskimo organization. One of the spokespersons urging unification was William Paul, grand
president emeritus of the ANB. While the Rampart Dam proposal was not a
focal point of his story, Snapp did get Army Corps of Engineer Colonel Sawyer to back off of his previous public claim that the relocation and compensation of Native people would not cost much. Sawyer admitted that his estimate had been based on a "'shotgun' guess," and that it had been made
without knowledge of large blanket ancestral land claims by the villages in
the Rampart area (*Tundra Times* June 17, 1963, 1).

Later in the summer, the *Tundra Times* covered Gruening's visits to villages in the Rampart footprint with a far different frame than Gruening had
in his newsletter to constituents. Rather than claiming enthusiastic Native
support for the project, the paper's headline and lead stressed Gruening's

dismissal of Natives' fears as "groundless." The story noted that Gruening "brushed aside as trivial stated objections to the project, and said the advantages and resources gained would far outweigh the disadvantages and resources lost." The article noted Gruening's characterization of the Natives' subsistence economy as poor, with some trapping, hunting, fishing, and some relief. As to large blanket Native land claims, the article quoted Gruening's suggestion that the Natives might be able to get a monetary award in the Indian Court of Claims since the dam authorization would constitute a "taking." He thought "it might be possible for these claims to be negotiated as a part of the cost of the dam since the amount for claims settlement would only be a small fraction of the total cost of the project" (August 5, 1963, 1, 5). Given Sawyer's remarks on land claims to the Tanana Chiefs in June, Gruening's remarks in July, and *Tundra Times* accounts in August, the evidence indicates that Athabascan opposition to Rampart was beginning to harden just as Gruening was claiming quite the opposite.

Gruening's lack of respect for the Athabascans' subsistence economy, coupled with similar remarks from members of the Committee for the Promotion of Rampart Dam, further fueled Native displeasure over what they were hearing and reading. For example, the *Tundra Times* reprinted an article from the *Valdez News* in order to illustrate the misinformation being circulated by Rampart supporters in public arenas around the state. In this reprint, Thomas Paskvan, speaking as a member of the Rampart promotional committee, told the Valdez Chamber of Commerce that two thousand Natives from eleven villages had agreed to relocate to the Minto area where there will be no conflict because they live off the land. In his editor's note following this story, Rock writes: "To relocate the entire population of the inundation area to Minto area seems inconceivable to us. For one thing, the ecology of Minto area would not support 2,000 more people. Villages are always located in areas where animal and fish resources will support them adequately" (*Tundra Times* August 5, 1963, 2). Of course this was not the first time that Rampart proponents had given short shrift to subsistence practices and to fundamental ecological principles concerning the land and water's carrying capacity to support human, animal, aquatic, and bird life.

For Athabascans, the threat to subsistence posed by Rampart Dam was never far from their minds as evidenced by this *Tundra Times*'s lead early in the fall of 1963: "Four Yukon Flat Athabascan Indian villages have compiled and turned in maps showing ancestral and current use of the Flats for subsistence." Each of the maps plotted the routes of old and current trap trails, the sites of cabins, the location of moose trap pens, the grounds for burial, the positions of fish camps and other locations that the people of Beaver, Stevens Village, Birch Creek, and Canyon village used to make a living (*Tundra Times* September 23, 1963, 1). These were the "memory places" Athabascans had not had to plot until recently in order, now, to demonstrate their use and occupancy of the land. They were the landforms whose spirits watched over them as much as they, in turn, watched them. As Nelson notes, traditional Athabascan people "live in a world that watches, in a forest of eyes . . . the surroundings are aware, sensate, personified. They feel. They can be offended. And they must, at every moment, be treated with proper respect" (1983, 14).

While the Athabascans were clearly beginning to understand that Senator Gruening was their enemy and a major threat to their way of life, Gruening's rhetorical sights were set on conservationists. In order to ratchet up the volume on the public relations battle for Rampart, Gruening, Anchorage Mayor George Sharrock, and Fairbanks Mayor Darrel Brewington called a conference at Mt. McKinley Park Hotel for September 7 and invited 103 Alaskan business, civic, and political leaders. Since the REAB had ceased to exist in August 1962 with its approval of the DRC report, the pro-Rampart public relations effort had been ad hoc and outflanked nationally by growing anti-Rampart conservationist sentiment. Consequently, Operation Rampart was born at this meeting as a statewide organization to push for construction of Rampart Dam "at the earliest possible moment." In covering this meeting for the *Tundra Times,* Snapp's lead bypassed the formation of Operation Rampart and instead framed Gruening and Sundborg's "all out attack" against conservationists, particularly those associated with the Interior Department. Snapp's story highlighted Sundborg's description of Secretary of the Interior Stewart Udall "as a man too busy climbing Mt. Kilamanjaro [*sic*] in Africa to attend a meeting in Alaska regarding the proposed hydro project." Referring to conservationists, Sundborg said, "Rampart has its enemies, waiting with a loaded shotgun and a red hot mimeograph machine." But the most vicious attack was reserved for Ira Gabrielson, head of the Wildlife Management Institute and the country's first director of the Fish and Wildlife Service in 1940. Gruening quoted a speech Gabrielson had given in March to the North American Wildlife and Natural Resources Conference in which he said that Rampart Dam would dwarf "all previous projects in unprecedented magnitude of fish and wildlife habitat that would be destroyed. . . . These are not the words of a scientist," Gruening said, "these are the words of a fanatic" (*Tundra Times* September 23, 1963, 5).

Operation Rampart was renamed Yukon Power for America (YPA) in

October. Taxpayer money and business support were quickly pledged for YPA's national campaign "to sell Rampart Dam to Congress and the rest of the nation." On October 9, the *Anchorage Daily Times* reported that the Anchorage City Council had unanimously voted to transfer $10,000 in city funds to YPA, that Fairbanks was expected to authorize $5,000, and that the state would be asked to contribute $100,000. Earlier, the *Fairbanks Daily News-Miner* ran stories noting that Natives along the Yukon River supported the Rampart project and that the Alaska State Chamber of Commerce had passed a resolution requesting the United States Chamber of Commerce to come out in favor of Rampart Dam (October 3, 1963). Nearly six weeks of pro-Rampart coverage in the mainstream press culminated on October 28 with a banner headline in the *Anchorage Daily Times* announcing a $100,000 budget for YPA with $50,000 coming from the Alaska legislature (Ross 2000, 126). The article added that the budget included $10,000 for participation in the upcoming New York World's Fair and that C. W. Snedden, publisher of the *Fairbanks Daily News-Miner,* had been named president of the organization.

However, while the money was pouring in and the bandwagon of pro-Rampart supporters was mounting a concerted effort to increase its numbers and to speed up its campaign for a positive decision, the road suddenly turned bumpy and the wheels began to fall off the wagon. The first bump came in a letter to the editor of the *Fairbanks Daily News-Miner,* dated November 15, from a Rampart resident. The writer took the paper to task for printing and editorially praising the intelligence of a letter writer by the name of Sam John whose favorable "letter" in support of Rampart Dam development had originally been run in the paper on April 4, 1963. In this letter, reprinted by the *News-Miner* on November 13, Sam John "wrote," "If I like live in swamp trap I go to Minto Flats, much miles swamp land there. Good to fish and trap. Ducks and geese can go there. No one cares. Alaska Big. Lots land. Who cares about little piece flooded? I for Rampart. Peoples against Rampart don't look in future" (*Fairbanks Daily News-Miner* November 13, 1963). The letter writer revealed that Sam John was a fictitious Indian and the paper had been easily hoodwinked because of its wish to find Natives supporting the project (*Fairbanks Daily News-Miner* November 16, 1963).

Two days later, the *Tundra Times*'s lead story (see figure 8) featured a recent meeting of Yukon Flats villagers who, with only one exception, spoke out against Rampart, an attitude, the reporter wrote, "in apparent contradiction to published reports of [N]ative feelings, as released in recent months by pro-Rampart politicians who have traveled in the Yukon region." The story was replete with Native oppositional views on Rampart of which the

Figure 8. This *Tundra Times* banner headline rejecting Rampart Dam in the fall of 1963 flew in the face of Alaskan mainstream newspaper accounts of villagers' sentiments toward the project in their Yukon Flats homeland. (Courtesy of Ukpeagvik Inupiat Corporation and the Tuzzy Consortium Library in Barrow, Alaska)

following was typical: "I am against it because a way of life would be changed. Should the dam be built, how will we make a living if all the fish and game are destroyed. I do not want to relocate" (*Tundra Times* November 18, 1963, 1). Rock's editorial in the same issue took up the apparent contradiction referred to in the aforementioned news story, charging that, "Senator [Gruening] Contradicts Self." Rock asked readers from Yukon Flats villages to contemplate their possible level of compensation for lands taken, given the following statement by Gruening: "The construction of Rampart would be in an area remote from the state's greatest scenic values and would flood an area about as worthless from the standpoint of human habitation as any that can be found on earth" (*Tundra Times* November 18, 1963, 8). The *Fairbanks Daily News-Miner* ran a story on the same event, but was much more equivocal about Native feelings, saying that "reports drifting in from the Fort Yukon area" suggest that villagers might "be having a change of heart in regards to the Rampart Dam project" (November 16, 1963).

Given these apparently contradictory statements by prominent politicians and YPA promoters together with, at best, equivocal reports about Native sentiment in the mainstream press, the *Tundra Times*, in early December 1963, embarked on a fact-finding campaign to level the public opinion playing field and to contest the one-dimensionality of the public discourse. The editor and his staff prepared ten questions and sent them to twenty-five Yukon River village councils to gauge the Natives' level of knowledge concerning Rampart Dam. For example, the questionnaire asked Athabascans about their subsistence practices, their level of understanding about what would happen to those practices should the dam be built, and whether promises of payment had been made to them for losses in actual property, fish and game, and culture. The last question asked them whether they were in favor of Rampart Dam construction.

In its December 23 edition, the paper reported thirteen responses: ten villages opposed the dam, one was undecided, one was scheduled to have a village-wide referendum, and one village was for the dam, provided that the dam's construction would mean work for the men of the village. The *Tundra Times* ran letters from village councils and individuals that accompanied the returned questionnaires. Almost every respondent, collectively or individually, voiced objections to the proposed dam on the grounds of damage to land, wildlife, and culture. One letter writer put it this way: "We do not think the mighty Yukon, which in our Athabascan language means 'broad and wide river' should be tampered with. The dam would only ruin the river. We do not like to think about what backed up water would do to our villages, and most important of all to our cemetery's [*sic*], our sacred resting place for our people since time immemorial. Besides nothing would want to live on a man-made lake. The moose and bear, beaver, muskrat along with a long list of other fur bearers would be endangered of [being] committed to outright extinction" (*Tundra Times* December 23, 1963, 6).

The villagers' responses and letters gave eloquent testimony to their desires to save their sacred lands and waters and to be heard on their own cultural terms. Over a period of months, their public discourse had reinforced Rock's discursive shift in the *Tundra Times* away from the mainstream press's preoccupation with capitalist economics to a grounding in the political economy of subsistence, with particular emphasis on Athabascan cultural and moral authority. Even with all the political legitimacy and economic power behind YPA, the battle for the high moral ground was just beginning for, as Stuart Hall reminds us, the winning of hegemony is not achieved simply in the economic and administrative fields, but it also "encompasses the critical domains of cultural, moral, ethical, and intellectual leadership" (1986, 17).

Early in 1964, Rock criticized the engineering of public consent for Rampart with state and local tax dollars and "suggest[ed] that public officials make more of an effort to know the people they are talking to, and that they travel to these areas with an open mind, to learn, so they can return with real impressions of what happened while they were there" (*Tundra Times* January 6, 1964). While this was a thinly veiled stab at Gruening's tour of Yukon Flats villages the previous summer, it was also a more general complaint on the cavalier manner in which bureaucrats and public officials had long dealt with Alaska Natives. As *Tundra Times* reporter Tom Snapp put it, "A government official flies into a village and has a general meeting in which he gives a brief talk and asks for questions. The [N]atives are perplexed, confused. Then the [few] non-[N]ative men in the village and [the] politicians take over. They use devious methods to misinform the [N]atives. Very little of . . . the interests of the [N]atives . . . is ever put in papers for general dissemination" (Snapp 1962, 3). In the same issue in which Rock called for more honest and open communication, an Athabascan villager reinforced Snapp's view of the traditional one-sidedness of political communication, saying, "Don't let Senator Ernest Gruening convince you that the land is worthless. It may be to him but not the Natives. He never stops long enough in the villages above Rampart area to discuss with them their land problems" (*Tundra Times* January 6, 1964, 5).

In January 1964, Fort Yukon villagers—the largest Athabascan settlement in Alaska's interior—made headline news when they rejected Rampart dam by a resounding vote of eighty-one to eighteen (*Tundra Times* January 20, 1964, 1). The referendum had been held to answer the last of the *Tundra Times*'s ten questions. But the biggest news coming out of the Yukon Flats area in 1964 was the organization of a multivillage association designed, as the *Tundra Times*'s lead story put it, "to thwart the construction of Rampart Dam." Called the Gwitchya Gwitchin Ginkhye, the association's Athabascan name meant "the Yukon Flats People Speak" (*Tundra Times* February 3, 1964, 1).

While the Yukon Flats people were speaking, YPA publicists and Alaska's political leaders were not listening, in part because they were simply deaf, dumb, and blind to any cultural authority other than their own. This inability to understand other cultures rang out loudly in a letter to the editor of the *Tundra Times* from Irene Ryan, published under the headline, "Why Are You Against Rampart When It Means Better Homes?" Ryan was a mining engineer, state legislator, former member of the REAB, and the executive secretary of the YPA. While her question underscored YPA's narrow economic inducement of a new home for villagers, it fundamentally failed to acknowledge any understanding of the larger cultural significance and sacredness of homelands for Athabascan peoples. Her letter's promise of jobs bypassed the negative consequences those jobs might have on the land and on wildlife resources.

Senator Gruening was not listening to the Athabascans either and his refusal to do so furthered their resistance at a land withdrawal hearing at Fort Yukon. In its lead story on February 17, the *Tundra Times* framed the proposal to withdraw nearly 9 million acres in the upper Yukon River area as being "thoroughly blasted," with sixteen people speaking against withdrawal and a lone official of the U.S. Geological Survey speaking in favor. The reporter contrasted this "blasting" with Gruening's muteness, noting that he "refused to stay in Fort Yukon an extra hour after the hearing" to talk with local people who "wanted to question him on his statement of last summer that the people of the Flats are not opposed to the dam" (*Tundra Times* February 17, 1964, 1). Gruening's refusal was not out of character, for, as his biographer puts it, he "always maintained a certain distance from the reality of the common man," particularly when he was not able to command the terms of the dialogue (Johnson 1998, 49). On the other hand, the Gwichya Gwitchin Ginkhye organization did have something to say about the land withdrawal petition, issuing a statement declaring that they were the rightful owners of the land. "This land is dear to us," its statement said, and "it has provided life for our fathers. It provided the means of life to us and would provide the means of life for our children. It is the resting place of our loved ones. . . . It is worth more than money to us" (*Tundra Times* February 17, 1964, 8). As a communicative vehicle for the Yukon Flats People, the *Tundra Times* was giving voice to indigenous communities, enabling them to articulate opposition to potential disruptions to their homelands from outside economic interests. By offering readers a mediated connection to the Athabascans' sacred places, the *Tundra Times* gave heartfelt expression to their sources' sense of place as a generator of cultural belongingness.

On February 22, the *Fairbanks Daily News-Miner* editorial writer criticized the *Tundra Times* for advocating smaller dams as an alternative to Rampart Dam. Using racist language hitting at indigenous practitioners of subsistence economies, the writer said, "you don't buy electrical power and gasoline with moose meat and duck feathers." Then, playing the anti-Native welfare card, the writer argued that those who say that it would cost the federal government a lot of money to build such a dam need to estimate how much it will cost the federal government "to run a welfare state up here for the next thirty years" (February 22, 1964).

Meanwhile, Rock praised the solidarity of Athabascans in the Rampart area. He suggested that other Alaska Native groups should follow their example and form strategic alliances to force politicians to keep their promises (*Tundra Times* February 3, 1964, 1–2). Heeding his call, Alaska Native groups began to unite. The first major affiliation of Alaska Native groups was organized by Steven Hotch, vice-president of the Alaska Native Brotherhood. On June 26–27, 1964, seven Native organizations—Cook Inlet Native Association, Alaska Native Brotherhood, Inupiat Paitot, Fairbanks Native Association, Gwitchya Gwichin Ginkhye, Arctic Native Brotherhood, and Dena Nena Henash—met in Fairbanks in a show of unity. For the first time ever, representatives from the entire Native population of 43,000 assembled for what was billed as the Conference of Native Organizations (*Tundra Times* July 6, 1964, 1, 4–5).

With their show of unity and call for increased communication, these seven Native groups posed additional difficulties for Rampart proponents already bedeviled by two serious developments in March and April—one an act of nature and the other a governmental report. On March 27, 1964, the second largest earthquake ever recorded struck Alaska with its epicenter just ninety miles east of Anchorage, the state's largest city. The earthquake took 115 lives in Alaska and sixteen more in California and Oregon. Damages were estimated at $400 million (*Alaska Almanac,* 1982, 49–50). Prominent members of YPA, including its president, C. W. Snedden, wondered whether Congress would have money for relief assistance *and* Rampart Dam (*Tundra Times* April 20, 1964, 1). Then, in April, the U.S. Fish and Wildlife Service issued a devastating assessment of Rampart's potential environmental consequences. According to its calculations, 36,000 ponds, 400 miles of rivers, and 2.4 million acres of prime waterfowl nesting area would be drowned. The subsistence costs to Athabascans and Yup'ik Eskimos were estimated to be severe with 200,000 to 400,000 salmon topping the list of losses. In addition, the report speculated that 1.5 million ducks, 12,500 geese, 10,000 cranes, 20,000 loons, 10,000 grebes, and an undetermined number of ptarmigan and grouse would be severely threatened. Mammals affected would include moose, black and brown bears, beaver, otter, mink, muskrat, red fox, marten, lynx, wolverine, and weasel in the thousands. Echoing the Gabrielson speech that had drawn such enmity in Alaska, the report said, "Nowhere in the history of water development in America have the fish and wildlife losses anticipated to result from a single project been so overwhelming" (Ross 2000, 129).

Privately, Gruening understood what a devastating blow this report was, and when he failed to find a competent biologist to counter the charges, he made the case himself, arguing that "experience with other great river development projects has shown an improvement in wildlife habitat and of recreational values ..." (Johnson 1998, 250). Despite the "bad news," Alaska's congressional delegation and its governor were steadfast in their support for Rampart Dam. In September, Governor Egan addressed a Pacific Trade Association Conference in British Columbia, expressing no doubt that Rampart Dam would be built. He maintained that "a fish and wildlife report that recommended against the project showed only that the department's research arm was weak" (*Fairbanks Daily News-Miner* September 14, 1964). And in Fairbanks, eight local unions and the chamber of commerce reacted by sending letters of support to YPA (*Fairbanks Daily News-Miner* September 26, 1964, October 6, 1964).

While continued local support for Rampart Dam was important, the Alaska congressional delegation and YPA had always placed a premium on cultivating the support of national political and economic leaders. So, when the nation's most prestigious newspaper, the *New York Times*, editorially lambasted the proposed dam as the world's biggest boondoggle, Rampart supporters had clear cause for alarm. Citing America's fascination with bigness, the *Times*'s editorial writer wondered if "the sheer size of the proposed Rampart Dam ... may so overawe Federal engineers and some members of Congress that they will fail to insist on answers to questions that must be answered before more than a *billion* dollars are poured into this remote Alaskan project" (*New York Times* March 8, 1965, 28). With his depth of press experience and his near obsession with Rampart, Gruening was not about to let this editorial slip by without a strong response (see Johnson 1998, 272). In a letter dated four days after the *Times's* editorial, Gruening wrote a rebuttal, attacking the *Times* for its lack of populist concern for low-cost power and for its failure to realize that, "Rampart will bring wildlife resource increases . . . simultaneously with increased prosperity for the people of Alaska and the nation" (*New York Times* March 17, 1965, 44).

A few months later, Gruening again sharpened his journalistic skills, prompted, this time, by an *Atlantic Monthly* essay by Paul Brooks, a conservation-minded writer with wilderness experiences in Alaska. Brooks, the coauthor of "The Disturbing Story of Project Chariot" in *Harper's* three years before, laid out the conservationist's case with precision and wit. Reminding his readers that waterfowl nest in shallow waters, he asked them to evaluate the carrying capacity of breeding areas that were believed to be replacements for the old nesting grounds (Brooks 1965, 56–57). Brooks's critique also indicted the Rampart sales campaign as a "promoter's dream," and highlighted the arrogance Rampart supporters articulated in attacks on conservationists. As he puts it, "Rampart supporters are impatient with what they call 'the old, old arguments of professional conservationists'—as if somehow the truth decayed with age. Others brushed off 'this duck business' with wisecracks such as 'Did you ever see a duck drown? Anyway, if the ducks don't like it, they are smart enough to go elsewhere'" (56). Gruening's demand for a right to reply was granted and appeared in the July issue under the title, "The Plot to Strangle Alaska" (*Atlantic Monthly* July 1965, 56–59; also reprinted in the *Congressional Record* July 21, 1965). In his typically breezy way, Gruening noted that moose would migrate to other parts of Alaska and that birds would do the same, flying to "ample duck nesting grounds in the vast swamps of northern, central, and western Alaska." As to salmon, he said that there is no certainty that they would be destroyed and that they had never before been deemed important (*Atlantic Monthly* July 1965, 58). Gruening's criterion of importance turned on commercial value, rather than as sustenance in subsistence practices, which, he dismissed three paragraphs later as a "bare subsistence economy supplemented by relief." He accused Athabascans of making representations that were not their own, intimating that words had been put in their mouths—words that repeat all the Fish and Wildlife allegations "not utterable by these [N]atives" (58). Finally, Gruening closed with a telling comment on his estimate of the value of the Athabascan's homeland, writing that the "Yukon Flats—a mammoth swamp—from the standpoint of human habitability is about as worthless and useless an area as can be found in the path of any hydroelectric development. Scenically it is zero. In fact, it is one of the few ugly areas in a land prodigal with sensational beauty" (59). Once again, this essay underlined Gruening's unwillingness to face genuine opposition, forged on different, yet legitimate, cultural grounds—those that recognized that humans are a part of nature. Without addressing Gruening in particular, Rock summed up this Euro-American arrogance when he wrote that "one of the most glaring discrepancies in dealing with Native cultures has been an almost total lack of respect for them by the people of the Western civilization" (*Tundra Times* April 19, 1965, 2).

Opposition to Rampart climaxed in 1966 when both conservationists and Alaska Natives turned up the pressure. First, a coalition of environmental groups called the National Resources Council sponsored an economic assessment of Rampart Dam conducted by Stephen Spurr, a resource economist and graduate dean at the University of Michigan. The environmental coalition included the Audubon Society, Sierra Club, Isaak Walton League, Boone and Crockett, and the National Wildlife Federation (Ross 2000, 130). Released in March of 1966, the Spurr report amplified many of the points about Alaska's energy needs and development potential made five years before by the Alaska Conservation Society. It noted that Alaska had urgent power needs best served by a small dam that could be built quickly, rather than a huge dam whose usefulness would be dependent on dubious claims for industrial development given Alaska's distance from markets, lack of raw materials, poor climate, unsuitable terrain, and high labor, transportation, and living expenses (Ross 2000, 130). Because of the detrimental impact a megaproject such as Rampart Dam would have on the Native population, the Spurr report recommended three less intrusive energy sources: natural gas development from the Kenai Peninsula and Cook Inlet, extraction of coal from rich seams in the Matanuska Valley, and hydroelectricity from Devil's Canyon (Coates 1991, 152).

In October, nearly four years to the day since the advent of the *Tundra Times* as a statewide Native newspaper, the paper's banner headline touted Native unity with the establishment of a statewide Native organization, the Alaska Federation of Native Associations and soon thereafter called the Alaska Federation of Natives (*Tundra Times* October 28, 1966, 1). Its greatest concern was the resolution of land claims. Its members prevailed upon Secretary of Interior Stewart Udall to freeze land claims in late 1966, thus stopping the state's land selections in furtherance of development projects such as Rampart Dam (McNickle 1973, 157; Berry 1975, 49). Four months later, the *Tundra Times*'s headline announced anticipation of the Interior Department's recommendation to forego construction plans on the Yukon River, an announcement confirmed by Rampart supporter George Sundborg. In his editorial in the same issue, Rock cited the importance of communications—especially the *Tundra Times*—with bridging the gap between Native peoples and Caucasian friends, especially, Rock wrote, "in posing our people's problems that were generally unknown before we came on the newspaper scene" (*Tundra Times* March 24, 1967, 1–2).

Conclusion

Clearly the cultural values of the different Alaska Native groups were not the values of a capitalist, industrial society in the 1950s and 1960s. In particular, different conceptions of land underlined these cultural differences. While Western capitalists treat land as a commodity to be surveyed, fenced, exploited, and sold, indigenous peoples see land as a place of cultural belonging with historical and religious meaning. Most of all, they treat the land with respect for it holds the bounty they harvest and distribute in shared patterns of communal exchange. Consequently, the dispute over the taking of eider ducks for subsistence was subjected to the vacillations of bureaucratic and state functionaries whose rules rationalized resource control to ensure sporting and recreational needs but denied indigenous people's most fundamental needs to survive. Local wisdom in the interests of resource reproduction gave way to the rigid steering mechanisms of imperial control through scientific resource management.

Project Chariot and Rampart Dam were efforts to engineer geography and people. Efforts to engineer geography were products of minds who compartmentalized knowledge in the narrow interests of instrumental rationality and the unquestioned assumption of peoples' right to dominate nature. Efforts to engineer people sought to use narrow political and economic power together with scientific expertise to trump informed debate and shape public opinion by controlling news agendas and framing the narratives that grew out of them. As one of the fathers of public relations, Edward Bernays, had once rather cynically put it, public consent needed to be engineered in the best traditions of Jeffersonian democracy (1947, 114–15). Alaska's political elite implicitly assumed that, here, amidst a sparse population—20 percent of whom were indigenous residents with minimal Western education—the citizenry could be handled as silent economic partners. When the silence was broken by indigenous organizations and indigenous media, shoddy, albeit well-financed, public relations campaigns sought to shore up a shaky consensus and to quiet rising dissent. The mainstream newspapers in Alaska legitimated the Western industrial model of development by unquestioningly quoting official, "scientific" versions of reality. As Hall has taught us, such official monopolies on public knowledge and expertise can go a long way toward constructing popular consent and reinforcing a dominating hegemony. When the economic benefits of Project Chariot were exposed as mere political inducement and when Rampart Dam came to be seen as more a force for destruction than production, then both of them began their own slow death marches, choked by the ineptitude of a technological imperative to do something grandiose without regard for different political economies and different cultural values and beliefs.

While technocratic hegemony momentarily stumbled on Project Chariot and Rampart Dam, state and multinational corporate hegemony over Native land rights maintained its powerful edge. Not surprisingly, the discovery of oil prompted an examination of Native land claims, in large part so that the state and these private economic juggernauts could gain access to vast energy reserves and the enormous profits they portended. But the point we have been making throughout this chapter is that indigenous voices from Barrow to Ketchikan articulated their resistance to these economic, political, and culturally homogenizing forces through sheer cultural persistence, communication, and organization. The *Tundra Times* was born in resistance to Project Chariot and enforcement of the Migratory Bird Treaty Act and it came to quick maturation in various land claim disputes, most prominently versus Rampart Dam's vast impoundment plan. As a man "in-between" cultures, Howard Rock was able, with others, to carve out political spaces to bring indigenous voices into political and cultural representation. He articulated this cultural persistence eloquently in an editorial late in 1966: "In the past, education of our Native people[s] was largely done from textbooks that tended to downgrade our cultural values. The result was the destruction of self image . . . making our children ashamed of what they were. . . . They could not look the world in the face because their identity had been downtrodden methodically. . . . One blessing for this may have been that many of us have grimly held on to our old values and this has given us strength to combat the onslaught of methodic submission of our cultures" (*Tundra Times* November 25, 1966, 1). The *Tundra Times* has often been credited with playing a key role in congressional passage of the 1971 Alaska Native Claims Settlement Act (ANCSA). Indeed, Rock hailed it as the beginning of a new era for Native peoples, but that view was not celebrated by all Alaska Natives. As we saw in the introduction, beginning in March 1973 and continuing for eight more months, Fred Bigjim (an Alaska Native) and James Ito-Adler (a Peace Corp volunteer) wrote "letters to Howard" in the *Tundra Times,* arguing that ANCSA was not a measure of self-determination but instead "one more step in the plan for termination of the Native way of life (Bigjim and Ito-Adler 1974, 77; see also Langdon 1986, 33). Bigjim and Ito-Adler's criticism turned, in part, on the irony of establishing Native corporations to "protect" land and assets. So, despite ANCSA's alleged "generosity," serious arguments have been raised over whether power and authority should reside in corporations, economic institutions born of cultural and historical situations far removed from the experiences of most Alaska Natives.

While the *Tundra Times* continued to be published under both Native and White editorial control until its death in 1997, its most important battles were fought in the 1960s. While it was in its heyday, a new medium emerged in the 1970s in southwest Alaska as an outgrowth of the federal government's "War on Poverty." Buoyed by indigenous organizational and communicative protests in the 1960s, a savvy group of Yup'ik Eskimos began to build on the gains of the 1960s. In the next chapter, we examine how the development of community radio in Alaska was a fundamental act of cultural assertion for, as one Yup'ik elder (M. Gregory 1997) told us, we had "to kick open some doors" in Washington to get our radio station started.

NOTES

1. For a comprehensive and well-researched account of the scientific disputes and the questions of academic freedom that followed, see Dan O'Neill's *The Firecracker Boys.*

2. While the villagers asked important questions after the AEC presentation, some of the early and pointed questions came from Keith Lawton, Point Hope's Episcopal minister. Lawton questioned the "suitability of the site's geology, the seismic effects of the blast, and the time of year of the detonation." He also wanted to know about the time it would take for radionuclides to decay and the extent of the injuries to people and marine life at Eniwetok, the AEC's nuclear test facility in the Marshall Islands (O'Neill 1994, 119–21).

3. The 1915 conference had been organized by Alaska's congressional delegate, James Wickersham. Congress had authorized the construction of a railroad linking Fairbanks with the Gulf of Alaska, and the government hoped to resolve the issue of Native land claims before the expected influx of white homesteaders (see Patty, 2–18).

4. While the Fish and Wildlife Service seemed to back off of curtailing Native sub-sistence harvests of eider ducks, Native hunters remained unsure of when enforce-ment officials might have a change of heart. Each spring, the *Tundra Times* carried stories wondering what direction federal agents would take that year. Typical of these stories was a special by Barrow Native Guy Okakok under the headline, "Barrow Has No Crops, Needs Ducks." Okakok wrote, "We people in Barrow need them [ducks]. We don't kill them for sport. There's no waste on duck. . . . The people will need the ducks now because whalers didn't get whales this spring. . . . We Eskimos don't raise crops like the people who are living outside of north. The game of any kind up here is our crops" (June 3, 1963, 3). The Eskimos continued to follow closely a subsistence case in Canada that reached its Supreme Court with a decision adverse to subsistence hunters in the fall of 1964, again throwing open the question of strict enforcement of the Migratory Bird Treaty Act (*Tundra Times* October 26, 1964, 1). It was only in 1995 that Canadian and United States officials finally amended the treaty to permit regulated subsistence hunting by indigenous residents in the spring and summer months (Ross 2000, 38).

5. In his study of the Indians of interior Alaska, Nelson uses the term Athapascan to refer to these peoples. In order to keep references from other sources consistent, we have chosen to use the term, Athabascan, simply because it was used more often by most other sources. We have also substituted the adjective Athabascan for Nel-son's more geographically precise designation of the Koyukon peoples, those who live around the confluence of the Kobuk and the Yukon rivers.

4   Warming the Arctic Air: Cultural Politics
     and Alaska Native Radio

IN THE 1970S, Alaska Natives embarked on a communications revolution
with the introduction of community radio into the isolated villages of rural
Alaska. Its origination in 1971 occurred in perhaps the most unlikely area in
the vast reaches of tundra Alaska: at Bethel, the Yup'ik village hub of the
lower Yukon–Kuskokwim Delta in southwest Alaska and by all accounts, the
poorest region in the United States. Following the establishment of KYUK
in Bethel, a similar station was launched in 1973 in the Inupiaq community
of Kotzebue (Qikiqtagruk), located on a spit of land extending into the Chuk-
chi Sea. In just fifteen years, the system would comprise ten full-service stations located in communities with populations under 2,500.

    In part, these developments were the outcome of a general cultural re-
naissance among Alaska Natives. Indeed, the story of community radio in
Alaska is most significant insofar as it is bound up in struggles for cultural
control and revitalization among Alaska's diverse indigenous groups. While
the fight for control over land and subsistence rights is ongoing, the Alaska
Native Claims Settlement Act of 1971 was a pivotal attempt at a resolution of
the profoundly conflicting cultural interests of Alaska Natives and Caucasians
in the far north. Many Alaska Natives have criticized the act, for it set up a
capitalist corporate structure for disbursing $1 billion and 44 million acres
of land in compensation for the loss of ancestral territories. But it had one
positive cultural consequence. As Wendell Oswalt maintains, cultural renewal
was an inevitable result of the terms of the agreement: "*It could not have been
otherwise.* For individuals and groups to be recognized under the act's terms
they were *required* to prove their Native heritage in overlapping biological,

historical, and legal contexts. . . . Successful claims conferred membership in a regional and village corporation plus rights to land and money. Because of these advantages a personal identity as a Native Alaskan became a favorable status for the first time in this century" (1990, 189).

As we saw in chapter 3, Alaska Native groups had organized themselves into regional and local associations on their own terms before this settlement. Some of these associations were direct outcomes of the federal government's Office of Economic Opportunity with its philosophy of local control of policy by low-income people. As this chapter shows, the development of community radio was partly a consequence of regional gatherings of villagers brought together by President Lyndon Johnson's War on Poverty programs. Its establishment was also a matter of enterprising and resourceful state bureaucrats responding to the federal government's Public Broadcasting Act of 1967 at a time when money was beginning to flow to the state from its lease of land for oil extraction.

But beyond the actions of federal or state policy makers, the inauguration of community radio was fundamentally an act of cultural assertion. Oswalt (1990, xiii) uses the phrase "bashful no longer" to describe the growing militancy of Yup'ik Eskimos over the years in response to economic and cultural conflicts with Westerners. As one of our informants, a Yup'ik elder, told us, community leaders had to "kick open some doors" in Washington to get KYUK started (M. Gregory, 1997). In defying the stereotype of Eskimos as reticent and passive, this Yup'ik elder confirmed Oswalt's recognition of their new cultural attitude, where deference to Westerners has been replaced by a sense of equality, and where confrontation, when necessary, is practiced.

The purpose of this chapter is to explore the cultural significance of community radio in Alaska by analyzing its origination and early development in Bethel and its extension to Kotzebue. After a brief theoretical introduction, the chapter proceeds as follows: First, in order to understand resistance as cultural persistence for Yup'iks in particular, and for indigenous Alaskans in general, we begin with a brief overview of Native-Caucasian contact in the Yukon-Kuskokwim region of southwest Alaska. Missionaries were of particular importance in the early years, while the U.S. military, with its Armed Forces Radio Network, was an acculturating force during World War II and the ensuing cold war. Second, we consider how programs connected with the War on Poverty in the 1960s and early 1970s stimulated grass-roots efforts at infrastructural development, including local radio, in Native communities. Third, we sketch the development of the Alaska Educational Broadcasting Commission (AEBC), the state agency responsible for community radio. Fourth, we examine the radio stations themselves, focusing primarily on the philosophy and purposes underpinning their establishment and operation. In the chapter's conclusion, we assess the future of community radio in Alaska in the face of a decade-long decline in state funding due to falling oil revenues.

Theorizing the Research Problems

As we noted in the introduction, any study of indigenous peoples must begin with the recognition that this is not a problem in multicultural identity politics with different settler groups sorting out their identities in the national imagination. Instead, it is a question of indigenous cultural politics based in the land and justified in political and cultural claims for self-determination (Bennett and Blundell 1995, 2; Fraser 1997, 12). In the first three chapters, we have seen numerous examples of cultural domination, including people being subjected to patterns of interpretation alien to their own culture, people being marginalized or made "invisible" by the authoritative norms and interpretive practices of elite settlers, and people being demeaned and degraded through stereotypical public representations by political leaders and economic developers (see Fraser 1997, 14). In this chapter we are particularly concerned with culture and communication in indigenous communities. Citing the fundamental principle of people's right to speak in their own cultural voices, James Carey writes that "people live in qualitatively distinct zones of experience that cultural forms organize in different ways" (1989, 66). Carey's ritual view of communication recognizes the centrality of the communicative process in creating, modifying, and transforming a shared culture. This definition of "communication as culture" resonates with the Yup'iks' self-identification of their traditional culture as one that emphasizes "speaking out to create, maintain, and perpetuate a well-governed society" (Fienup-Riordan 1990, 198).

Of course, the problems of cultural representation are particularly complex in Alaska, given the multiplicity of indigenous groups. In this chapter, we will deal principally with two groups—Yup'ik and Inupiat Eskimos. Yup'ik Eskimos speak Yup'ik and live along the Bering Sea and inland along the Kuskokwim River. They subsist on a wide variety of coastal marine and riverine life together with lowland mammals and vegetation, and maintain their customs and beliefs through storytelling, ceremonies, dances, and everyday subsistence practices. Inupiat Eskimos speak Inupiaq. They live mainly along the coast north of the Arctic Circle and center their traditional storytelling, ceremonies, and everyday subsistence practices on the coastal marine environment and its bounty, particularly the bowhead whale.

The tension between tradition and innovation is a critical issue in any study of indigenous groups (Bennett and Blundell 1995, 4). In Western discursive practices, this issue has too often been posed as a matter of polar opposites, where First Peoples are either lodged in the iron cage of a timeless essential past or bound for assimilation into mainstream Western life. As we noted in the introduction, we follow an alternative conceptual path articulated by Canadian communication scholar Gail Valaskakis. She argues that for First Peoples, "resistance is cultural persistence; the social memory and lived experience continually negotiated in the discourse and practice of everyday life" (1993, 293). With respect to the development of community radio, we suggest that cultural persistence has been effected through the exertion of control over programming by indigenous peoples. In so doing, Alaska Natives have minimized the cultural power of Western mass media to export alien ideas from centers of political and cultural authority. However, funding community radio in rural Alaska has always been problematic. Any loss of local symbolic control increases the threat posed by homogenized centralizing messages from afar and this remains one of the enduring problems Alaska Natives face in maintaining and adapting their cultures.

Early Western Contacts

Western contact with the indigenous peoples of Alaska has historically turned on access to commercially exploitable resources. Starting with the eighteenth-century Russian harvest of sea otters in the Aleutians, the commercial exploitation of natural resources has been enormously disruptive to subsistence cultures, leading in some instances to mass starvation and the near-extinction of particular indigenous groups. Ironically, the Yup'ik Eskimos of the Kuskokwim region experienced minimal disruption because the area lacked any significant exploitable resources (Fienup-Riordan 1990, 25–26; Oswalt 1990, 94). As a consequence of these "resource deficits," the first significant Western influences on the Yup'iks were Moravian missionaries, led by John and Edith Kilbuck, who established Bethel in 1885 (Fienup-Riordan 1991, 33).

Ann Fienup-Riordan suggests that the Kilbucks were probably more empathetic to Native ways than most missionaries because John Kilbuck was a Delaware Indian (1991, 11–12). As a result, the Kilbucks learned Yup'ik cultural practices and preached in Yup'ik. Still, there were many features of Yup'ik culture that the Kilbucks sought to eradicate. A prime target was the qasgiq, the communal living quarters for men where the oral traditions were passed on. The Kilbucks persuaded Yup'ik men to move into single-family homes, but the values underlying the qasgiq and other traditional institutions remained. In a sense, the role of the qasgiq has been assumed by the village council and, in many villages, it is making a reappearance with the sovereignty movement in southwest Alaska (Fienup-Riordan 1990, 215). For our purposes, the continuing role of the qasgiq is important because, as Fienup-Riordan's (1990, 216–17) work so clearly shows, the communicative style that it embodies is the discursive practice of speaking out, voicing opinions, and listening to the advice of others—all practices which get played out as well in the environment shaped by community radio. In short, the traditions of Yup'ik culture faded, but were not erased, under the missionary influence of the Kilbucks. To this day, the Moravian Church in Bethel conducts services in both Yup'ik and English and these services have, periodically, been carried by KYUK.

The Kilbucks also spent almost five years among the Inupiat Eskimos in the Arctic. By the time they arrived at the northernmost community in Alaska, in 1904, Yankee whaling and trading practices had significantly altered Inupiat subsistence economies from the Bering Strait past Kotzebue and Point Hope to their destination at Barrow. Thus, they encountered a culture altered by the commercial environment and a people who had some facility with the English language acquired in two decades of contact with Yankee whalers and traders (Fienup-Riordan 1991, 243–45). The demand for whales was sharply reduced by the second decade of the twentieth century, but commercial scouts were never far from the region around Barrow. Scientific explorations around the turn of the century led to a presidential executive order in 1923 reserving 37,000 square miles in northern Alaska as Petroleum Reserve #4 (Federal Field Committee 1968, 406).

The Military and Communication Technologies

Movies were introduced to Bethel in 1924, with the cost of admission being one dried salmon (Lenz 1985, 45). Still, major cultural changes did not take place in Bethel in particular, nor Alaska generally, until World War II. With the bombing of Pearl Harbor, as Gerald McBeath and Thomas Morehouse put it, colonial Alaska was catapulted into the twentieth century (1994, 78).

Bethel's strategic location with respect to the Pacific theater resulted in the establishment of an Army Airfield there in 1942 and the arrival of more than three hundred soldiers, nearly equaling Bethel's population.

A year later, radio appeared with the licensing of military station WXLB. According to John Duncan, Alaska was probably the birthplace of the Armed Forces Radio Service. By the war's end, there were some twenty-three Armed Forces stations operating in Alaska, but most of them—including WXLB—were discontinued when the military installations they served were dismantled (1982, 81–91). However, Alaska's proximity to the Soviet Union hastened the development of a telecommunications infrastructure in support of military objectives during the cold war. The Distant Early Warning System (DEW Line), a chain of radar stations stretching across the North American continent to the east coast of Greenland, was built in the mid-1950s to detect any intrusion by Russian aircraft. A more benign system, code-named White Alice, implemented a radio interconnection project run by the Air Force for military and civilian telephonic communication throughout Alaska from the mid-1950s until 1969 when it was sold to RCA. A military radio repeater station was online in Bethel by 1959 as part of the White Alice project. Kotzebue probably had an illicit radio station in operation as early as 1945 under the direction of a U.S. Weather Bureau employee. It was officially sanctioned as a military repeater station in 1959, serving military personnel posted at a DEW Line installation near Kotzebue (117, 166).

Thus, it was Alaska's strategic geopolitical position that "delivered" limited broadcasting to much of the indigenous population of rural Alaska. The strange-looking transmitting dishes, receiving screens, and white domes of the White Alice and DEW Line systems were the surveillance eyes and ears of the military, but the Yup'ik and Inupiat ears they reached through their repeater stations were not particularly attentive. In our interviews with people familiar with these stations, we were told that, for young people, the military stations provided more reliable access to popular music than the occasional nighttime signals from Radio Luxembourg or commercial stations in Anchorage, Fairbanks, or Nome. The stations also provided valuable weather reports. But for most villagers, the stations were of minimal importance.

The War against Poverty

Bethel, Kotzebue, and Barrow were by far the largest Native villages in the 1960s, but their populations—mainly subsistence-oriented—remained extremely poor by Western economic standards. However, because of welfare legislation and the national security state, the operative mechanisms of social control in rural Alaska increasingly emanated from federal and state governmental agencies. In a centennial history of Bethel, Mary Jane Lenz writes that while "the Yup'ik way of life remained intact far longer than that of almost any other Native American people in the United States," Bethel became the staging area of social service agencies in the 1960s. With bureaucracy one of the town's main industries, she adds, "children grew so used to references like the B.I.A., F.A.A., and L.K.S.D., they called the local ice cream parlor, the I.C.P." (1985, 5).

Launched in 1964, President Johnson's War on Poverty provided programs as well as ideological positions that facilitated the cultural and political revitalization of Alaska Natives. A prime player in this renaissance was a young Inupiat Eskimo from Barrow, Charles Edwardsen Jr. As a student at Sitka's Mt. Edgecumbe boarding school—not far from the state capital in Juneau—Edwardsen had come of age on news of the civil rights movement. His role in raising Native consciousness was played out after the passage of Johnson's landmark civil rights and poverty legislation. The premises underlying the Office of Economic Opportunity (OEO) Act of 1964 were of enormous significance for Native activism: that poor Americans lacked control over programs that were supposed to help them, and lacked access to the agencies shaping policy directed at them. Thus, establishment of local control over economic opportunity programs and access to policy-making agencies marked the cornerstones of the OEO's Community Action programs aimed at eliminating poverty (Smith 1982, 102).

Edwardsen's activist orientation advantageously meshed with the OEO initiatives that would soon dominate Alaska's rural landscape. He believed that they offered Alaska Natives the opportunity to pursue their interests with federal aid, without—for the first time ever—having to go through the despised Bureau of Indian Affairs. Land was his central concern. Edwardsen was intent on regaining the Arctic North for the Inupiat, putting into action a principle he had learned from reading the historian Hubert Bancroft when he was sixteen: that the United States could not buy what the Russians never owned (Gallagher 1974, 17).

Consequently, in late 1965, Edwardsen mapped out the area of Alaska historically occupied and used by the Inupiat and invited villagers within its boundaries to file a joint land claim. Most agreed, although Willie Hensley, a community leader in Kotzebue, said that the villagers in the Kotzebue Sound region wanted to file their own claim (Gallagher 1974, 118–19). While

Hensley was an important player in both the land claims movement and in community radio development, his dissent did little to slow Edwardsen down. By January 1966, Edwardsen had organized the Arctic Slope Native Association (ASNA), arguably the most important group in the Eskimo-Indian movement for historic land rights. The organization claimed that 96 million acres of land—an area slightly smaller than California—was theirs by right of historic use and occupancy. The growing confidence and assertiveness of Inupiat activists was reflected in a *Tundra Times* editorial about the ASNA movement: "Its leaders are young men who are not afraid to speak out. Their utterances are succinct, terse and to the point. The statements they make publicly are hashed out at meetings and these sessions are not always sweetness and light but are often heated. This, contrary to the belief that Eskimos are placid in nature" (May 27, 1966).

Poverty-related programs exerted considerable influence throughout rural Alaska, impacting prominently on the emergence of community radio. Most radio transmission in the "bush" had involved point-to-point transmissions aimed at handling emergencies. A Federal Field Committee investigating conditions in rural Alaska pursuant to settling indigenous land claims summarized the status of communication in 1968: "Communication with most villages is by letter or radio, for only twenty-three native villages [out of a total of about two hundred] have telephone service linking them to other places (another seventy places can be reached by radio telephone link-ups). Not all of the villages have radio transmitters and receivers, and even if they do, communication may be made uncertain by climatic conditions. And since most of the transmitters and receivers are in state or federal schools, their use is limited to official business and emergencies" (Federal Field Committee 1968, 43). In other words, what little communication infrastructure there was rested firmly in the hands of professional educators or medical personnel. Communication was oriented to individual survival, not the shared, communal orientation that would soon come to characterize community radio.

The Institutional Setting for Public Radio in Alaska

Sargent Shriver, director of the OEO, visited Bethel in the summer of 1967 and declared the region's poverty as "deep, tragic, and appalling as any in the world" (*Tundra Times* July 7, 1967). This impoverished region was home to one-fourth of the state's indigenous peoples. Yup'ik villagers were, however, using War on Poverty programs to attack their problems. About a year after

Shriver's visit, southwest Alaska's Association of Village Council Presidents (AVCP) issued a declaration calling for village electrification, safe water supplies, sanitary waste disposal systems, and improved communication. They envisioned locally controlled radio as critical to addressing the problems of forty-eight villages (over a 55,000 square mile area) with more than 12,000 total residents. The AVCP adopted a resolution calling for the establishment of a station that would provide employment, supplement education, and enhance local thinking (*Tundra Times* September 27, 1968).

Elsewhere, state officials were trying to institutionalize control over educational broadcasting. The eventual outcome was the Alaska Educational Broadcasting Commission (AEBC), later renamed the Alaska Public Broadcasting Commission (APBC). Its development was complicated, tied to evolving national policies regarding satellite communications and the eventual merger of ad hoc state committees that dealt with educational broadcasting and satellite communication. The national 1967 Public Broadcasting Act settled disputes among several contenders for the control of satellite delivery of educational broadcasting, granting this right to the Communication Satellite Corporation (COMSAT) (Gibson 1977, 120–22, 139–40). Upset that Alaska was outside COMSAT's footprint, Alaska senator Bob Bartlett called for a state commission to develop policy on communication satellites (*Tundra Times* September 8, 1967). In response, Governor Walter Hickel formed the Satellite Communication Task Force, which later became a subcommittee of the AEBC (*Tundra Times* April 5, 1968; APBC 1990, 12). A second relevant committee was assembled by Commissioner of Education Cliff Hartman to draft legislation for a state broadcasting system. The committee's draft legislation went nowhere in either the 1967 or 1968 Alaska legislatures. However, in 1969, Republican governor Keith Miller reenergized the dormant committee. Charles Northrip, general manager of Alaska's only public radio station, KUAC, in Fairbanks, was named executive director, a position he would hold off and on for thirteen years. In 1970, the state legislature formally recognized the task force as the AEBC.

In the meantime, with federal assistance, community leaders in Bethel had formed an Economic Development Committee. High on its list of priorities was the 1968 charge from the AVCP to start a radio station capable of serving the communicative needs of the region (*Kuskokwim Kronicle* December 7, 1969). The Committee talked with Northrip about possible state funding, and in the winter of 1969, he made a presentation about radio to a Bethel community gathering.

Northrip (1998) told us that his philosophy on public radio underwent a sea change in the course of that visit. He had gone to Bethel with a kind of mainstream, urban view of public radio—that it did what commercial radio failed to do, by programming classical music, public affairs discussions, and highbrow features. A story told by a public health nurse from an outlying village made him reassess his elitism. She described her encounter with a Yup'ik mother who said her baby's ears needed checking. Finding the baby's ears to be normal, the nurse reassured the woman. But the woman insisted that she check again, because, she said, her other four children had had fluid running out of their ears when they were babies. The nurse's poignant story drove home the dire need for a forum to talk to people about wellness. Urban Alaska had facilities to handle such problems, but rural Alaska was another world. Northrip realized that radio *had* to be local or regional at the very least. Right from its beginnings, then, the AEBC adhered to a philosophy of local control, voiced repeatedly in its official statements (see AEBC August and September 1973). Its philosophy meshed with the desires of the region's village council presidents expressed on a number of occasions during the previous twelve months.

The Formation of KYUK

Bethel was at the top of the AEBC's list of priorities. Northrip believes that it was slated to get the first station for a number of reasons: (1) the fact that education commissioner and AEBC member Hartman was well aware of the low level of educational achievements in the area measured by Western standards, (2) the fact that talks about the establishment of radio had been in progress for some time among community leaders in Bethel, and (3) the fact that Bethel state representative George Hohman and other key legislators were solidly behind the initiative. However, everyone understood that Bethel was just the start (Northrip 1998).

The first meeting of Bethel Broadcasting, Incorporated (BBI), was held on March 25, 1970, in the Bethel offices of the Alaska Legal Services, an OEO-sponsored agency. Ray Christiansen, representing the Kuskokwim Valley Native Association, was named president. Moses Paukan, a representative of the AVCP, was named vice-president. Hohman, also representing the Kuskokwim Valley Native Association, was named secretary-treasurer. The board's articles of incorporation provided for local control of policy, equipment, personnel, and operation, and outlined the station's purpose: "through its program preparation and broadcasting services to encourage and assist all people, but particularly the poor people, in areas reached by its broadcasts to raise their social and economic level and generally to enrich the quality of their lives" (FCC 1970).

In its FCC construction permit application, the BBI noted that "education levels in this region are among the lowest in the entire United States. Median school years completed average 1.9 for Natives in the area, compared with an average of 12.9 years for non-[N]atives" (FCC 1970). While further justifications cited the assistance the station would offer in employment, health and nutrition, news, and community improvement, its most compelling justification dealt with Eskimo culture: "KICY [Nome], the only radio station which programs in Eskimo, serves . . . an area in which the dialect of Eskimo spoken cannot be understood by peoples of Southwestern Alaska. The proposed radio station, programming in both English and in the Yup'ik dialect of the Southwestern region, would provide a much-needed outlet for the region's cultural heritage. This could be an important factor in maintaining cultural pride and respect for the Natives in the area. The influence of early [W]hite settlers has done much to make Native Alaskans ashamed of their birthright rather than justifiably proud of belonging to a culture which survived thousands of years in hostile climates long before the modern conveniences of living were available" (FCC 1970).

With $30,000 worth of state money, a small contribution from the City of Bethel, and a matching grant of $33,000 from the federal Department of Health, Education, and Welfare, KYUK-AM went on the air May 13, 1971, as the first Native-owned-and-operated public radio station in the United States (FCC 1970). Right from its outset, KYUK's operations, programming, and tone were decidedly local. A comparison of KYUK with aboriginal Australian radio is instructive here, for they exemplified local, community access media in similar ways. Writing about the Central Australian Aboriginal Media Association, Eric Michaels notes that its community focus did not always show up in content, but that it emerged on air through the station's format, announcers' styles, and call-in cheerios, all of which gave the station authority and resonance for its Aboriginal audience (1994, 29). Reflecting a similar tone, KYUK-AM's bilingual announcer began his broadcasts with "Angelanaqvaa [Oh, what fun!] . . . KYUK . . . On the air now"—all said, according to a *Tundra Times*'s characterization, with an Eskimo dance rhythm (June 23, 1971).

The *Tundra Times* article gives a sense of how well the station resonated with the community in its early days. Even before the transmitting tower had been put up—when the signal only reached 10 percent of its expected range, KYUK was getting sixty fan letters a day. For a nonliterate population under

2,500, the volume of letters spoke loudly to the community ethos, which the station generated. One listener wrote in, "You can't imagine what a difference the station makes in our lives. . . . Little things, like before if we wanted to get word around town that a meeting was canceled we had to knock on doors. Now we just phone the station." The article's description of the response to KYUK's "Eskimo Story Hour" in which local legends were told in Yup'ik provides further evidence of the participatory ethos fostered through the station's programming: readers were informed that "Villagers along the Kuskokwim are so enthusiastic about it that they are making tapes of their own stories and the station hopes to use them if it can resolve problems with sound quality" (*Tundra Times* June 23, 1971).

Beneath the surface tranquility, however, KYUK faced problems. Less than a month after the station went on line, the local *Kuskokwim Kronicle* reported that, "Bethel has been totally involved in its latest innovation Radio Station KYUK for nearly three weeks now, and loving every minute of it. [However], that love affair may come to an end in July . . . if funding for the station's continued operation is not forthcoming from the state." What is important here is not so much the financial crisis—this particular emergency would be averted—but the community's impassioned response. In the words of Bethel Economic Development Committee spokesperson Charlie Guinn, "This is our station. I think we have a sense of pride and ownership. . . . We also need to keep this station. To do everything within our power to insure its future . . . because it is changing all of our lives" (*Kuskokwim Kronicle* June 1, 1971).

A second problem involved a fractious debate over station management between Yup'iks and Caucasians. According to the *Tundra Times,* KYUK's bilingual announcer was an unexpected find by the station's White manager, Dave Moore, who had told the BBI's board that finding an experienced radio announcer who spoke Yup'ik was an "impossibility" (June 23, 1971). Aside from the implicit advocacy of Western professionalism or the rejection of indigenous production as amateurish, this comment foreshadowed trouble that would erupt two months later, when the BBI board replaced Moore with a Yup'ik Eskimo.[1] The director of the BBI board was quoted as saying that the move was an effort "to improve program quality to give us a greater insurance [*sic*] that Bethel radio . . . is going to meet the needs of the people in the area" (*Kuskokwim Kronicle* September 8, 1971).

In his history of Alaska broadcasting, Duncan claims that the BBI board overmanaged operations, thereby hamstringing its manager. The evidence clearly points in the opposite direction. First, close management was exactly the task with which BBI was charged in its articles of incorporation and in keeping with the AEBC philosophy of local control. A laissez-faire approach would have played into the control mechanisms characteristic of Caucasian-oriented policies so common in the region prior to the 1960s and whose legacy was still so strong. For example, in 1968 Yup'ik Eskimos comprised more than 85 percent of Bethel's population but its city council was nearly all Caucasian and most of its meetings were conducted in English, despite the fact that this disenfranchised many elders.

The Caucasian editor of the *Kuskokwim Kronicle* maintained that the firing of the manager was a "travesty" because the "majority of the programming prior to the coup was Upik oriented" (September 8, 1971, 4). While content is not unimportant, the more basic question is who was in control? As Michaels maintains, "aboriginal content" cannot be defined in the abstract. Culture, he reminds us, is not about skin color or blood type, but about communication and the maintenance of tradition, so that content becomes "aboriginal" only when the means of communication become the aboriginals' media (1994, 44–45). The BBI's close management was a classic example of resistance as cultural persistence where the only solution to the centralized biases of mass communication is localism, where communal, land-based systems work against hierarchy and authoritarianism (see Michaels 1994, 42).

Recent Assessments of KYUK's Contributions

By the mid-1970s, KYUK had a Yup'ik general manager and at least five announcers who could speak Yup'ik. As a result, the news was broadcast in Yup'ik three times a day, in fifteen-minute segments. However, getting Native speakers had not been easy. Volunteers had filled news positions off and on since the station's start, but John Active, a Yup'ik news director hired in 1974, found himself constantly working to keep them. Our conversations with cultural workers and former members of the board who have lived in Bethel since KYUK's early days indicated that "keeping Yup'ik programming on the air has been a struggle every day" (Hamilton 1997). One long-time board member, Paul Gregory, maintains that it was his understanding in the early days that 75 percent of the airtime would be either traditional Yup'ik or educational programming, but that over the last few years, it has become more and more Gussak (a term derived from "Cossack" used to refer to Caucasians) (P. Gregory 1997). A human resources specialist at the regional hospital in Bethel, Gregory himself originated "Yuk to Yuk" ("Person to Person"), a one-hour call-in talk show that has been a mainstay of the station for most of its existence (Bethel Broadcasting 1991).

In a 1974 interview in the *Tundra Drums*, Gregory espoused the position that all public institutions in Bethel should be oriented to Eskimo ways if they were to be of any meaning to the villagers (April 29, 1974). Over the years, Yup'ik-speaking journalists sought to provide culturally relevant broadcasts. Alexie Isaac, a newscaster with a wide range of audio and video production experience at KYUK over a twenty-year period, explained to us that Western news stories made little sense to elders, because they were too fast and because the elders were used to stories that built up gradually and that then had endings (Isaac 1997). Throughout his career at KYUK, Isaac has sought to counteract a growing presumption among community elders that what they have to say no longer matters. He does so by interviewing elders about topics that interest them—"Arctic survival tips, family values, old stories" (Bethel Broadcasting 1991).

Similarly, Peter Twitchell, who was hired as a news translator in 1971 and remained at KYUK for twenty-three years, said that his "news translations were never for the benefit of the Western world. They were always geared to the Yup'ik out there—those who only spoke Yup'ik." Like Gregory and Isaac, Twitchell understood that radio needed to address Yup'ik traditions and customs, "So I was making sure that we had a lot of voices because I think radio is about a lot of voices. It's not just my voice, or Alexie's voice, but many voices. . . . Our values are different . . . the way we look at things is different. Our streams are full of fish. You walk on the tundra and there is growth: berries, moss, roots. You respect that. You can look at the tundra and say, 'Hey, there's nothing here. Just flat tundra.' But there's food under there; there's food seasonally. We got our moose, our birds, our bears, our birds. That's our culture. Very simple, but hard to understand. So we have to get our rights to subsistence respected. We're pretty lucky because I just have to jump in my boat to go get my dinner" (Twitchell 1997). Twitchell's Yup'ik broadcasts were highly appreciated by the elders. Because of their positive reception and the importance of the language to Yup'ik culture, Twitchell and his fellow radio workers vowed to do even more cultural programming: "We said, 'Our elders are dying with all this wisdom. Since time immemorial, elders have instructed us: how to live, how to survive. And they're dying with all this knowledge.' So we decided to get some monies to go out and record the stories and the mores and just profile some of our elders" (Twitchell 1997).

Twitchell collected more than five hundred profiles, stories, and recordings of Native folkways from villagers throughout the region, most of which have been aired on KYUK. Twitchell is happy to have been a part of this process for, as he put it, this knowledge is an invaluable oral record for a people who suffer from an identity crisis and for whom ancestral knowledge about the land and subsistence is still vital.

Throughout the 1970s, KYUK set the tone and tenor of community radio in Alaska, and it was far and away the leader in Native language broadcasting. Its sister station, KOTZ in Kotzebue, modeled its operations after KYUK, duplicating its articles of incorporation to the letter and even hiring Dave Moore, its deposed manager, in March of 1972, about six months after the Bethel "coup" (*Kotzebue News* March 22, 1972; FCC 1972). We now turn our attention to KOTZ in Kotzebue.

The Formation of KOTZ

In the late 1960s, a group of Kotzebue educators and community leaders began investigating the possibilities of starting an educational radio station in the local, BIA-run high school. While the group included several teachers, a member of the school board, and the mayor of Kotzebue, June Nelson was its central figure. Nelson was a Native educator, the first president of Kotzebue Broadcasting Incorporated (KBI), and later a member of the AEBC. An early member of KBI's board suggests that the positive demonstration of Bethel's station and the unique opportunity to have a station of its own stirred interest in Kotzebue. Local leaders were encouraged and assisted legislatively by Willie Hensley, who by that time represented Kotzebue in the Alaska Senate (Tiepelman 1997).

As he had done in Bethel fourteen months earlier, AEBC's executive director, Charles Northrip, made a presentation to the community on public radio in January 1971. In keeping with AEBC's policy of local control, Northrip advised citizens to set up a local committee and then have it decide what to do, because, as he put it, "You're the boss . . . it's your station, not the FCC's and not the AEBC's" (1998). By late spring, Hensley had secured a $50,000 legislative appropriation, guaranteeing a federal match. In August, June Nelson posted a notice in the *Kotzebue News* inviting people in the region to join the group working toward bringing "local radio to all of us." By the end of the month, the KBI board had been organized. One year later, its local emphasis was underscored by Dave Moore in a letter to the editor of the *Kotzebue News:* "This will be your radio station," he wrote, "so we will be contacting you in a few weeks after you think about this matter. We hope you will have some thoughts, ideas, and answers on this matter" (September 27, 1972).

Six months later, in March 1973, the fledgling Kotzebue radio station went on-air as KICE, but not before a technological problem common to community radio stations in Alaska had to be overcome (APBC 1990, 17). Rural Alaska has few roads outside of village limits. Consequently, transmitting towers, which must be located near the power grid, are often erected close to airport towers. Two towers in close proximity often meant both safety and signal interference problems. In Kotzebue, the station's debut was put on hold while the engineer, the FAA, and the FCC worked out a tower-sharing arrangement (*Kotzebue News* November 22, 1972; FCC 1972). Shortly after going on air, KICE experienced another setback when its transmitter was destroyed by fire. After repairs, the station reopened in July with a new general manager and a new set of call letters, the originally requested KOTZ (APBC 1990, 17).[2]

As with KYUK, KOTZ's early programming was concerned with bilingual broadcasts of indigenous oral traditions. In his book on oral societies and the electronic media, anthropologist Edmund Carpenter notes the effect of radio in furthering the binding power of the oral tradition (1973, 53–54). Inupiat columnist Andy Cleveland gave poignant evidence of this binding power when he lamented the temporary interruption in "Eskimo Stories" after the fire. Cleveland wrote, "We sure like to listen to KOTZ radio station. Only we miss the Eskimo stories, even old people buy radio to listen to 'Eskimo Talking.' We are wishing to hear 'Eskimo Talking' again, cause there's more Eskimo listening to this radio station" (*Kotzebue News* July 20, 1973). While Cleveland's commentary conflated "Eskimo Stories" and "Elder Talks," two KOTZ features which together aired five nights a week, his remarks nevertheless provided significant testimony to the popularity of radio's place in the maintenance of the oral tradition.

The cultural vitalization furthered by KOTZ was particularly important in the outlying villages, because their residents had not been as assimilated into the English language and Western culture as villagers from Kotzebue had. The villages of Kivalina, Noatak, Ambler, Shungnak, Kobuk, Kiana, Noorvik, Selawik, Buckland, Candle, Deering, and Point Hope[3] were spread out over an area the size of Illinois, where the median level of education was below the fourth grade (FCC 1972). Nevertheless, there were far fewer Inupiaq speakers in the northern Arctic in the mid-1970s than there were Yup'ik speakers in the southwest. Michael Krauss's linguistic mapping project in

Alaska notes that there were 5,000 Inupiaq speakers out of a population of
12,500 in 1974 whereas Yup'ik speakers numbered 13,000 out of a population
of 18,000 (1974).

Despite (or perhaps because of) the declining numbers of Inupiaq speakers, one of KOTZ's preeminent goals was bilingual programming. Linguistic and cultural revitalization had been federally funded in southwest Alaska by cultural heritage programs in Bethel and several smaller communities
in 1974 and 1975 (Oswalt 1990, 191; *Tundra Drums* June 21, 1975, and September 20, 1975). Ironically, such programs were given added impetus by federal
and state Bicentennial commissions, which channeled money to communities to support heritage programs in celebration of the nation's anniversary.
In Kotzebue, these funds, together with grants from the NANA regional corporation,[4] supported the collection of oral histories among the elders. Many
of their recollections were broadcast by KOTZ as "Eskimo Stories." Former
KBI board member Dennis Tiepelman recalls the significance of the Bicentennial for Inupiat cultural awareness: "The Bicentennial was the first time
that the elders were able to collaborate on what information *they* thought was
important to themselves about what they wanted to pass on. The Bicentennial caused them to reflect on the fact that so many people who had been the
repositories of the oral history and traditions were no longer with them. They
understood that, as elders, they were still a very powerful influence in what
ought to be talked about" (1997).

Tiepelman singled out youthful bilingual broadcaster Ruthie Ramoth
Samson as a person who was particularly instrumental in KOTZ's oral documentation of the elders' wisdom. He described her work as a bridge linking the languages and generations. With her excellent command of Inupiaq,
her emphasis on Inupiat-oriented topics, and her on-air use of her Eskimo
name (Tatquvan), Samson blended her knowledge of contemporary music
with a deft sense of the organic and evolving Inupiat culture rooted firmly
in certain timeless traditions (Tiepelman 1997).

Because KOTZ began its operations in the BIA school, it initially attracted
the interest of the youth. One of its most diversified practitioners was Nellie
Ward, a student at the school when talk of KOTZ was still in the community
planning stages. After graduation, Ward worked at the local newspaper before moving over to KOTZ, where she held a number of positions, including its news director. Now the host and producer of Independent Native
News, a weekday five-minute national Native news radio program, Nellie
Ward Moore still believes strongly in the importance of local radio as a means
of cultural preservation. She recalls her days at KOTZ and how she would

bring Inupiaq elders into the studio and set them before the microphone with no other instructions than to tell their stories. Such productions, she believes, are far more valuable for maintaining the culture than large-scale, professional productions (1997).

Recent Assessments of KOTZ's Contributions

Tiepelman maintains that KOTZ's cultural contributions in the early years were inseparable from certain political and social developments affecting Native identities and practices. Specifically, the Indian Self-Determination Act of 1975 decentralized the administration of federal Indian programs, strengthening and expanding the role of Alaska Native regional associations in education, job training, health, and welfare (see also McBeath and Morehouse 1994, 270). While the Self-Determination Act had material consequences for local sovereignty, the American Indian Movement (AIM) in the contiguous forty-eight states also had important if more amorphous repercussions for Alaska Natives. Tiepelman believes that the national movement certainly caused Inupiat Eskimos to question their status, though in less militant forms than AIM. Against the backdrop of these developments, Tiepelman notes, "radio helped to reinforce in us our traditional sense of who we were—showing respect for our elders and reacting against the boarding school concept which had threatened our culture and language in the name of assimilation" (1997).

KOTZ's persistent emphasis on local news was an important means of resisting assimilation. Suzy Erlich, a former member of KBI's board, explained how the station's extensive coverage of local events helped residents understand that the station reflected the community's aspirations (1997). Local coverage included live reports of City Council meetings, or public hearings on the land selection process following the 1971 Alaska Native Claims Settlement Act. Throughout the late 1970s, KOTZ covered debates over another critical piece of legislation, the Alaska National Interest Lands Conservation Act (ANILCA). With the passage of this act in 1980, Congress delivered on promises made in the Alaska Native Claims Settlement Act to set aside land for a vast federal conservation system of forests, parks, wildlife refuges, preserves, and wild and scenic rivers. ANILCA reversed the clause in ANCSA extinguishing Native subsistence rights by establishing preferences for rural— though not exclusively Native—hunters and fishermen (McBeath and Morehouse 1994, 86, 112). For Erlich, there is no question about the centrality of the subsistence economy to Inupiat Eskimo lives. She states, "I came from a subsistence family; I grew up that way. I am very proud of it. I want my children to grow up that way. I want my great-great-great grandchildren to grow up that way and be proud of it because it brings strength to us as Inupiats. It is something different than going to AC [Alaska Commercial store], or Hansen's. Our grocery store is millions of acres wide, not just a few thousand feet, and it brings us pride" (quoted in Berger 1985, 53).

As KOTZ moved into the oil-prosperous years of the 1980s, it and other Alaska community radio stations fared extremely well. However, two events—one national and the other international—would profoundly affect community radio in Alaska. The first was the ascendancy of national conservative forces with the election of Ronald Reagan to the presidency in 1980. Consistent with Reagan's philosophy of privatization, Congress cut federal support for public broadcasting by 20 percent for the biennium beginning in 1983 (Engelman 1996, 102–3). Additionally, the FCC approved enhanced underwriting, thereby allowing sponsors of public broadcasting to say more for their dollars. This change precipitated commercial-like audience research and marketing practices for many public broadcasting outlets (Engelman 1996, 76). It is important to remember that Alaska's rural communities are particularly ill suited to the kind of commercial practices common in most rural areas of America.

Secondly, public broadcasting in Alaska was shaken by the worldwide plunge in oil prices in the mid-1980s. By 1985, oil prices were at one-third of their 1982 levels. With declining tax revenues, Alaska's Governor William Sheffield proposed eliminating the public broadcasting budget in 1986. Public broadcasting survived the decade only because its community orientation gave it a solid political base. As Northrip puts it, "To localize the stations meant that you created a political base in the legislature that protected the system from budget cuts, because any potential cuts were not aimed at some amorphous state program, but instead it was 'our' station that was threatened with being cut" (1998). By the late 1980s, worldwide oil prices regained some of their earlier losses and this market fluctuation allowed public radio to survive with level funding.

Conclusion

Throughout this chapter we have consistently described public broadcasting in Alaska as community-oriented. This choice of terms is rooted in a fundamental distinction between federal forms of public broadcasting associated with mainstream expression and highly local forms of broadcasting rooted in decentralized and participatory forms of cultural expression (Engelman 1996, 6, 67–68). While these two forms of public broadcasting are not mutually exclusive they clearly articulate different ideological frameworks for understanding the future of public broadcasting in Alaska. The federal form subscribes to a Western pluralist model of broadcasting articulated by National Public Radio mission statements and programming standards that accept the individual as the basic unit of analysis (Engelman 1996, 89–92). Furthermore, this individualism is couched in the context of an informational model of the media that tacitly assumes an acceptance of the advanced capitalist order and the individual consumer choices that are made available under it by the professional norms of its practitioners (see Curran 1991, 100). In Alaska, when these individually oriented discourses are aired over community radio, they are often at odds with the collectively oriented subsistence economies that are fundamentally grounded in an ideology of sharing. To highlight differences between these two models of public broadcasting we conclude with an examination of how funding problems were dealt with through most of the 1990s and ask how things might have been handled differently.

When the Republicans swept the 1994 national midterm elections, their "Contract with America" contained a provision for eliminating federal funding for public broadcasting (Engelman 1996, 3). In Alaska, legislators from both sides of the aisle had been wielding the ax on state support for broadcasting ever since 1986. Between 1986 and 1994, state funding had decreased by 40 percent even though the number of stations had increased. Additionally, federal funding had declined by 18 percent (Public Broadcasting Endowment Trust minutes April 7, 1994, 3).

Members of the APBC had to deal strategically with a real crisis. They reviewed what they called a "panoply of alternatives for reorganizing the system" (APBC document 1994, 1). However, in our examination of APBC documentation, we did not see any mention, for example, of European public service–oriented models with their programming safeguards for specific groups. Instead, faced with another 50 percent cut in 1995, the APBC devised plans for a satellite interconnection project, whereby stations would receive program streams that they could 'mix and match' to produce an ersatz version of local service. The project was approved and funded by a 1995 grant from the U.S. Commerce Department's Public Telecommunications Facilities Program.

Additionally, the APBC mandated that stations apply for funds by accepting a grouping of stations under a new set of regional schemes. The largest region, the Associated Alaska Public Broadcasting Stations (AAPBS), would comprise eleven stations, including those of Barrow, Bethel, and Kotzebue. Obviously, any shared programming would have to be in English since Yup'ik and Inupiaq are mutually unintelligible languages. Hence, the bicultural/bilingual features of community radio were substantially weakened by the system imperatives of cost-cutting efficiencies. Furthermore, the *delivery* of information over a superhighway to recipients at the state level is culturally incongruent with communicative forms that imply community or group interaction rather than passive individual reception. This solution is a classic example of what Carey criticizes as a transmission model of communication (1989). The unidirectional movement of packaged cultural goods has nothing in common with communicative forms that revolve around collective interaction.

To their credit, APBC members have recognized and acknowledged the grave threat to localism posed by restructuring (APBC 1996, 1). Obviously, financially hard-pressed stations would find it advantageous to tap into what were described as "a 24-hour national, international, and state news stream and an entertainment stream consisting of popular music from national sources and original 'dee-jay' record programs" (APBC 1994, 2). For indigenous peoples in rural Alaska, community radio remains very important. Recent documentation in support of a grant application submitted by KOTZ shows that its listeners "overwhelmingly requested more Inupiat cultural, educational and entertainment programming. . . . Listeners praised KOTZ's efforts to produce cultural programming featuring Inupiat oral history and traditional dance music as well as newscasts and language instruction in the Inupiaq language" (KOTZ-AM Program Narrative 1997, 2).

The contradictions posed by these funding crises raise the fundamental question of how far one can take a medium down an instrumentally driven highway before it loses its substantive, cultural raison d'être. We have argued that with community radio, citizens have an intimate part to play in their image- and discursive-making practices, a situation all too uncommon with most contemporary forms of media. Recognizing that this discursive process is politically inflected, we need to ask what political and communicative forms in the Alaskan cultural landscape are amenable to Alaska Native groups and their ideologies of sharing. For Alaska Natives, the answer requires a restoration of local control over their media so that they can carry on their oral traditions with the complement of radio technology facilitating village gatherings, much like a new version of the old Yup'ik qasgiq.

NOTES

1. As an engineer, Moore was actually given a raise and removed from his managerial duties, but when he declined this horizontal "promotion," he was fired.

2. The call letters KICE had been assigned because KOTZ was already taken by a Coast Guard cutter. The ship was mothballed shortly thereafter.

3. Point Hope, Deering, Candle, and Buckland were either on the coast or close enough to it to have been drawn into, or affected by, the acculturative influences of the whaling industry in the late nineteenth and early twentieth centuries. This was particularly true of Point Hope. In fact, none of the villages reached by KOTZ was untouched by commercial whaling, which disrupted Native trading practices among the inland, upriver people as well as those who lived along the coast.

4. NANA is one of the twelve regional corporations established to administer the Alaska Native Claims Settlement Act.

5   Whose Vision Is It, Anyway?:
Technology, Community Television,
and Cultural Politics

THE STORY of the development of community television in rural Alaska,
where most of Alaska's seven culturally distinct Native groups live in 278
communities, is extraordinarily complex and contradictory. Today, most of
the estimated 98,000 Alaska Natives live in communities with populations
under 2,500. Since 1977, the state has at least partially supported a system of
satellite-delivered television to any community with a population over
twenty-five. By 1990, the Rural Alaska Television Network (RATNET) was
serving 248 communities (Boucher and MacLean 1990, 6). The uniqueness
of the system was the result of a confluence of factors, including the vast geographical distances separating communities, the tremendous diversity of to-
pography and climate, and the small population bases that were insufficient
to support commercially driven television stations common to the rest of the
United States.

The contradictions in the development of rural Alaskan community television turn on the dialectics of local control and cultural integrity versus
the imperializing and homogenizing forces of technological authority exercised from afar in state and national political, economic, and entertainment capitals. Conceptually, our understanding and explanation of the
consequences of these dialectical struggles of "communication as culture"
will follow James Carey's perceptive essays on the limitations of communications technologies articulated through the work of Canadian scholar
Harold Adams Innis.

While the power of television as a consciousness industry has long been
recognized, Alaska Native groups have made concerted efforts to negotiate

the introduction of this ideological force into their homelands on their own terms (Enzensberger 1974; Gouldner 1976; Horkheimer and Adorno 1972; Schiller 1973). In chapter 4 we explained the introduction of community radio in Alaska Native communities by following another Innis scholar, Gail Valaskakis, who argues that "for First Peoples, resistance is cultural persistence" (1993, 293). With respect to the development of community television in Alaska, we suggest that cultural persistence has been manifested in a wide range of culturally expressive forms, from film and video documentation of the past to the use of video and television for contemporary problem-solving to a very attenuated form of program decision making essentially dictated by statutory legislation and Hollywood producers.

In our documentation of these cultural struggles, we follow Carey's communicative notion of cultural reality as that which is "formed and sustained, repaired and transformed, worshiped and celebrated in the ordinary business of living" (1989, 87). With this in mind, we heed Carey's warning to researchers of other cultures: "an analysis that does not develop on [N]ative grounds is simply a pose" (97). Indeed, it is neither our intent nor our place to judge the content of Native programming. Instead, following the work of Michaels on Australian aboriginal video and Valaskakis on Canadian indigenous broadcasting, we contend that the crucial question turns on Native control of scheduling and programming (Michaels 1994; Valaskakis 1992). Drawing upon the 1990 Canadian Native Broadcasting Policy, Valaskakis says that a Native undertaking should be defined "not in relation to 'the preservation of aboriginal languages and cultures' . . . but in relation to [N]ative ownership and control, [N]ative target audiences, and [N]ative-oriented programming" (Valaskakis 1992, 78).

The chapter unfolds as follows: First, as evidence of the viability and value of local control, we will begin in the middle of the chronology of the development of community television in Alaska to show the high point of local television production and programming. Second, we will establish some theoretical tools to think through the historical struggles to control television in bush Alaska through Carey's articulation of Innis's ideas on space- and time-biased media. Third, we will describe the historical dialectics of these struggles by setting the post–World War II political and technological context in Alaska. Fourth, we will critically analyze a number of pivotal episodes in the development of community television, including: (1) the establishment of Yup'ik community-run television station, KYUK-TV, Bethel; (2) the novel Alaskan development of mini-TV sites and associations; (3) the Applied Technology Satellite-6 project (ATS-6), with its initiation of "representative" consumer committees; and (4) the state's Satellite Television Demonstration Project (SATVDP) and its evolution into what came to be called RATNET, the Rural Alaska Television Network. Finally, we will assess the status of community television in the bush in light of declining state support and offer recommendations for a Native media policy in light of the lessons of this history.

Cultural Documentary Production: The Middle of the Story

To focus attention on Valaskakis's notion of cultural persistence and Carey's imperative of grounding cultural analysis on Native grounds, we begin with a Yup'ik-informed description of an extremely rich period of video documentary production. Beginning in 1980, a largely Yup'ik Eskimo video production team at Native-operated public television station KYUK-TV in Bethel, began producing thirty- and sixty-minute documentaries on their culture. These productions were meant to counter the usual representations of indigenous peoples in the "White man's image." The first video, "They Never Asked Our Fathers" (1980), loudly affirmed Native voices against the imperializing and silencing actions of more than one hundred years of American ideological hegemony in the far north. In this video, the documentary's producers give voice to the Yup'ik Eskimos of Nunivak Island who lament the fact that Russian and American missionaries, traders, and government officials "erased forever a whole way of seeing and being as humans." The Yup'ik narrator, John Active, explained how his cultural ancestors "lived off the land and felt a part of it, but had no conception that they possessed it." With the coming of the White man, that relationship was profoundly disrupted, as alien animal species—reindeer, caribou, and musk oxen—were introduced to the island by companies located thousands of miles away, and as the taking of fish and game became subject to a host of regulations imposed from afar. The alienation of the islanders culminated in the designation of the island as a National Wildlife Refuge.

In the next four years, this group of documentary filmmakers produced six more videos celebrating the folklore of their culture and contributing to the continuity of their lived traditions. Perhaps the most poignant example of their cultural work was the 1983 documentary, "Eyes of the Spirit." It celebrated the return of the carving of the eyes in Yup'ik masks together with the performance of masked dancing by the Bethel Native Dancers. For the Yupiit, the importance of the masks went beyond their status as mere physical objects to the magical claims of what they enabled their people to do. As Alexie Isaac, the director of the documentary, told us, "masked dancing used to play a big part for Yupiit in asking the Creator to make the animals they hunted plentiful" (Isaac 1997). The video crew documented this experience not only for the apprentice mask-makers *within* the video but also for all other receptive Yup'ik eyes who saw the broadcasts over KYUK-TV. Indeed, the documentary emphasized the rediscovery of carved eyes in the creative mask-making process after their nearly centuries-long prohibition by Moravian missionaries. According to Yup'ik beliefs, the eyes of the mask offered a form of magical access to other worlds, other human beings, and to the animals and stories of the dream world. The documentary's thematic focus on the return to the carving of the eyes in Yup'ik dancing masks signified for them a spiritual reawakening of their Yup'ik cosmology. For the Yupiit, cultural persistence was a joyful resistance against the structures of authority represented by the Western culture of Moravian missionaries. As explained in the video, the Bethel Native Dancers wanted to return the masks to a community purpose, to reclaim the masks and their mythic significance for themselves (see Fienup-Riordan 1990, 48–67).

Within both the performance and its recording on videotape, the Yup'ik people of the Bethel region experienced genuine wonder and awe. The documentary and its broadcast over KYUK-TV revivified Yup'ik culture in a form that was obviously nontraditional, what Valaskakis would call an example of the use of modern technology as "cultural persistence." Clearly, the documentary was not a frozen celluloid image imposed by alien filmmakers capturing ethnic exoticisms, but instead was a cultural self-representation of the Yup'ik peoples, an important marker in the continuity of their lived traditions.

Ironically, when KYUK-TV's video documentary team chose to produce videos in just the Yup'ik language, or with little English translation, they were barred from being shown on the statewide RATNET because of a policy of programming for general audiences. This programming policy underscores how disruptive alien authority structures were to Alaska Native peoples' storytelling capacities, despite the efforts of well-intentioned bureaucrats simply to "serve" Native peoples. We will see how this culturally destructive policy arose in a later section of the chapter. To make sense of how these contradictions could arise and to understand the reasons behind the erosion of local control, we now turn to Carey's refinement of conceptual tools articulated by Innis.

Conceptualizing the Research Problems

In a 1975 essay on Canadian communication theory, Carey explains Innis's dialectical positions on the media as either space-biased or time-biased. As Carey puts it, space-biased media reduce the time in which a message is sent and received by increasing the speed of communication over greater and greater distances while at the same time decreasing the costs of its transmission. Carey calls this a "high communication policy" and argues that it has characterized American thinking on communication and its technology since the advent of the railroad and the telegraph. Invoking Innis's ideas, Carey maintains that this communication policy has had consequences for the physical and social relationships among people by its creation of new forms of social organization and new relations of power and control (1975, 30–31).

In his explanation of Innis's positions, Carey maintains that long-distance and short-distance communication have different physical, structural, and cultural dimensions. For example, time-biased media favor physical forms of communication that don't carry far, that emphasize community relations, and that foster intimate ties rooted in a shared historical culture (Carey 1975, 30, 36). Space-biased media, in contrast, favor mechanical—particularly electronic—forms of message distribution from centralized locations distributed over wider and wider areas leading to imperial structures of authority and conditions of inequality and dependency (42).

In their two-part essay called "The Mythos of the Electronic Revolution," Carey and John Quirk trace the historical development of space-biased media in the United States and explain how they were conceptualized through a set of rationalized and romantic notions that they call the "rhetoric of the electrical sublime" (1970, 396). According to them, this late-nineteenth-century rhetoric invests electricity with divine, democratic consequences and promises a return to community. Carey and Quirk suggest that Americans convinced themselves that they could have Europe's industrial revolution without any of its degrading, dirty, and exploitative consequences. The key to this benevolent rhetoric is a faith in a neutral technology. Carey and Quirk utilize Innis to deromanticize the rhetoric of the technological sublime. As they put it, "the least dramatic, most serious problem posed by electric and electronic technology of communications and transportation, however, is its erosion of organic cultures and cultural institutions. The space-binding bias of the television networks . . . disregard[s] in tone and coverage local and regional developments and . . . ignore[s] the cultural diversity of ethnic groups and nationalities" (413–14). Multiculturalism notwithstanding, the power of commercial television is to present one relatively homogeneous culture as *the* American culture and to offer it unproblematically as just entertainment.

Finally, it is important to recall, through Carey, Innis's refutation of Frederick Jackson Turner's frontier thesis. Turner had held that the *peripheries* of Western cultures were the source of democracy, social action, and community. For Innis, the opposite was the case: The *centers* of empires were served by the frontiers, which provided the staples that fed the interests of the industrial, commercial machine (Carey and Quirk 1970, 238; Carey 1981, 75). Indeed, Mary Louise Pratt uses the term "contact zones" in part because it avoids the concept of frontier, terminology that only makes sense to expansionist forces (1992, 6–7). Carey maintains that when the transportation and communications costs of the frontier are high, the staples and the people on the margins tend to be left alone, but when these costs are lessened or strategic interests are increased, then domination and control are intensified (1975, 33).

In the far north, the strategic interests posed by the geopolitics of World War II brought Alaska into the high communications policy of the United States. The discovery of vast reserves of oil in the late 1960s furthered these strategic interests and heightened this policy. As Carey reminds us, Innis's work documented several major transformations in social organization in Western history, the most recent of which were "American and Russian empires founded upon neotechnics: electronics and electricity, petroleum and jet aircraft" (1975, 48). Alaska would play a significant role in the provision of the staple necessary for this transformation—oil—and the development of electronic communication would be its necessary "reward."

For Alaska, satellite communication was a tremendous engineering feat in the 1970s that revolutionized the delivery of television to some of the most remote villages on the globe. As one RATNET Council member proclaimed, "this was a great project . . . used as a model for rural communities across the world" (Nelson, 1999). Nevertheless, a critical analysis of this optimism raises anew the technocratic limitations that Carey's elaboration of Innis's insights posed. To paraphrase Carey, we need to question apolitical technocrats who offer "neutral" technologies as solutions to every problem, even loneliness and isolation (1975, 53). Writing at a time when the last "frontier" of space was about to be colonized with satellite technology, Carey and Quirk warned us about the international ramifications and the globalizing rhetoric "expressed in various documents published by the Carnegie Commission on public television, the Ford Foundation on broadcasting, and the United States' review panel on communications policies. Invariably, these papers reflect a spatial bias toward the focus and scope of communications media and an elitist bias of *noblesse oblige* toward the receivers and subjects of the media within the United States" (1970, 413).

The Public Broadcasting Act of 1967 and the public debate surrounding a domestic satellite policy formed the backdrop in Alaska for a great deal of agitation at the state level for a public broadcasting system that would extend far beyond the state's sole public radio station in Fairbanks (Northrip 1998). The culmination of this agitation was a number of communicative experiments funded by both state and federal agencies.

The Political and Technological Context in Alaska

State involvement in a rural television network in Alaska in the 1970s had ample justification and precedent, for the vast distances, the difficult terrain and weather, and the high costs of construction had long warranted government involvement in telecommunications. In fact, the telephone system in Alaska traces its development to a 1900 congressional authorization of $450,000 for a 2,500–mile telegraph line connecting military outposts in Alaska with Seattle via a submerged cable. The political imperative behind this Washington-Alaska Military Cable and Telegraph System (WAMCATS) illustrates the suitability of space-biased media to authoritative control over vast distances. The military had established a number of outposts in the Klondike and around Nome following the discovery of gold in 1897, and the telegraph line was a tool to keep order in the territory. It allowed instantaneous communication year-round, where, previously, the military outposts had been cut off from the outside world for more than five months of the year (Mitchell 1904; Jenne and Mitchell 1982).

One of the provisions of WAMCATS was that it be made available to commercial users whenever this service would not adversely affect military traffic (Jenne and Mitchell 1982, 14). Over the years, the U.S. Army Signal Corps continued to develop WAMCATS. Wireless communication replaced some of the cable that deteriorated under Arctic conditions, although this "advancement" actually weakened communication, for intense auroral activity frequently caused signal interference (Duncan 1982, 15–18). In 1936, Congress and the War Department changed the name of WAMCATS to the Alaska Communication System (Pearson and Barry 1987, 1).

Alaska's importance as a strategic link to the Pacific Theater during World War II led to federal improvement and expansion of the Alaska Communication System's long-distance lines when an open wire was strung along the Alcan Highway connecting Alaska to the contiguous forty-eight states in 1943 (Melody 1978, 16). Cold war tensions prompted the Air Force to invest $100 million between 1955 and 1958 in what was called the White Alice project to upgrade military and civilian long-distance telephone and telegraphic communication and to interconnect twenty-three Armed Forces radio stations with high frequency tropospheric scatter signals distributed from transmitting dishes. The White Alice system provided a few bush communities with their first reliable long-distance telephone service (Duncan 1982, 163).

But after this federal investment in the Alaska Communication System the Pentagon repeatedly ignored the system's civilian and military requests for direct-distance dialing and other telecommunication improvements. Private telecommunication suppliers such as AT&T regarded Alaska as a military- and government-supported economy whose potential was dependent on a continued military presence (Ely, Boesch, and Cornman 1965, 21, 58–59). By the late 1960s, it was clear that the Defense Department wanted out of the Alaska Communication System and that something would have to be done to improve Alaska's communications infrastructure. Concerned over the federal government's apparent indifference to these problems, Alaska senator Bob Bartlett turned his attention to the Communication Satellite Corporation's (COMSAT) plans for a national satellite system following the 1967 passage of the Public Broadcasting Act and the strong recommendation of the Carnegie Commission on Public Television that a satellite-linked public television system be developed (Carnegie Commission 1967, 53). When Bartlett learned that COMSAT's pilot program for such a system did not include Alaska in its footprint, he intensified his negotiations with its board of directors, arguing that "it would be extremely shortsighted if COMSAT were to help bring improved communications to an emerging nation without first having attempted to do the same for Alaska" (*Tundra Times* January 19, 1968).

At Bartlett's urging, Governor Walter Hickel established a Satellite Communications Task Force to study the potential use of satellites to solve problems posed by the state's vast distances and rugged terrain (APBC 1990, 12). Late in 1968, COMSAT announced that it would build a satellite ground station near the village of Talkeetna, an announcement hailed by Hickel "as the most important breakthrough in communications in Alaska in a generation." Hickel's enthusiasm reverberated with the rhetoric of the electronic sublime, as he proclaimed that "the ground station will prove the key to an educational TV system reaching all points of rural Alaska and will provide a breakthrough of major significance in the state's efforts to help rural Alaskans to full employment through education" (*Tundra Times* December 13, 1968).

Centralized, federal military control of Alaska's communications was substantially reduced in 1969 when Bartlett introduced legislation in Congress authorizing the Department of Defense to sell the Alaska Communication System while retaining the White Alice Communication System and the Distant Early Warning radar stations because of their continued military importance. RCA Global Communications purchased the system. The terms of the sale included half-ownership in COMSAT's Talkeetna ground station and a promise to extend telephone service to 142 remote communities while reducing intrastate toll rates (Melody 1978, 10–18).

Meanwhile, legislation creating the Alaska Educational Broadcasting Commission (AEBC) was passed in 1970. The Commission played a central role in the development of community television in Alaska, and one of its early projects involved assisting community leaders in Bethel in their efforts to establish a local television station.

The Advent of KYUK-TV (Bethel)

While KYUK-TV would not go on air until two and a half years after radio's appearance, public planning for it was simultaneous with that of radio. Not surprisingly, the respective philosophies underpinning community radio and television in Bethel were more or less identical. AEBC executive director Charles Northrip assured Yup'iks that the commission's philosophy of local control over radio broadcasting extended to television. In 1969, a Yup'ik leader of the Bethel Economic Development Committee outlined the group's ten goals, including "radio and television to provide entertainment and education and [to] relieve the communication gap that presently exists in the area" (*Kuskokwim Kronicle* December 1969). Then, in 1971, at the urging of the southwest region's state representative George Hohman, the legislature added $627,000 to the AEBC's fiscal year 1972 budget for an educational television station to be run by Bethel Broadcasting, Inc. The station went on the air in August 1973, featuring a mix of local and public programming (APBC 1990, 17–18; Northrip 1998).

In its first year, KYUK-TV had an abbreviated schedule of five hours of programming a day, six days a week. Even with a small, local staff lacking formal production training, the station offered 20–25 percent local programming, including musical performances by the high school band, theatrical performances written and performed by elementary school students, mixed entertainment productions by Native guitarists, singers, and dancers, and news programs in both Yup'ik and English. In addition, a half-hour interview program often featured political and economic topics discussed by representatives of the Native, profit-oriented regional corporation (Calista), the nonprofit regional corporation (Yupitak Bista), and the Association of Village Council Presidents. In addition, KYUK-TV produced a live two-hour talent show hosted by Yup'ik speaker Mary Gregory. The show featured fifty-five performers, including the Chevak dancers, an elder Yup'ik storyteller, and Yup'ik Eskimo drummers (AEBC February 1974a, 1).

In April 1974, the inaugural issue of the *Tundra Drums,* a self-supporting publication of the KYUK radio and television stations, provided news gathered by its staff, and guides to the upcoming radio and television schedules. According to the *Tundra Drums,* during KYUK-TV's second year of operation, it increased its programming hours significantly with local output ranging from 15–30 percent of its weekly scheduling. Less than two years into its on-air status, KYUK-TV was offering approximately fourteen hours of daily programming (*Tundra Drums* March 15, 1975). Then, in the summer of 1974, KYUK increased the reach of its signal when the FCC approved construction of translators at Tuntuliak, Nightmute, Tuluksak, Kalskag, and Marshall (*Tundra Drums* June 3, 1974; Bethel Broadcasting Incorporated 1991).

An examination of the *Tundra Drums*'s television schedule reveals a programming profile highlighting local programs and imported feature films. The November 3, 1974, issue touted its new "Program Guide" with a full-page advertisement emphasizing local programming: "The changes in the program log . . . represent the anticipated change to fall programming from PBS [Public Broadcasting System] to KYUK. A number of new shows do not come from PBS, but originate in the studios of KYUK-TV. It is our pleasure to offer you new locally produced shows such as 'Pat's Corner,' a twice weekly peek into the world of women's activity. . . . Joe Coolidge and Irene Reed will introduce a University of Alaska videotape of Joe narrating in Yup'ik the story of 'Peter and the Wolf.' . . . A very special treat is in store for you when you view Maggie Lind and Josh Weiser performing traditional Eskimo stories and the 'Sound of the Drum' will return to KYUK Saturday Evening programming." Feature films were also shown over KYUK under the aegis of the

Bethel Film Club, a separate entity from KYUK-TV composed of Bethel individuals and businesses who contracted with Screen Gems for films to fill up additional air time (*Tundra Drums* April 29, 1974 and October 19, 1974).

The Mini-TV Experiments

While the AEBC was assisting KYUK-TV with its construction permit application to the FCC in 1971, it was also involved in a number of experiments to extend television to other parts of rural Alaska. AEBC members were struggling with the problem of how to provide television economically throughout the state, while adhering to the policy of local control. Charles Northrip, the commission's executive director, was toying with the idea of using low-power VHF television transmission with half-inch videotape recorders in remote communities. In 1971, Northrip's efforts landed a grant from the Corporation for Public Broadcasting (CPB) to pay for a study on the feasibility of low-power television transmission in three remote communities, Angoon, Fort Yukon, and Togiak. Unlike the AEBC's discussions with the Bethel Economic Development Committee about its support for public television in Bethel, the AEBC went unannounced into these communities in the spring of 1972.

Northrip explained the experiment's objective to us: "There was no organized program, just random choice programming. The whole idea was to demonstrate the technical feasibility of low-power transmission" (Northrip 1985). Technically, the equipment worked perfectly in two of the three sites (Northrip and Dowling 1972, 3). In their project report, Northrip and Richard Dowling explored the costs of an expanded system, arbitrarily basing their speculations on fifty sites (7). They envisioned using educational film from the Alaska State-Operated School System (ASOSS) and videotaped programming from PBS. They estimated duplication costs at more than $232,000 a year, but reasoned that "future distribution by satellite could well reduce the cost of this service" (6, 9). While community input on the structure of the system was perhaps beyond the bounds of this report, its absence underscored the mistake of importing an alien technology first and then dealing with the community at some future point. Indeed, the mistake of elevating technical concerns over community matters was further exacerbated by anticipated reliance on programming from the ASOSS, which had historically been at odds with local communities (Anthropos 1974, 19).

In the fall of 1972, the AEBC sought CPB funding to establish a network of mini-TV transmitters to deliver public television programming to Unalaska, St. Paul, and Fort Yukon. The purpose of this experiment was "to gain necessary information for the eventual establishment of a system of delivering public television to all remote areas" using bicycled videotapes (Anthropos 1974, 2). In spring 1973, the CPB awarded the AEBC $22,400 to cover the purchase of cassette tapes and equipment, the duplication of tapes at KYUK-TV, Bethel, and the necessary travel for project support. A subsequent supplement by the CPB brought the total to nearly $30,000. The first programs aired in January 1974 (AEBC 1974b, 1).[1]

As in the earlier pilot project, the major objective in launching this small network was to answer technical questions—whether the system could be extended to all remote areas. The operational focus of this latest test was clear from the AEBC report. The findings were divided into eight categories, only the last two of which dealt with audiences or program content. The first six categories dealt with problems and progress in equipment, videocassette distribution, FCC licensing requirements for operators, and the durability of shipping containers. On programming and community utilization of the station, the report noted that each station supplemented the network's public television offerings with its own collection of cassettes or dubs of television programs obtained elsewhere. In its last finding, the report optimistically noted the origination of local programming, particularly in Unalaska: "Perhaps the most notable accomplishment of the mini-TV licensees is their wide-ranging utilization of their recorders to originate programming important to the communities they serve. At Unalaska . . . 57 hours of broadcast time in January had been locally originated. Activities in English and history classes, instructions in pottery-making and fishing and presentations of the Unalaska band and chorus have been recorded and broadcast. . . . News, weather, and local announcements are also broadcast by the school's class of video students" (AEBC 1974b, 6–7).

An independent evaluation of the project noted that the opportunity for local, cultural programming went largely unfulfilled in the other two villages. Evaluators traced the unrealized potential to differing managerial structures. At Fort Yukon and St. Paul, the city held the license and therefore the city manager set policy. Station managers made what they considered to be routine programming decisions within the structure that had been established for them. In contrast, the locally controlled school district held the license in Unalaska, and the school functioned as an inviting community center. The cultural milieu for the station's operation was further enriched by a media advisory committee that represented the village's five hundred mainly Aleut residents. In assessing the patterns of control, the evaluators maintained that the people in Fort Yukon and St. Paul may have been satisfied with what they received, but that there was no encouragement, financing, technical assistance, or planning to help them develop programs on local issues or their indigenous cultures (Anthropos 1974, 17, 19–20).

Except for help providing public broadcasting material through KYUK-TV, the AEBC maintained its policy of noninterference in programming and operations. But this "neutral" stance was an implicit affirmation of the soundness of the existing media model, and the Anthropos evaluation team took the AEBC to task for its casual approach. It prophetically warned that "there is a critical difference between laissez-faire and accepting responsibility for helping communities to help themselves. If this is not done, it is not unlikely that we shall see some replication in rural Alaska of the adverse aspects of television viewing so frequently documented in the nation at large" (Anthropos 1974, 26). In its self-analysis, AEBC said the major difficulty in this small network was the erratic distribution of videocassettes, including the often-unsequential programming that resulted. While there were problems in a distribution system that was necessarily convoluted by Alaska's airline and bush plane schedules, the AEBC's unflagging interest in technical efficiency remained paramount.

Over the next several years, the AEBC established mini-TV stations in a number of other communities; by the end of 1976 there were thirty-nine of them in operation. While one of the greatest virtues of the mini-TV stations was the absence of a centralized, homogenizing network in any but the crudest sense, it was increasingly clear that the state was headed in the direction of satellite distribution of communication. In 1972, the AEBC had submitted a plan to the U.S. Department of Health, Education, and Welfare to use NASA's proposed Applied Technology Satellite-6 (ATS-6) for health and educational programming in rural Alaska. As we will see, the ATS-6 project paved the way for a Satellite Television Demonstration Project (SATVDP) that would link the mini-TV stations together. To the credit of their planners, ATS-6 experiments did try to inject some measure of local control over programming with the initiation of consumer committees, a structural feature later adopted by the facilitators of the SATVDP. We now turn our attention to the reasons why those efforts failed.

The ATS-6 Experiments and Their Consumer Committees

According to the state's mission statement, the primary objective of the ATS-6 experiments was to acquire technical experience applicable to future statewide satellite communication systems.[2] The Governor's Office of Telecommunications (GOT) oversaw the project, and described this goal in its final report: "The state's objective was not to determine if satellites can be useful, but how to most effectively use them" (1975, 1:12–13). The satellite's footprint covered southeast, south-central, and interior regions of the state. Of the sixty-three communities within this region, nineteen were chosen to participate on the basis of their remoteness and their lack of prior experience with television. They included Athabascan, Tlingit, and Yup'ik communities.

The experiment's planners were well aware of the state's cultural diversity, and in their efforts to provide culturally relevant programming, they sought "to involve users in all phases of actual program content selection and development" through the establishment of consumer committees (GOT 1975, 1:15). The GOT asked each participating village to select one resident to serve on consumer committees for three educational programming ventures: Basic Oral Language Development, Health Education, and Early Childhood Education.[3] State bureaucrats from the Division of Public Health and the ASOSS were also asked to participate. The village representatives tended to come from school staffs. As a result, nine of the nineteen villagers selected were non-Natives, raising questions about the ability of the committees to ensure cultural relevancy and authenticity of programming. In addition, the formal charter drawing up the committees' responsibilities reveals the aptness of the passive term, *consumer* committee. Because of this consumer orientation, the decision-making responsibilities of committee members were attenuated.

Before a contract had been let for the instructional programming component of the experiment, the GOT's educational coordinator met several times with the Center for Northern Educational Research (CNER) in Fairbanks concerning its interest in the project. In a fall 1973 meeting between representatives of public television station KUAC in Fairbanks, the CNER, and the GOT, participants agreed on the desirability of visiting villages to talk with Natives regarding program development. Considerable discussion turned on the availability of half-inch portable video equipment because, as filmmaker Sarah Elder of the CNER put it, this would enable people to produce their own programs. Furthermore, local production would provide audiences with an intimate emotional connection to the programming (GOT 1975 3:H, 2–3). Upon returning to Juneau, the GOT's Education Experiment manager sent a letter to Elder the following day, expressing "a need for further clarification for what is meant by the terms content design and production," adding that he "would like to reiterate that the subject matter areas have already been selected, and while we want the greatest possible participation from the remote site users, there is an urban component as well" (GOT 1975, 3:H.1, 5–6). A couple of months later, the CNER's director sent a letter to GOT, pulling out of the instructional programming bidding process because of "the need for extensive lead time to assure adequate local involvement." He endorsed the proposals of the CNER's competitor, the Northwest Regional Educational Laboratory (NWREL) based in Portland, Oregon, because he said it had "a large sophisticated staff where equipment facilities have already been established" (GOT 1975, 3:H.3, 8).

After NWREL was awarded the contract, a memorandum of understanding was drawn up between GOT, NWREL, and the production team of the University of Alaska (Fairbanks) Division of Media Services, which indicated the degree to which the consumer committees' decisions would be "engineered" as much as any technical aspect of the experiment. The memorandum said that "the charge of these committees is to approve, disapprove, or alter the material presented to them at scheduled times by the NWREL" (GOT 1975, 3:H.6, 23). The first meeting of the Basic Oral Language Development Consumer Committee was indicative of this engineering. According to the minutes of the meeting, "One member felt that possibly the programs were too 'commercial' and not culturally relevant. This concern was discussed and the committee decided that trying to put in too much so-called cultural relevancy would alter the basic design and destroy its effectiveness." Another item in that same report reflected the trivial nature of the "cultural relevancy" that did get accepted: The characters in one of the children's programs wore hats. The committee accepted a proposal to supplement the standard cowboy and fireman hats with hats "from the different cultural areas of Alaska, for example, a beaver hat, a spruce hat" (GOT 1975, 3:H.9, 43).

Several months into the project, the GOT decided to supplement the educational programming with "Alaska Native Magazine" (ANM), a public affairs program targeted toward adults. Once again, a consumer committee was constituted, but in a manner that favored assimilated, urban Natives. Following the suggestion of the Alaska Federation of Natives (AFN), now a statewide arm of the regional corporations, the ANM consumer committee was drawn from the four Native regional corporations within the satellite footprint (the Chugach and Cook Inlet Native Associations and the Calista and Sealaska Corporations) and from two noncorporate organizations (the Tanana Chiefs Conference and the AFN).

The initial meetings of the ANM's consumer committee in the summer of 1974 focused on the program's format, topics, and production values. At the first meeting, state planners suggested a format of reports on salient topics by the program's host, followed by interaction between people in the studio and the villages. The committee agreed upon a list of topics for the first several programs that included civil rights issues, Native land claims, environmental protection, fisheries, and profiles of prominent Natives (GOT 1975 3:H.29, 130–31). At the second meeting, the committee agreed to sponsor slow-paced programs that avoided bureaucratic language. The committee advised film crews to keep an open mind about how subjects ought to be treated when they went into the villages on their shoots (GOT 1975, 3:H.30, 132–33).

But despite this sensitivity, cinematographer Mark Badger, in an interview a number of years later (1985), identified several communicative problems in the ANM production process. First, he recalled that when he went into the villages he was surprised at how little attention had been given to involving local people in the process of program planning. While the consumer committee served as a formal representative structure, it evidently lacked any mechanisms for grass-roots villagers' involvement. Badger noted that it was up to the film crew to ascertain villagers' views of the project and to determine whether it met their needs. Second, he maintained that the tight production schedule "was a meatgrinder." He believed that because the project involved a "delicate and critical" intrusion into another culture, the production crew should have had much more time to work with, and learn from, villagers.

The ATS-6 experiments lasted almost nine months. Ironically, one of the last ANM programs featured Leonard Kamerling's film of Inupiat women's role in whaling. About a year before, Kamerling had begun "The Alaska Native Heritage Project" with Sarah Elder, mentioned previously as the CNER filmmaker who crossed swords with the GOT's Education Experiment manager over her desire to let villagers produce their own films. According to film scholar Steven Leuthold, the Alaska Native Heritage Project "exemplifies co-produced films in which [N]ative perspectives are central. Co-production is a form of collaborative ethnography based upon shared decisions of the film team and the communities. Films by Kamerling and Elder . . . depart from traditional ethnographic and fiction film because of their 'lack of any overt message, a leisurely pacing that allows cultural processes to unfold at their own rate, and an episodic structure in which there is no clear beginning or end'" (1998, 72; see also Collier and Collier 1986, 157).

Following its completion, the ATS-6 project was externally evaluated for the National Institute of Education by Practical Concepts, Incorporated, with assistance from the CNER. After the release of their official report, the CNER issued its own paper, refining and analyzing the evaluators' broad recommendations "as they relate to Alaska's multi-cultural population" (Darnell 1976, iii). The authors explained that their recommendations were being issued in response to the state legislature's decision to move forward with plans to provide television through satellite to the bush. Specifically, the legislation provided funding "for a satellite transponder lease project to demonstrate the feasibility of satellite communications in Alaska, priority being given to satellite television" (cited in Pittman and Orvik 1976, v).

The CNER recommendations epitomized a model for local control of television programming with regional networks. The authors urged that money be appropriated for programming purchases by representative committees, and that Natives be trained in the media so that they could make their own culturally relevant programming. According to the CNER, the consumer committees may have been a valuable investment in consumer education, but, these evaluators argued, "they do not represent a model for villager control of rural media" (Pittman and Orvik 1976, 13, 17, 20). Despite the CNER's recommendations, the state pushed ahead with plans that had little to do with either local control or culturally relevant programming.

The State's Satellite Television Demonstration Project

In December 1975, a legislative subcommittee hearing on the distribution of television programming brought together commercial and public broadcasters, cable operators, the state Division of Communication, the AEBC, and the GOT. A Television Advisory Group of mainly commercial broadcasters was appointed to look into financing and programming problems (GOT 1978, 2:Section 12, 12–13). This Television Advisory Group met with the legislative subcommittee again in February 1976 to decide whether private enterprise or the state should provide entertainment television to the bush. The state wanted to stay clear of programming, but was, as in the past, willing to finance the necessary technological hardware. Indeed, hoping to resolve a long-running dispute with RCA's subsidiary, Alascom, about its slowness in providing telephone service to the bush, the state had appropriated $5 million in 1975 for the construction of small, two-way earth stations in one hundred villages. The ATS-6 project had shown that, with small modifications, these earth stations were capable of video reception (Dowling 1982, 32).

Despite initial opposition by the Alaska Broadcasters Association to a process in which the state would deliver entertainment programming, one of the state's pioneer commercial broadcasters, A. G. Hiebert, led negotiations among the state, the networks, and the FCC (GOT 1978, 2:16). An agreement forged between PBS and the three commercial networks and their Anchorage affiliates allowed programs to be taped in their entirety and then retransmitted to rural Alaska from a Tape Delay Center operated by the Alaska Public Broadcasting Commission in Anchorage (APBC).[4] The arrangement benefited all parties. As an incentive for cooperation by networks and commercial broadcasters, the state allowed commercial broadcasters to use its leased transponder for live delivery of network news and sports to urban audiences.

The SATVDP went into operation in January 1977, with twenty-three rural communities receiving signals through modified small earth stations and then rebroadcasting them locally though ten-watt transmitters. Before the SATVDP went into operation, the state continually and emphatically stated that it should not and would not be involved in programming, and that it was imperative that an "independent, identifiable consumer group be given the responsibility of making program selections" (GOT 1978, 1:35). But what the state never recognized, or at least never acknowledged, was that its laissez-faire approach to programming made the commercial system the de facto control agent. In addition, from the standpoint of its intended audience, the GOT saw its users as falling into three categories: (1) commercial television network affiliates, (2) public service agencies, and (3) individual viewers of network programming during prime time hours (GOT 1975, 1:66). By categorizing users as individual viewers rather than as members of distinct cultural groups, the state had, for purposes of its operations, effectively assimilated rural Natives into the mainstream of American life. As Innis had warned, space-biased communication systems centralize structures of authority, homogenize communication, and in the process, injure organic communities.

The responsibility for the selection of programs was placed in the hands of the AFN's Telecommunications Committee, formed in late 1975 in anticipation of the project. This committee was simply an enlargement of the ANM consumer committee, including representatives from each of the twelve Native regional corporations (GOT 1978, 2:Section 12, 35). For the most part, the committee made its program selections from *TV Guide* and *Gambit*, a magazine listing PBS programs. Flawed as the committee was in its largely urban composition, some members, nevertheless, questioned the relevance of their participation within the strictures of mainstream television fare. For example, the GOT was asked about the availability of Alaska Native or Canadian Native programming, but the idea was shot down on the dubious grounds of quality control, broadcast restrictions, and lack of interest among villagers.

The GOT's final report did acknowledge that the "Kamerling/Elder series, perhaps the finest film footage of rural life today, was available for broadcast at $400 per film" (GOT 1978, 2:Section 5, 18). The report made no further comment about this cost, but it was certainly reasonable, for the Carnegie Commission had estimated that, with $2,000 weekly, an average station could produce one hour of superior programming a week (1967, 50). Again, the GOT report was unequivocal about reproducing the commercial system in Alaska rather than in assisting indigenous production for the needs and desires of local cultures. In answer to its rhetorically posed question whether villagers wanted to watch commercial programming or indigenous programming, the report stated, "it appears that the biggest fuss over Alaskan produced material is being made from people with either a vested interest in locally produced materials or those people living outside the villages obsessed with 'saving the culture'" (GOT 1978, 2:Section 5, 2).

While the SATVDP was supposed to end after one year, the legislature continued to appropriate funds to keep RATNET going. Having invested more than five years in television experiments and demonstrations, the state was not in a political position to pull back. Then, when the trans-Alaska oil pipeline went online in 1977, the state's treasury was sufficiently flush to ensure continued support, although Governor Jay Hammond used line-item vetoes to slash a nearly $11 million legislative appropriation for television in fiscal year 1978 to just over $2 million (McIntire 1984, 1). Hammond's wariness about state involvement in a usually private matter led him to hire a Los Angeles contractor to run the system, but this action inspired complaints from Natives who felt that this outside company had little understanding of rural Alaska Native needs (Isett 1995, 24–25).

Meanwhile, indigenous receivers of the system were often confused over who was responsible for programming. While the AFN Committee had its "menu" from which to choose, its structured decisions were majoritarian, not pluralist, ignoring all Alaska's different language groups and ethnic traditions (Northrip 1998). The practice of programming for a mass audience drew the wrath of other interests as well. The Alaska Department of Education (DOE), the nominal bureaucratic home of the APBC, was perhaps the most vocal. In 1979, the legislature passed a resolution asking state agencies to study the feasibility of telecommunications for instruction in the state. In a 1980 report prepared primarily by the DOE with contributions from the University of Alaska System and the APBC, instructional telecommunication planners pointed out that successful systems include "services to a wide variety of specialized users (not a general or mass audience)" (DOE 1980, 18).

Following a national trend, though, Alaska's noncommercial broadcasters had moved away from educational programming toward popular, general interest fare, a movement reflected in the state's renaming of the Alaska Educational Broadcasting Commission in 1976 as the Alaska Public Broadcasting Commission. The DOE's Jennifer Wilke lamented this turn away from education and the growing desire to appeal "to the largest possible general audience" (DOE 1980 Appendix C1, 12). Consequently, the DOE's instructional television feasibility report made numerous references to the need for Alaskan subject matter, for programming of local relevance, and for a production system that would enable all Alaskans, including Alaska Natives, to share their perceptions and viewpoints (DOE 1980, 25, and Appendix C1, 28, 31). While these suggestions seemed meritorious, the DOE never mentioned any specific cultural needs of Alaska Native communities. Its call for Alaska television production was firmly lodged in the institutional sector where educators determine instructional objectives (DOE 1980 Appendix C1, 28–30). In short, the DOE's potential telecommunications clientele was a wide range of students for whom educational producers were required to maintain academic integrity in an efficient manner (DOE 1980 Appendix C2, 1). For the DOE, communication was a pipeline or transmission belt with some possibilities for interaction, but not in the sense of communication as a cultural or intercultural process. The dominant culture was always the invisible presence making its ideological mark on decision-making processes as if it were a natural process.

RATNET and LEARN/Alaska Programming

In response to the DOE's feasibility study, the state legislature established a second rural satellite television channel, LEARN/Alaska, in 1980. This channel was run mainly by the DOE and the University of Alaska Instructional Telecommunications Services. LEARN/Alaska went on line in 1982, feeding imported as well as self-produced programming to more than two hundred communities. Before the advent of LEARN/Alaska, some instructional programming had been aired over RATNET during the daytime hours. LEARN/Alaska freed up more time for commercial programming, including soap operas, over RATNET. Paradoxically, this programming shift would increase

RATNET's popularity, but make it more susceptible to cuts by political leaders who questioned state involvement in commercial broadcasting.

Telecommunication services were restructured and clarified through executive orders issued, and legislation adopted, in 1981. The name RATNET, long used to refer to the system that had evolved out of the SATVDP, was officially adopted (Isett 1995, 27). Control of the Tape Delay Center was transferred out of the APBC to the Division of Telecommunications Systems, housed in the state's Department of Administration. The APBC was given autonomous status within the Department of Administration and relocated to the state capital, Juneau, where its funding source could be better pumped (Northrip 1998). Most important for programming purposes, the RATNET Council, a carryover from the SATVDP's user committee, was formally recognized as twelve appointees of the regional nonprofit associations and two appointees by the governor. The decision-making powers of the Council were ratified, and the Council adopted a set of policy guidelines, making de jure what had been de facto practices.

Three guidelines proved especially pertinent to the RATNET Council's programming practices. They dealt with the source of entertainment programming, with the programming rights of so-called special interest groups, and with the airing of programs produced in Alaska. Codifying past practice, the guideline entitled "Entertainment Program Selection" stated that, "Entertainment programs will be selected from the four major networks (ABC, CBS, NBC, PBS) and independent program producers (if permission to carry programs is available)" (RATNET Council 1984, 4). The guideline on "Special Interest Groups" stated that, "Special interest groups and organizations requesting to present programs over the state of Alaska Satellite Television Project, which are controversial subjects or programs for selective audiences only, must obtain approval of the RATNET Council" (5).

Under this provision, programs with regional appeal produced in a Native language were judged as special interest programming. Peter Twitchell, a sixteen-year member of the RATNET Council and a Yup'ik speaker himself, said the Council did not want programming solely in one Native language, "but we accepted programming which was interwoven with the language of the people who produced it, as long as it was presented in English for the benefit of all our viewers" (Twitchell 1999). Documentaries produced at KYUK-TV during the efflorescence of Native videography in the 1980s apparently fell into the special interest category as well. There is no evidence, or independent recollection, that these Yup'ik-oriented documentaries were ever aired on RATNET (Flintoff 1999; Isaac 1997; Nelson 1999; Twitchell 1999; see also Isett 1995). Why KYUK's documentaries were apparently not broadcast by RATNET is unclear, but this guideline was probably determinative. Corey Flintoff, a non-Native producer of many of these videos, says he consciously chose to produce narration in both languages and often he overtly emphasized Yup'ik not only because he wanted it available to Yup'ik speakers but also because he wanted the White audience to hear the sound of Yup'ik (Flintoff 1999). Because there was no production money available at RATNET, there was no opportunity to subtitle the programming in English so that it could have been available for statewide audiences while still promoting local and regional cultures. As this example shows, the guideline on special interest groups clearly privileged English speakers over Native speakers. Ironically, an effort to be sensitive to diverse cultural needs ended up enshrining the values and language of the dominant culture. The upshot of the guideline was that "special interest" programming was consigned to the ghetto of the competing, and far less popular, LEARN/Alaska network.

In its guideline on "Alaska-Produced Programs," the RATNET Council encouraged locally produced programs for the Alaska statewide audience if they met technical standards as approved by the Tape Delay Center (RATNET Council 1984, 5). This guideline implicitly raised the question of whose technical standards were important in a medium that had its "professional" development in Western aesthetic structures and practices. Most of the technicians at the Tape Delay Center were urban professionals who grew up with Western narratives, conventions, and fast-paced production practices. Would different narratives, different conventions, and different pacing—such as the coproductions of Kamerling/Elder—have met their technical standards? Most Alaska Native viewers and RATNET Council members favored local productions, but the institutional mechanisms to promote them in any serious way were lacking. As a former RATNET Council president put it, "There was never any money for production. The Council favored local productions and live broadcasts over canned programs [but] there were never enough produced for the liking of the [rural] public and the Council. We all wished there was more Alaskan produced programming, . . . [And] we didn't have a mechanism or procedure for soliciting programs from Canada. The TV stations (commercial network affiliates) offered us their programming and so did private producers. We chose from what was offered" (Nelson 1999). Even with its expressed preference for local programming, the RATNET Council consistently refused to carry KYUK-TV's daily Yup'ik news program because it aired in Yup'ik and because of its regional flavor. The fact that

Yup'ik Eskimos comprise the largest group of Alaska Natives was apparently an insufficient reason to override the Council's guidelines (Isett 1995, 38–39). Thus, as with other television experiments, demonstrations, projects, and even instructional programming, RATNET guidelines never countenanced the diverse cultural needs in rural Alaska.

The Beginning of the End?

In 1986, Alaska's heavily petrodollar-dependent economy took a severe hit when the global oil market collapsed. The legislature's budget reductions claimed LEARN/Alaska in the summer. By the late fall, some instructional material was sent over the RATNET system after its entertainment-laden, eighteen-hour programming day had concluded. Rural educators largely ignored it. Democratic governor-elect Steve Cowper's transition team recommended eliminating RATNET in 1987, but powerful rural legislators withstood this challenge by forming coalitions with Fairbanks area legislators and holding off Anchorage conservatives. In the face of a continuing recession in the oil market, each legislative session in the late 1980s continued to threaten RATNET's existence while cutting its budget. Rural versus urban legislators formed the battle lines over RATNET with many non-Native urban legislators exhibiting little understanding of the system, its council, or even of life in rural Alaska (Boucher and MacLean 1990, 6; Isett 1995, 40; Nelson 1999). From fiscal year 1987 to fiscal year 1990, RATNET system funding decreased nearly 37 percent. By 1990, there was barely enough money available to pay for the transponder lease time on Alascom's Aurora satellite (Boucher and MacLean 1990, 10).

From 1989 to 1991, the Center for Information Technology at the University of Alaska/Anchorage held three conferences on communications issues. At the first of these Chugach Conferences, participants concluded that Native and rural Alaskans needed to be more actively involved in developing a vision "of where [they] want to go with telecommunications in Alaska" (Pearson 1990, 1). Indigenous respondents focused on the bias of satellite technology that sends messages, as Innis would have put it, from afar while changing the quality of communication close at hand. As one Tlingit commentator put it, "there is a real need to develop a reverse transmission system that will direct programming from the rural areas of the state . . . the satellite should be broadcasting in both directions" (Kito quoted in Pearson 1990, 9). D'Anne Hamilton, an Inupiat Eskimo with significant broadcasting experience asked, "how much say do Natives actually have in deciding what actually goes on the air? . . . is there any way we can offer more culturally relevant options to the 'Wheel of Fortune' and 'The Price is Right?' What are we saying to young people when we show them the bliss of winning a Mercedes but not the honor and dignity of bringing home a caribou to put on the family table?" (Hamilton quoted in Pearson 1990, 6). Agreeing with Hamilton's focus on the need for media decision making by Alaska Natives, Gail Valaskakis, an indigenous communication scholar whose work we have foregrounded in this book, maintained that "the issue is control" (Valaskakis quoted in Pearson 1990, 16).

Less than five years later, in June 1995, RATNET went "dark" for more than a month during the summer subsistence season in order to save money. The 1995 legislature had just pared $400,000 from RATNET's $1.25 million budget, eliminating all six positions at the Tape Delay Center. A cable company that had been receiving its signals from Anchorage affiliates through RATNET equipment volunteered to continue feeding signals to the system. The rest of RATNET's operations were transferred to KYUK-TV and were organized under the new name of Alaska Rural Communications Service (ARCS) (*Anchorage Daily News* June 15, 1995).

As a consequence of this reconfiguration, Alaska's four public television stations, including KYUK, were folded into one operation known as Alaska One. This merger created one public television superstation, eliminating four separate purchases of PBS programming. However, in this money-saving consolidation, KYUK's local control was sacrificed and with it, its ability to produce programming in the Yup'ik language (Isaac 1997). KYUK-TV's identity was further diminished by the promotion and underwriting responsibilities it assumed under the new ARCS arrangement. Public and private partnerships became a common solution to what was perceived as the "problem" in public broadcasting in Alaska following the Republican sweep in the midterm national elections in 1994. In Alaska, as in the nation at large, privatization was the resurrected buzzword from the Reagan deregulation era as Republican leaders began to call for the elimination of federal funding for public broadcasting (Engelman 1996, 3).

On the regional level in southwest Alaska, the silencing and blinding of Yup'ik programming by these consolidations were every bit as powerful as the loss of Yup'ik vision effected by the authority structures of Moravian missionaries in the late nineteenth century and the technological systems of generally well-intentioned state bureaucrats in the past two decades. In both cases, the centralizing effects of these structures have threatened the vitality of indigenous peoples' cultures. By promoting high technology over more locally advantageous forms of communication, the state opted for the economic solution of a Satellite Interconnection Project using digital technologies. In fiscal year 1998, public/rural television suffered another 12 percent decline. With digital technology, the Satellite Interconnection Project can offer more channels over what was once the lone RATNET channel (APBC 1996, 5–6). However, with rare exceptions, control over programming and scheduling remains centralized.[5] In the face of these continuing technological fixes, one must ask the seemingly melancholy question of whether the vision supplied by modern media to rural Alaska has been irrevocably occluded by its centralizing and homogenizing aspects or, more optimistically, whether, with resistance as cultural persistence, the magic, the "spirit of the eyes," can be reinvigorated?

Conclusion

In a perceptive ten-year retrospective on telecommunications in Alaska, one of the bureaucrats heavily involved in these experiments put it well when he said, "where progress has been made in Alaska, we have generally erred on the side of *doing,* rather than *planning*" (Walp 1982, vi). Indeed, the rarity of this admission underscores the primacy of the rhetoric of the electronic sublime. But it was a rhetoric that was never equally shared among Alaska's indigenous peoples. The Chugach Conferences were emblematic of the technological and cultural divide between Alaska Natives and non-Natives. While Alaska Natives understood full well the biases of technology, non-Native bureaucrats were at best equivocal about these biases. Whenever this equivocation threatened to surface, it was quickly submerged by the rhetoric of the electronic sublime and a concomitant experiment, program, or demonstration. Intentionally or not, political, economic, and bureaucratic leaders in Alaska have used various forms of technology, and the authority structures which underwrite them, to attempt to assimilate Alaska Natives into the relatively homogeneous commercial mainstream of American life.

However, as we have tried to show, Alaska Natives have continually engaged in practices of "resistance as cultural persistence." Forms of cultural expressiveness recalling spiritual beliefs and practices tied to the land and to subsistence have been central to this resistance. At times, Alaska Native groups have utilized film, video, and television productions for their own purposes. When they have been most successful, the key component in their cultural expressiveness has been indigenous control over the means of communication. As we noted in the book's introduction, the vitality of Alaska Native cultures is dependent upon their control over both the material and symbolic dimensions of justice. This revitalization must include media policies in which Alaska Natives are the architects. Neither privatization nor a laissez-faire policy offers sound cultural solutions. Instead, the state must recognize that communication is a cultural process and that communication systems must be regarded as essential services if indigenous cultures are going to survive.

We reiterate the recommendations offered by Theda Sue Pittman and James Orvik more than a quarter of a century ago. Alaska Natives should receive funding to produce and purchase their own programming so that they might be able to strike some balance between the reception of space-biased communication and the production of time-biased communication. The point is not that television should be strictly indigenous, but rather that Alaska Native groups must be provided the opportunity to strike the appropriate balance between the consumption of other cultures and the production and reception of their own. Native groups and state officials must exercise care to see that satellite interconnection projects do not recapitulate the centralizing and homogenizing effects on the state level that have already taken place at the national level. In order to produce their own programming, Alaska Native groups need financial assistance to set up media training centers for Native youth, where instruction is firmly grounded in the context of regional cultures and Native languages.[6] In 1998 Alaska voters approved an English-Only ballot measure further endangering Native languages. If Alaska Native peoples and their cultures are to persist, they must have their multiple voices heard and their own visions recognized with their own cultural definitions over their own media on their own time-honored terms.

NOTES

1. Northrip left the AEBC in 1971, when a new administration in Juneau changed the commission's composition. The CPB's grant followed Northrip to the University of Alaska where he resumed his old position as Director of the Division of Media Services. Northrip's report (coauthored with Project Engineer Richard Dowling) on the mini-TV project was submitted to the appropriate agencies in November 1972.

2. Much of our description of this and subsequent satellite projects follows an account published as James and Daley, 1987.

3. The Early Childhood Education program was never developed.

4. The FCC needed a lot of persuasion. However, there were precedents. For example, in 1975, KYUK-TV in Bethel had begun showing some commercial videotaped

programs over its publicly licensed station without getting appropriate clearance or apparently without paying for rebroadcast rights. This resulted in a visit to the station by the FBI in 1976. In March 1977, the FCC granted KYUK a waiver of FCC rules, allowing its commercial programming. In its applications for renewal of the waiver, KYUK maintained that its programming of commercial fare never exceeded 20 percent of its total airtime and that it did not conflict with RATNET's commercial programming (FCC licensing files, KYUK-TV).

5. Ironically, just as the state was pulling the funding out from under RATNET's feet, two Alaska Native women were producing very popular programming for the channel. Jeannie Greene's "Heartbeat Alaska" independently solicited amateur videos and produced programming from them, "sometimes just slow-moving video postcards." As one Native reporter put it, "I think for the first time the general public is about to see just who we are by our own definition" (*Anchorage Daily News* December 9, 1993).

In addition, Sharon McConnell's "North Country News" was a television news magazine originally produced for public television. Perhaps acknowledging the hybrid nature of her programs, which seek to use modern technology while living with traditional values, McConnell says she has "learn[ed] to walk in two worlds with one spirit" (*Anchorage Daily News,* vertical file of Anchorage Public Library, date unknown).

6. Koahnic Broadcasting Incorporated in Anchorage has been running a week-long Alaska Native Youth Media Institute every summer for the past few years. A small number of high school students receive scholarships and are trained in print, radio, and television principles and practices. Most of its classes are conducted at Koahnic's KBNA studios. While the students seem to learn a lot in a short period of time, their learning situations in an urban setting and with a station with increasing reliance on corporate underwriting raise some pedagogical warning flags. We address additional concerns about Western professional norms in the book's conclusion.

CONCLUSION: Cultural Politics and
Indigenous Public Spheres

IN THIS BOOK we have presented a series of case studies on how various Alaska Native groups' everyday cultural practices could be understood in terms of Gail Valaskakis's concept of resistance as cultural persistence. In particular, we emphasized how her concept elegantly accounts for the ways in which traditional oral societies appropriated the new media of mass communication as a means to counter the imposition of Western cultural ideas and practices. As with all forms of appropriation, there were adverse as well as positive cultural consequences for Alaska Natives. To paraphrase James Carey, in order to be heard and to "control" their own narratives, Alaska Natives had to accept the multiplying means and forms of communication that dislodged their cultures from the places in which they were created (1989, 2). Community radio stations offer the best illustration of the successes and failures in Alaska Native media building. On the one hand, their establishment provided the means for the articulation of collective voices in community-oriented discursive democracies. On the other hand, their development was forged within national and state systems of public radio where the production of news and views adheres to professional standards of objectivity and a liberal pluralist tradition serving an audience predicated on individual consumer choices.

In other words, the cultural crises posed by many of these earlier material struggles required that Alaska Natives be heard in public spheres controlled and dominated by others. Under these circumstances, Western news narratives clashed with Alaska Native cultures and their collectively oriented subsistence economies grounded in ideologies of sharing. Our historical case studies show that Alaska Natives understood news as a particular cultural construction demanding challenges from them for, as William Paul put it in 1926, "a group of people without the power of telling what they have done can be robbed." In the course of their material struggles, Alaska Natives increasingly recognized that all of their storytelling practices—including the indigenous production of news—were cultural activities that produced and reaffirmed their traditional values and beliefs. However, when Alaska Natives tried to tell their stories in the dominant news media, they found reporters framing their words with adverse cultural constructions under the professional mantle of objectivity.

In academic circles, professional journalistic claims to objectivity have been challenged for a number of decades now by scholars who have emphasized routine news practices and processes in which reporters filter events through capitalist organizational requirements and a repertoire of implicit story formulas (Cohen and Young 1973; Darnton 1975; Schudson 1978; Tuchman 1978; Gans 1979; Fishman 1980; Ericson, Baranek, and Chan 1987; Carey 1989; Lule 2001). In his description of "storytelling in the age of mass culture," Robert Fulford reminds us that "there is no such thing as just a story. A story is always charged with meaning; otherwise it is not a story, merely a sequence of events" (1999, 6).

Of course storytelling in the age of mass culture has roots in oral traditions common to many peoples. Scholars have long emphasized storytelling as central to the human experience. Walter Ong, for instance, tells us that "narrative is everywhere a major genre of verbal art, occurring all the way from primary oral cultures into high literacy and electronic information processing" (1982, 139–40). In his seminal work on the narrative paradigm, Walter Fisher "sees people as storytellers—authors and coauthors who creatively read and evaluate the texts of life and literature" (1985, 86). And, in his *Daily News, Eternal Stories,* Jack Lule highlights the connections between ancient myths and contemporary news stories by invoking the commonality of flood stories told by Choctaw elders, by Incan high priests, by the Biblical story of Genesis, and by a reporter for the *New York Times.* "Journalists," he tells us, "are part of a long storytelling tradition that includes fleet-footed messengers, minstrels, troubadours, carriers, couriers, criers, poets, chief priests, missionaries, rabbis, and medicine men" (2001, 1–6).

Despite the journalistic claim to Olympian detachment and the apparent structural uniformity between myths and some news stories, all storytellers are situated in a particular time and place. From their space- and time-bound locations, storytellers creatively craft language into dramatic action that gives voice and stability to their cultural values and beliefs. In this book, we have emphasized that indigenous peoples' communicative practices resonate with a strong cultural sense of place located in the natural environment and intimately connected with political economies of subsistence. In the American journalistic profession, reporters, as storytellers, operate from the mythic position of objectivity and the allegedly neutral category of information while echoing what sociologist Herbert Gans identifies as the enduring values of order, individualism, responsible capitalism, moderatism, leadership, small-town pastoralism, altruistic democracy, and ethnocentrism (1979). As we have shown, Alaska's mainstream press resonated with news narratives and editorial views that reproduced these enduring values and represented events and issues in the state from a monocultural position. In its crassest moments, the ideological blind spots of the mainstream press and the dominant Western culture enabled seemingly enlightened political leaders such as Senator Ernest Gruening to devalue all that was dear to Alaska Natives, calling their lands ugly and worthless and labeling their subsistence practices as welfare traps. Most of the time, however, the political frames articulated by public officials in new stories were more implicit than Gruening's outspokenness, thus protecting their ideological claims from outright racist challenges but not reducing the ongoing threats to indigenous peoples embedded in them (see Bennett and Edelman 1985, 165).

Therefore, while Alaska Natives continue to achieve some success in their everyday practices of resistance as cultural persistence, they do so in the face of hegemonic news media and a unitary public sphere that undermine their abilities to tell their own stories, particularly those stories that emphasize their relationships to nature, to place, and to their subsistence practices. As we noted in the introduction, Fred Bigjim, an Alaska Native, wrote a series of "letters to Howard [Rock]" in the early 1970s challenging the Alaska Native Claims Settlement Act (ANCSA) as just a continuation of the story of termination of the Native way of life because of its reorganization of Natives into corporations and its extinguishment of their subsistence rights. As he put it, "what is happening to Native people in Alaska is not a *new* story; it is a new chapter in an *old* story" (Bigjim and Ito-Adler 1974, 8). In essence, all the past failures of federal Indian policies attempting to transform Indians into assimilated White people now seemed redesigned in Alaska in a major effort at social engineering by legislative fiat. ANCSA in effect smuggled alien ideologies into the villages of Native Alaska in the form of corporate dividend checks and individualized hunting and fishing licenses.

As Bigjim puts it in another letter to Howard, "we don't want to become better [W]hite men or beat them at their own game. We just want a chance to develop our traditional values into a satisfying way of life that we can understand. . . . [ANCSA] is based on *competition;* the Native way is based on *cooperation*" (Bigjim and Ito-Adler 1974, 82–83). With its antagonistic corporate boardrooms and its accompanying capitalistic discourses threatening subsistence, ANCSA has become the lightning rod for many Alaska Natives for resistance as cultural persistence in this continuing old story. As political policy scholar John Dryzek maintains, ANCSA's "goal was thoroughly insensitive to the culture, abilities, and concerns of Natives on the receiving end" (1990, 118). In the mainstream media, ANCSA has been consistently and positively framed under the enduring values of responsible capitalism and possessive individualism.

In response to this insensitivity, a sovereignty movement in Alaska quickly gained momentum in the 1980s as Alaska Native groups recognized that the language of ANCSA spoke with an accent of termination and assimilation, attempting to turn all of them into businesspersons with no regard for traditional cultures (see McBeath and Morehouse 1994, 112). In 1983, the villagers of Akiachak, Akiak, and Tuluksak in the Yukon-Kuskokwim Delta declared themselves citizens of Yupiit Nation (Fienup-Riordan 1990, 193). That same year the Inuit Circumpolar Conference, an international organization of Eskimos from Alaska, Canada, and Greenland, appointed Canadian judge Thomas Berger head of an Alaska Native Review Commission to interview Natives all over the state and to discuss with them the ideological implications of ANCSA. After public meetings with people in sixty-two villages, Berger concluded that the ideas and sentiments expressed by villagers coalesced around desires for sovereign tribal governments in the form of Indian, Eskimo, or Aleut Country (Berger 1985, 170). Dryzek suggests that the Alaska Native Review Commission constituted new public spaces in which ordinary citizens articulated, shared, and judged their respective views concerning questions of "community development, protection and assertion of Native access to subsistence resources, renewable resource development, cultural renewal, and opposition to large-scale oil and mineral exploitation" (Dryzek 1990, 121, 127).

Dryzek's claim that new public spaces were opened up by the Review Commission calls to mind Nancy Fraser's criticism of Jürgen Habermas's unitary public sphere, especially his contention that discursive multicultural interaction can take place with the bracketing of social and cultural inequalities. As Fraser puts it, Habermas's misplaced faith in the efficacy of social and cultural bracketing results in a public sphere that is "so utterly bereft of any specific ethos as to accommodate with perfect neutrality and equal ease interventions expressive of any and every cultural ethos" (1993, 11). Over and over again, we have shown that when the indigenous peoples of Alaska have had to argue for, and defend, their subsistence rights in what Fraser and David Morley call a zero-degree culture, then their arguments were almost always seen through the metaphoric lenses of the dominant normative system with its privileging of capitalist resource development and possessive individualism as organizing precepts. For Alaska Native groups, communal subsistence practices are intertwined with cultural beliefs and understandings. However, whenever their subsistence practices were understood through the lenses of the dominant normative system, indigenous cultures were inevitably framed as deviant, abnormal, primitive, or outdated. As Fraser argues, these cultural differences and social inequalities must be thematized, rather than bracketed or assumed away, if political, economic, and cultural justice is to be maintained and perpetuated (1993, 17–18).

We maintain that the failure to thematize Alaska Native differences represents a cultural loss, or as William Paul might put it, a form of cultural thievery. Arguably, this cultural thievery has been at least partially responsible for an acute anomie in diverse Alaska Native communities with often-severe pathological consequences, including stunning rates of alcoholism, drug addiction, spouse abuse, child molestation, and suicide. In his book *The Way of the Human Being,* historian Calvin Martin documents some of the cases he encountered while working at a hospital and a prison among the Yup'ik peoples in southwest Alaska. In his prison work, he met Robert and Charlie. Robert, he tells us, was from a village amidst the ponds and sloughs by the Bering Sea, "a place of human conversation with the sea and tundra that goes back thousands of years" (1999, 123). Robert vehemently maintained that "hunting and gathering were the Eskimo's *religion,* not *subsistence.*" Robert said that if he were not in prison, he would be out at sea, which he considers heaven (124–25).

In a class session at the prison, Martin encountered a man whom the guards called "Charlie." As was his custom whenever he addressed a class, Martin would go around the room and ask every man to give his name. When he came to "Charlie," the man said, Qavcicuaq. Even though Martin had difficulty pronouncing Quavcicuaq, the young Yup'ik man insisted that he wanted to be called by his given name. He had lost not only his freedom, but also his name and a good part of his culture. Martin taught Qavcicuaq the "concept of living by a Story—that we all live a certain story." Qavciquaq said he liked his "Story," but the next time that Martin encountered Qavcicuaq after his release from prison, he was drunk and he said that his "Story was 'not well'" (1999, 128). For Martin, these painful cases illustrate the fact that too many Alaska Natives have lost their stories and that the mass media are partially responsible for these losses. As he puts it, facts only make sense within a certain paradigm of reality and there are now at least two very different realities percolating in North America: one Western and one Aboriginal (82, 121, 128).

Martin's poignant insights provide us with a stepping-off point by which to examine the ways that a few Alaska Natives began to reflexively interrogate and counter the paradigmatic dominance of Western cultures—as Tinker puts it, to come up with communal stories that could generate functional mythologies in new and vibrant ways for indigenous peoples (cited in Weaver 1997, 16, 33). In January 1987, six students and an instructor in a postsecondary broadcasting class at the North Slope Higher Education Center (NSHEC) began a critical investigation of news values at Barrow's community radio station, KBRW. The class, "Newswriting and Broadcasting in a Bilingual Context," was initiated by the acting general manager of the station.[1] While KBRW had begun broadcasting in December 1975, its early history had been punctuated by numerous ongoing problems, including allegations of financial mismanagement, high turnover of largely Caucasian station managers, a lack of full-time Native staff, conflicts with North Slope Borough organizations over news decisions, and a programming schedule that was insufficiently local (Duncan 1982, 276–79).

For instance, within the first two years of its operation, KBRW and its Caucasian manager were criticized by Borough officials for refusing to cover borough-initiated meetings on subsistence, specifically the international whaling controversy (*Anchorage Daily News* January 18, 1978, 24). These problems were endemic to the station's operations over the next decade and KBRW's acting station manager hoped that the class would offer some solutions to them. Specifically, she believed that the course might stimulate interest in radio work among Inupiat Eskimos in order to ameliorate long-standing borough criticisms about the lack of Native newscasters.[2]

The cultural makeup and size of the class was typical for courses taught under the auspices of the NSHEC. The six students included three Inupiat Eskimos, one Navajo Indian, and two Caucasians.[3] The instructor's class notes indicated that he outlined the course to conform with KBRW's wishes to instill more professionalism in its newscasts. As we noted in chapter 4, in rural Alaska, community-based systems of communication have been developed on public, nonprofit grounds, in part because of the absence of any viable commercial base. Thus, professionalism meant adherence to the professional standards outlined by National Public Radio (NPR), including neutrality and objectivity (NPR Program Standards 1973). Additionally, in keeping with the Western liberal pluralist tradition, national public radio conceived of its audience in individual terms. William Siemering, NPR's visionary first head, articulated this position as part of the organization's mission statement in 1970, writing that, "Public radio will serve the individual: it will promote personal growth; it will regard the individual differences among men with respect and joy rather than derision and hate" (Engleman 1996, 90). NPR's program standards are also situated in the context of an informational model that tacitly assumes an acceptance of the advanced capitalistic order and the individual consumer choices that are made available under it by the professional norms of its practitioners. NPR guidelines put it this way: "We cannot expect our listeners to obtain a better understanding of themselves and the world around them if the information we transmit does not conform to that world" (NPR Program Standards 1973).

From the outset, the class raised questions about the discursive differences of individualism and collectivism in the news. In a discussion about the gendered characteristics of Inupiat men and women as news sources, one student noted that Inupiat men always qualified their voices before the microphone as not being representative of what other people think. A female Inupiat student explained that "in our culture, there are no stars, just the team. Everything's for the team."

In the second class, the students used this collectively oriented cultural difference to raise a definitional question about news and about a bureaucratic agency from which Western reporters have traditionally gathered the news. The question turned on why KBRW lacked a criminal justice beat (actually one of its beats was the judicial district court). KBRW had been criticized for its overemphasis on soft news. For the Inupiat students the answer was clear: the Western criminal justice system was an inappropriate remedy to traditional notions of justice and the culture of shame that was used to redress wrongdoing in Inupiat circles. One of the Caucasian students insisted that preserving one's culture doesn't mean that one has to protect people from knowing that their kids are messing up. However, the Inupiat students assured this classmate that elders and mothers would have known about the wrongdoing through the many communal and interpersonal ways that people in oral cultures have of making negative matters known.

By the third meeting, the class recognized that the storytelling practices of broadcast news were dependent upon cultural preconceptions. Thus, one

Inupiat student keenly suggested classifying stories on cultural grounds. She said that if a story is an "English issue" (court cases, for example), then she would present the story all in English and provide a summary in Inupiaq. Conversely, in dealing with an Inupiat issue, say a whaling captains' convention, she would do the story in Inupiaq and provide a summary in English. When the class was visited by KBRW professionals—some of whom were newcomers to the community and on temporary contracts—the question of cultural competence leaped to the fore. One student noted that "the bicultural reporter in Alaska needs an understanding of the cultural mechanisms underlying the institutions that are in place on the North Slope." This discussion led to the more fundamental question of why KBRW was unable to attract Inupiat reporter trainees who already had the requisite cultural capital. While the class was unwilling to concede that "journalism was the domain of [W]hites," its students nevertheless acknowledged the double bind faced by a bilingual reporter who had to adopt Western standards and ethics in the face of community displeasure with Western news values. In short, the class recognized the catch-22 whereby White reporters were the dominant voices perpetuating Western journalistic values. As one student put it, "By always having White reporters, much of the listening audience is not being accurately presented or affected by the news."

Interestingly, the class compared the guidelines of NPR with those of KBRW, but evidently they did not relate them to a definition of community interests and values that was also available to them in course packets in the form of a document called the Inupiat Iltiqusiat, that is, the Inupiat way of life. Nowhere in KBRW's three pages of guidelines was there any reference to Inupiat people or their culture, although there were frequent references to matters that affect "the lives of the people who live on the North Slope." However, KBRW's (Silakkuagvik Communications, Inc.) mission statement—not included in the class handouts—does list cultural programming as its second most important priority behind information, its "most important product" (FCC Engineering Files 1989).

The most culturally revealing aspects about this class were its discussions and planning for the production of a program about cultural life in Barrow. The options presented the students offered them a window on different cultural discourses relevant to the project. They decided to adopt a documentary form, which allowed them to approach the topic from a historical perspective. However, they still faced questions about the character of the news they should present. The power of Western journalistic conventions and practices restrained them from adapting storytelling forms most appropriate for oral cultures. In their words, they wanted to produce the documentary in an "information context" and to avoid an "issue-oriented" program. Yet they admitted that they would be "investigating large, theoretical segments of life in Barrow—education, economy, government."

In short, the students had grappled with complex issues of intercultural communication up to that point in the semester, and now they were struggling with how to put into practice the lessons they had learned. Based on their desire to avoid issues, they chose to focus on the people of Barrow. This choice implicated the power that objectivity held over them. The ambivalence between what they had learned and the pull of Western journalistic standards was apparent in their discussion and conception of whom they should interview. They noted that "Barrow is, among other things, a bicultural community, and the perceptions of the various population segments must be given equal balance." Their response was to fit potential interviewees within the Fairness Doctrine as outlined in KBRW guidelines.

While they did not give a lot of attention to reworking the form of the traditional documentary to conform to indigenous values, they did raise some questions about presentational features, maintaining that five-minute segments were too limiting (KBRW news guidelines had stressed the fact that no story should exceed five minutes). They also wondered about how to handle the question of language usage—Inupiaq versus English—and whether they needed a consistent pattern across topical segments. Finally, they debated whether theme music should be Inupiat, raising questions whether indigenous musical ambience had been stereotypically overdone in other Native American documentaries.

While the form of their documentary did not weigh heavily in their deliberations, they were quite clear about how they wanted to frame and rank different cultural discourses. While the students wanted the entire documentary to show how patterns of Western educational control from boarding schools to BIA schools to those under local control had shaped Inupiat culture, they chose to place these patterns within a process, what Mary Louise Pratt calls transculturation, so that the Inupiats could be understood, as determining to some degree, what they absorbed into their own culture (1992, 6). The initial topical segment discursively framed traditional subsistence economy and culture from the perspective of an eighty-four-year-old elder. Not wanting to impose an interview schedule on her traditional storytelling practices, the students merely asked her to address changes in the subsistence economy affected by the introduction of mandatory school attendance and Western lessons early in the twentieth century. In three of the five segments, the students foregrounded Inupiaq identity and subsistence resources in terms of both physical and cultural sustenance, coming full circle at the end with a celebration of the importance of whales to Inupiat culture.

As a piece of broadcast journalism, the documentary's outline was rooted in cultural ideas and content relevant to the community's oral Inupiat traditions. In his critical history of public broadcasting, Ralph Engelman asks whether radio journalism should be rooted in traditions of oral storytelling or whether it should be conceived as an extension of the print media. This class seems to have answered that question for the Inupiat. The class notes revealed that this culturally heterogeneous mix of students struggled with the Western journalistic paradigm of objectivity, recognizing the cultural pain and dislocation it could bring to Inupiat Eskimos. Interrogating Western news values from an Inupiat cultural perspective, they began to see objectivity as a poseur—a masquerader hiding a storyteller's perspective. While the introductory nature of the class did not afford them the time to work out an indigenous model of news broadcasting, they realized that, for Inupiat storytellers, the important point is to narrate stories from those positions where their perspective on the land and nature is part and parcel of their cultural milieus—to fulfill what James Tully calls the "human aspiration to belong to a culture and place, to be at home in the world" (1995, 32).

The question confronting Alaska Native communicative possibilities in all of their institutional forms at the onset of the twenty-first century is what sort of guarantees are necessary in order for them to survive the political, cultural, and economic pressures now engulfing them. How does resistance as cultural persistence achieve its emancipation in the form of rights to speak in culture-affirming ways in public institutions and spheres free of imperial masters? We would suggest that this NSHEC class offers indigenous peoples an introductory step in establishing a form of communication free from domination. In their own ways, these students recognized what James Carey has so eloquently called communication as culture in all of its constitutive aspects (1989). For Alaska Natives, full citizenship rests on an unequivocal affirmation of the politics of cultural recognition (Fraser 1997, 12; Tully 1995, 3). As James Tully notes, the struggles of the Aboriginal peoples of the Americas "are exemplary of the 'strange multiplicity' of cultural voices that have come forward in the uncertain dawn of the twenty-first century to demand a hearing and a place in their own cultural forms and ways" (1995, 3). Thus cultural politics requires, as Tully argues, no less than the satisfaction of intercultural demands for expression in one's own language with publicly supported media under local control (2).

In 1992, 138 villages united to form the Alaska Inter-Tribal Council to provide a unified voice for tribal governments (McBeath and Morehouse 1994, 278). Two years later, a government panel known as the Alaska Natives Commission documented the cultural breakdown in rural Alaska, recommending that tribal status for Alaska Native groups was the blueprint for positive political change and that cultural empowerment was dependent on the guaranteed continuation of subsistence practices (Alaska Natives Commission Volume 2 1994, 57, 59). While the United States Supreme Court reversed a lower court's decision granting the Athabascan village of Venetie the status of Indian country in 1998 (*New York Times* February 26, 1998), many Alaska Native leaders had already affirmed their positions months before, that a Supreme Court reversal would have no bearing on their de facto practices of sovereignty (*Anchorage Daily News* July 5, 1997).

The political and cultural implications of this trend are clear and seemingly inexorable. Wendell Oswalt's claim that the Eskimos are "bashful no longer" can be extended to all Alaska Native groups (1990). Aboriginal cultures in the "far north" and elsewhere are engaged in what some of them have called a 'world reversal,' a "refus[al] to regard Aboriginal cultures as passive objects in an Eurocentric story of historical progress" and an avowal "to regard them[selves] from Aboriginal viewpoints, in interaction with European and other cultures" (Tully 1995, 21). Tully offers an intriguing symbol of what he calls a "post-imperial dialogue . . . in which the participants are recognized and speak in their own languages and customary ways" (24). That symbol of cultural diversity is a black bronze sculpture of a canoe with thirteen passengers from Haida mythology by Bill Reid, a renowned artist of Haida and Scottish ancestry. Three of these creatures bear special mention. First, there is "Hlkkyaan qqustaan, the frog, who symbolizes the ability to cross boundaries (xhaaidla) between worlds" and then there is "Xuuyaa, the legendary raven—the master of tricks, transformations and multiple identities [who] steers the canoe as his or her whim dictates" and finally, "holding the speaker's staff in his right hand, stands Kilstlaai, the chief or exemplar, whose identity, due to kinship to the raven is uncertain" (17–18). Reid, Tully says, consciously avoids the didactic position of telling us what it all means but he does ask us to think of the passengers as squabbling and vying for position each in his/her culturally distinct ways (24). In closing, we would suggest that perhaps the humble lesson to be drawn from these case studies and from Reid's sculpture is that we must set out to listen in order that Alaska Natives may speak—so they may be robbed no longer.

NOTES

1. All references to this class come from a memorandum and class notes provided to us by Dave Sims of the North Slope Higher Education Center at Barrow. Sims, an assistant professor of English and Communication Skills, taught "Newswriting and Broadcasting in a Bilingual Context" in the spring semester of 1987.

2. Both the acting general manager and her successor envisioned the course as an inducement to keep borough funds flowing to the station. As a percentage of total revenues, borough funds had varied between 11 percent and 17 percent from 1983 to 1987 (FCC Engineering Files, 1989).

3. Postsecondary students at NSHEC are generally older than typical college students. They usually work full-time and many of them raise families. For example, one of the Inupiat students was the public information officer for the North Slope Borough. One of the Caucasian students was the journalism instructor at Barrow High School. He was relatively new to the community. The other Caucasian student was the daughter of a man who had been a longtime resident of Barrow.

REFERENCES CITED

Adams, David Wallace. 1995. *Education for Extinction: American Indians and the Boarding School Experience, 1875–1928.* Lawrence: University Press of Kansas.

Alaska Almanac. 1982. Anchorage: Alaska Northwest.

Alaska Blue Book. 1963. Anchorage: Alaska Press Club.

Alaska Conservation Society News Bulletin. March 1961–May 1965. Archives, Alaska and Polar Regions Department, Rasmuson Library, University of Alaska Fairbanks. ACS Box 1, Folders 1–2.

Alaska Educational Broadcasting Commission. 1973. *Newsletter.* August and September. Juneau.

———. 1974a. *Newsletter.* February. Juneau.

———. 1974b. "A Pilot System of Mini-TV Transmitters to Provide Public Television to Rural Alaska." Prepared for the Corporation for Public Broadcasting, Juneau.

Alaska Natives Commission. 1994. *Final Report.* Volumes 1–3. Washington, D.C.: Alaska Natives Commission.

Alaska Public Broadcasting Commission. 1990. *Public Broadcasting in Alaska: A Long-Range Plan.* Juneau: Alaska Public Broadcasting Commission.

———. 1994. "Restructuring Public Broadcasting in Alaska: First Steps toward a New Future." Manuscript. April 7.

———. 1996. "APBC's Strategic Planning Process: A Compilation of Significant Documents, 1992–1996." Manuscript. September 23.

Alaska Territorial Resource Development Board. 1955. *Estimate of Alaska's Population, July 1, 1954, to June 30, 1955.* Juneau.

Alexander, Jeffrey C., and Paul Colomy, eds. 1990. *Differentiation Theory and Social Change: Comparative and Historical Perspectives.* New York: Columbia University Press.

Allen, Henry T. 1985. *An Expedition to the Copper, Tanana, and Koyukuk Rivers in 1885.* Anchorage: Alaska Northwest.

Anthropos. 1974. "Evaluation of the Impact of Mini TV Stations upon Three Remote Communities in Alaska." Mimeograph. Anchorage.

Arctic Health Research Center. 1959. "Project Chariot Environmental Program, Preliminary Report." November 23. Fairbanks.

Arnold, Robert. 1976. *Alaska Native Land Claims*. Anchorage: Alaska Native Foundation.

Ashcroft, Bill, Gareth Griffiths, and Helen Tiffin. 1995. Introduction to Part 7: "Ethnicity and Indigeneity." In *The Post-Colonial Studies Reader*, ed. Ashcroft, Griffiths, and Tiffin. 213–14. New York: Routledge.

Associated Alaska Public Broadcasting Stations. 1997. Proposal to the Alaska Broadcasting Commission. Manuscript.

Atomic Energy Commission. 1960. "Bioenvironmental Features of the Ogotoruk Creek Area, Cape Thompson, Alaska." First Summary by the U.S. Committee on Environmental Studies for Project Chariot Plowshare Program. December. Oak Ridge, Tennessee.

Badger, Mark. 1985. Personal interview, September 20. Fairbanks.

Bancroft, Hubert Howe. 1886. *The Works of Hubert Howe Bancroft*. Vol. 33: *History of Alaska, 1730–1885*. San Francisco: A. L. Bancroft and Co.

Barnard, Frederick M. 1967. "Lewis Henry Morgan." *Encyclopedia of Philosophy*. New York: Macmillan.

Bartlett, E. L. 1961. Memorandum to Bartlett's Staff, June 28. Archives, Elmer Rasmuson Library, University of Alaska Fairbanks. Bartlett Collection, Series XVI, Box 3, Folder 18.

Beck, Mary L. 1979. "Raven: Benefactor, Transformer, Trickster, Thief." *Indian Historian* 12.2 (Summer): 50–53, 62.

Bennett, Tony, and Valda Blundell. 1995. "Introduction: First Peoples." *Cultural Studies* 9.1 (January): 1–10.

Bennett, W. Lance, and Murray Edelman. 1985. "Toward a New Political Narrative." *Journal of Communication* 35.4 (Autumn): 156–71.

Berger, Thomas R. 1985. *Village Journey: The Report of the Alaska Review Commission*. New York: Hill and Wang.

———. 1991. *A Long and Terrible Shadow: White Values, Native Rights in the Americas, 1492–1992*. Seattle: University of Washington Press.

Berkhofer, Robert F., Jr. 1978. *The White Man's Indian: Images of the American Indian from Columbus to the Present*. New York: Alfred A. Knopf.

Bernays, Edward. 1947. "Engineering of Consent." *Annals of the American Academy of Political and Social Science* 250 (March): 113–20.

Berry, Mary Clay. 1975. *The Alaska Pipeline: The Politics of Oil and Native Lands Claims*. Bloomington: Indiana University Press.

Bethel Broadcasting Inc. 1991. "KYUK Anniversary Edition." September 26. Bethel, Alaska.

Bigjim, Frederick Seagayuk, and James Ito-Adler. 1974. *Letters to Howard: An Interpretation of the Alaska Native Land Claims*. Anchorage: Alaska Methodist University Press.

Boucher, H. A., and Eileen MacLean. 1990. "Rural Alaska Television Network—A Report to the Legislature by the House State Affairs Committee." Manuscript. Juneau.

Bridges, George, and Rosalind Brunt, eds. 1981. *Silver Linings: Some Strategies for the Eighties.* London: Lawrence and Wishart.

Brody, Hugh. 1982. *Maps and Dreams.* New York: Pantheon Books.

Brooks, Paul. 1965. "The Plot to Drown Alaska." *Atlantic Monthly,* May.

Brooks, Paul, and Joseph Foote. 1962. "The Disturbing Story of Project Chariot." *Harper's,* April.

Carey, James W. 1975. "Canadian Communication Theory: Extensions and Interpretations of Harold Innis." In *Studies in Canadian Communications,* ed. Robinson and Theall. 27–59.

———. 1981. "Culture, Geography, and Communications: The Work of Harold Innis in an American Context." In *Culture, Communication, and Dependency,* ed. Melody, Salter, and Heyer. 73–91.

———. 1989. *Communication as Culture: Essays on Media and Society.* Boston: Unwin Hyman.

Carey, James, and John J. Quirk. 1970. "The Mythos of the Electronic Revolution." *American Scholar* 39.2 (Spring): 219–41 and 39.3 (Summer): 395–424.

Carnegie Commission on Educational Television. 1967. *Public Television: A Program for Action.* New York: Carnegie Corporation.

Carpenter, Edmund. 1973. *Oh, What a Blow That Phantom Gave Me!* New York: Holt, Rinehart and Winston.

Chamberlin, J. E. 1975. *The Harrowing of Eden: White Attitudes toward Native Americans.* New York: Seabury Press.

Champagne, Duane. 1990. "Culture, Differentiation, and Environment: Social Change in Tlingit Society." In *Differentiation Theory and Social Change,* ed. Alexander and Colomy. 52–87.

Clifford, James. 1986. *Writing Culture: The Poetics and Politics of Ethnography.* Berkeley: University of California Press.

———. 1997. *Routes: Travel and Translation in the Late Twentieth Century.* Cambridge: Harvard University Press.

Coates, Peter A. 1991. *The Trans-Alaska Pipeline Controversy: Technology, Conservation, and the Frontier.* Bethlehem, Pa.: Lehigh University Press.

Cohen, Stanley, and Jock Young. 1973. *The Manufacture of News: Deviance, Social Problems, and the Mass Media.* Beverly Hills, Calif.: Sage.

Collier, John, Jr., and Malcolm Collier. 1986. *Visual Anthropology: Photography as a Research Method.* Albuquerque: University of New Mexico Press.

Collins, Richard, James Curran, Nicholas Garnham, Paddy Scannell, Philip Schlesinger, and Colin Sparks, eds. 1986. *Media, Culture, and Society.* Beverly Hills, Calif.: Sage.

Colt, Steve. 2000. "Salmon Fish Traps in Alaska: An Economic History Perspective." Institute for Social and Economic Research Working Paper 2000.2. <http://www.alaskool.org/projects/traditionalife/fishtrap>.

Cooley, Richard. 1963. *Politics and Conservation: The Decline of the Alaska Salmon.* New York: Harper and Row.

Coombes, Annie E. 1994. *Reinventing Africa: Museums, Material Culture, and Popular Imagination in Late Victorian and Edwardian England.* New Haven: Yale University Press.

Corey, Peter. 1987. "An Open Letter to Sheldon Jackson." In *Faces, Voices, and Dreams,* ed. Corey. xiii–xvii.

Corey, Peter, ed. 1987. *Faces, Voices, and Dreams: A Celebration of the Sheldon Jackson Museum, Sitka, Alaska, 1888–1988.* Seattle: Division of Alaska State Museums and the Friends of the Alaska State Museum.

Cornwell, Peter, and Gerald McBeath, eds. 1982. *Alaska's Rural Development.* Boulder, Colo.: Westview Press.

Curran, James. 1991. "Mass Media and Democracy: A Reappraisal." In *Mass Media and Society.* Ed. James Curran and Michael Gurevitch. 82–117. London: Edward Arnold.

Curran, James, Michael Gurevitch, and Janet Woollacott, eds. 1979. *Mass Communication and Society.* Beverly Hills, Calif.: Sage.

Daley, Patrick, and Dan O'Neill. 1993. "Howard Rock (Siqvoan Weyahok)." *Dictionary of Literary Biography.* Detroit: Gale Research.

Darnell, Frank. 1976. Introduction. In *ATS-6 and State Telecommunications Policy for Rural Alaska,* ed. Pittman and Orvik. iii–iv.

Darnton, Robert. 1975. "Writing News and Telling Stories." *Daedalus* 104.2 (Spring): 175–94.

Dauenhauer, Nora Marks, and Richard Dauenhauer, eds. 1987. *Haa Shuká, Our Ancestors: Tlingit Oral Narratives.* Juneau: Sealaska Heritage Foundation.

———. 1990. *Haa Tuwunáagu Yís, For Healing Our Spirit: Tlingit Oratory.* Seattle: University of Washington Press.

———. 1994. *Haa 'Kusteeyí, Our Culture: Tlingit Life Stories.* Seattle: University of Washington Press.

DeArmond, R. N. 1987. "The History of the Sheldon Jackson Museum." In *Faces, Voices, and Dreams,* ed. Corey. 3–19.

Demac, Donna. 1990. *Liberty Denied: The Current Rise of Censorship in America.* New Brunswick, N.J.: Rutgers University Press.

Dena Nena Henash. 1962. Transcript of Chiefs' Conference, June 24–26. Tanana, Alaska.

Department of Education, University of Alaska, and the Alaska Public Broadcasting Commission. 1980. "A Report on the Feasibility of Telecommunications for Instruction in the State of Alaska." Prepared for the Legislative Council, Senator George Hohman, Chair, February 15, in Response to Senate Concurrent Resolution 35. Juneau.

Dowling, R. P. 1982. "The Small Earth Station Program: Mitigating Isolation through Technology." In *Telecommunications in Alaska,* ed. Walp. 31–35.

Drucker, Philip. 1958. *The Native Brotherhoods: Modern Intertribal Organizations on the Northwest Coast.* Washington, D.C.: Government Printing Office.

———. 1965. *Cultures of the North Pacific Coast.* San Francisco: Chandler.

Drury, Clifford Merrill. 1952. *Presbyterian Panorama: One Hundred and Fifty Years of National Missions History.* Philadelphia: Board of Christian Education.

Dryzek, John S. 1990. *Discursive Democracy: Politics, Policy, and Political Science.* New York: Cambridge University Press.

Duncan, John Thomas. 1982. *Alaska Broadcasting, 1922–1977: An Examination of Government Influence.* Ann Arbor, Mich.: University Microfilms International.

Eagleton, Terry. 2000. *The Idea of Culture.* Malden, Mass.: Blackwell.

Ely, Robert, William Boesch, and John Cornman. 1965. "A Study of the Alaska Communication System: Its Past, Present, and Future." Prepared for Senator E. L. Bartlett.

Engelman, Ralph. 1996. *Public Radio and Television in America: A Political History.* Thousand Oaks, Calif.: Sage.

Enzensberger, Hans Magnus. 1974. *The Consciousness Industry.* New York: Seabury Press.

Ericson, Richard V., Patricia Baranek, and Janet B. L. Chan. 1987. *Visualizing Deviance: A Study of News Organization.* Toronto: University of Toronto Press.

Erlich, Suzy. 1997. Personal interview, June 20. Kotzebue, Alaska.

"Eyes of the Spirit" (videotape). 1983. KYUK-TV Productions, Bethel Broadcasting.

Federal Communications Commission. 1970. Engineering Files, KYUK-AM. Washington, D.C.

———. 1972. Engineering Files, KOTZ-AM, Materials in support of application for Construction Permit, September 1, October 17, and December 18. Washington, D.C.

———. 1989. Engineering Files, KBRW-AM. Washington, D.C.

———. 1991. Licensing Files, KYUK-TV. Washington, D.C.

Federal Field Committee for Development Planning in Alaska. 1968. *Alaska Natives and the Land.* Washington, D.C.: Government Printing Office.

Fienup-Riordan, Ann. 1990. *Eskimo Essays: Yup'ik Lives and How We See Them.* New Brunswick, N.J.: Rutgers University Press.

———. 1991. *The Real People and the Children of Thunder: The Yup'ik Eskimo Encounter with Moravian Missionaries John and Edith Kilbuck.* Norman: University of Oklahoma Press.

Fisher, Walter R. 1985. "The Narrative Paradigm: In the Beginning." *Journal of Communication* 35.4 (Autumn): 74–89.

Fishman, Mark. 1980. *Manufacturing the News.* Austin: University of Texas Press.

Flintoff, Corey. 1999. Personal correspondence.

Foote, Don Charles. 1961. Project Chariot and the Eskimo People of Point Hope, Alaska: Submitted to the United States Atomic Energy Commission in compliance with modification No. 2 Supplemental Agreement to Contract No. AT (04-3)—315, March. Archives, Alaska and Polar Regions Department, Rasmuson Library, University of Alaska Fairbanks. Project Chariot Collection.

Fraser, Nancy. 1993. "Rethinking the Public Sphere: A Contribution to the Critique of Actually Existing Democracy." In *The Phantom Public Sphere,* ed. Robbins. 1–32.

———. 1997. *Justice Interruptus: Critical Reflections on the "Postsocialist" Condition.* New York: Routledge.

Fulford, Robert. 1999. *The Triumph of Narrative: Storytelling in the Age of Mass Culture.* New York: Broadway Books.

Gallagher, Hugh G. 1974. *Etok: A Story of Eskimo Power.* New York: Putnam.

Gamson, William, and Andre Modigliani. 1989. "Media Discourse and Public Opinion on Nuclear Power: A Constructionist Approach." *American Journal of Sociology* 95.1 (July): 1–37.

Gans, Herbert. 1979. "Messages behind the News." *Columbia Journalism Review* 17.5 (January/February): 40–45.

Gibson, George H. 1977. *Public Broadcasting: The Role of the Federal Government, 1912–1976.* New York: Praeger.

Gibson, James R. 1976. *Imperial Russia in Frontier America: The Changing Geography of Supply of Russian America, 1784–1867.* New York: Oxford University Press.

Gilroy, Paul, Larry Grossberg, and Angela McRobbie, eds. 2000. *Without Guarantees: In Honour of Stuart Hall.* New York: Verso.

Goldin, Laurence A. 1996. "The Land Is Ours." Juneau: Aurora Films.

Goodall, Heather. 1993. "Border Wars: The Shifting Meanings of Boundaries in Aboriginal/Coloniser Relations in Southeastern Australia." *Communal/Plural* 2:65–94.

Goodykoontz, Colin Brummitt. 1939. *Home Missions on the American Frontier, with Particular Reference to the American Home Missionary Society.* Caldwell, Idaho: Caxton.

Gouldner, Alvin. 1976. *The Dialectic of Ideology and Technology.* New York: Seabury Press.

Governor's Office of Telecommunications. 1975. *ATS-6 Health/Education Telecommunications Experiment: Alaska Education Experiment Summary Final Report.* Volumes 1–3. Juneau.

———. 1978. *Satellite Television Demonstration Project (SATVDP) Final Report.* Volumes 1–2. Juneau.

Gramsci, Antonio. 1971. *Selections from the Prison Notebooks.* Ed. and trans. Quintin Hoare and Geoffrey Nowell Smith. New York: International Publishers.

Gregory, Mary. 1997. Personal interview, June 15. Bethel, Alaska.

Gregory, Paul. 1997. Personal interview, June 15. Bethel, Alaska.

Gruening, Ernest. 1954. *The State of Alaska.* New York: Random House.

———. 1961. "Alaska Has Shared in New Frontier Progress." *Congressional Record: Proceedings and Debates of the 87th Congress, First Session.* September 27. University of Alaska Anchorage Consortium Library. Alaska Vertical File, Rampart Dam.

———. 1962. Correspondence from Colonel Christian Hanburger. Archives, Alaska and Polar Regions Department, Rasmuson Library, University of Alaska Fairbanks, Gruening Collection, Box 4, M11H2, Folder: Public Works, Dams—2—Rampart—Century 21, February.

———. 1963. Reports of Meetings at Stevens Village and Rampart Village, July 27, 1963. Archives, Alaska and Polar Regions Department, Rasmuson Library, University of Alaska Fairbanks. Gruening Collection, Box 4, M11H2, Folder: Public Works—Rampart—Native—1963–65.

———. 1965. "The Plot to Strangle Alaska." *Atlantic Monthly,* July 1965. Reprinted in *Congressional Record: Proceedings and Debates of the 89th Congress, First Session,* July 27, 1965. University of Alaska Anchorage Consortium Library, Alaska Vertical File—Rampart Dam.

Gupta, Akhil, and James Ferguson, eds. 1997. *Culture, Power, Place: Explorations in Critical Anthropology.* Durham, N.C.: Duke University Press.

Gurevitch, Michael, Tony Bennett, James Curran, and Janet Woollacott, eds. 1982. *Culture, Society, and the Media.* New York: Methuen.

Hage, Ghassan, and Lesley Johnson, eds. 1993. *Communal/Plural* 2/1993. Nepean, NSW: University of West Sydney.

Hall, Stuart. 1979. "Culture, the Media, and the 'Ideological Effect.'" In *Mass Communication and Society*, ed. Curran, Gurevitch, and Woollacott. 315–48.

―――. 1981. "The Whites of Their Eyes: Racist Ideologies and the Media." In *Silver Linings*, ed. Bridges and Brunt. 28–52.

―――. 1982. "The Rediscovery of 'Ideology': Return of the Repressed in Media Studies." In *Culture, Society, and the Media*, ed. Gurevitch et al. 56–90.

―――. 1986a. "Cultural Studies: Two Paradigms." In *Media, Culture, and Society*, ed. Collins et al. 33–48.

―――. 1986b. "Gramsci's Relevance for the Study of Race and Ethnicity." *Journal of Communication Inquiry* 10.2 (Summer): 5–27.

―――. 1992. "The West and the Rest: Discourse and Power." In *Formations of Modernity*, book 1, ed. Hall and Gieben. 275–331.

―――. 1995. "New Cultures for Old." In *A Place in the World?* ed. Massey and Jess. 175–213.

Hall, Stuart, ed. 1997. *Representation: Cultural Representations and Signifying Practices*. London: Sage.

Hall, Stuart, and Bram Gieben, eds. 1992. *Formations of Modernity*. Book 1. London: Polity Press.

Hall, Stuart, Chas Critcher, Tony Jefferson, John Clarke, and Brian Roberts. 1978. *Policing the Crisis: Mugging, the State, and Law and Order*. London: Macmillan.

Hamilton, Joan. 1997. Personal interview, June 15. Bethel, Alaska.

Hamley, Jeffrey. 1994. "An Introduction to the Federal Indian Boarding School Movement." *North Dakota History* 61.2:2–9.

Hardt, Hanno. 1998. *Interactions: Critical Studies in Communication, Media, and Journalism*. Lanham, Md.: Rowman and Littlefield.

Haycox, Stephen. 1986–87. "William Paul Sr., and the Alaska Voters' Literacy Act of 1925." *Alaska History* 2.1 (Winter): 17–38. Citations in the text follow the Web version at <http://www.alaskool.org/native>.

―――. 1994. "William Lewis Paul/Shgundi [Shquindy]," May 7, 1885–March 4, 1977." In *Haa 'Kusteeyí, Our Culture*, ed. Dauenhauer and Dauenhauer. 503–24.

Hays, Samuel P. 1987. *Beauty, Health, and Permanence: Environmental Politics in the United States, 1955–1985*. New York: Cambridge University Press.

Hinckley, Ted C. 1965. "Publicist of the Forgotten Frontier." *Journal of the West* 4.1:27–40.

―――. 1966. "The Presbyterian Leadership in Pioneer Alaska." *Journal of American History* 52.4:742–56.

―――. 1972. *The Americanization of Alaska, 1867–1897*. Palo Alto, Calif.: Pacific Book.

―――. 1982. *Alaskan John G. Brady: Missionary, Businessman, Judge, and Governor, 1878–1918*. Columbus: Ohio State University Press.

Hinckley, Ted C., ed. 1970. "The Canoe Rocks—We Do Not Know What Will Become of Us." Complete transcript of a meeting between Governor John Green Brady of Alaska and a group of Tlingit chiefs, Juneau, December 14. *Western Historical Quarterly* 1.3:265–90.

Horkheimer, Max, and Theodor Adorno. 1972. *Dialectic of Enlightenment*. Trans. John Cumming. New York: Seabury Press.

Hulbert, Bette. 1987. "Note on the Mission of the Sheldon Jackson Museum." In *Faces, Voices, and Dreams,* ed. Corey. xi–xii.

Hyde, Lewis. 1998. *Trickster Makes This World: Mischief, Myth, and Art.* New York: Farrar, Straus and Giroux.

"Indian Country: Two Destinies, One Land." 1997. *Anchorage Daily News* (special series), June 29–July 5.

Inupiat Paitot. 1961. "The Statement of Policy and Recommendations Adopted by the Point Barrow Conference on Native Rights, Barrow, Alaska." November 17.

Isaac, Alexie. 1997. Personal interview, June 16. Bethel, Alaska.

Isett, Rosemary Alexander. 1995. "Publicly Funded Satellite Television in Alaska: Lost in Space." Ph.D. dissertation, Michigan State University.

Jackson, Sheldon. 1880. *Missions on the North Pacific Coast.* New York: Dodd, Mead.

———. 1886. *Report on Education in Alaska.* Washington, D.C.: Government Printing Office.

James, Beverly, and Patrick Daley. 1984. "The Development of the Alaskan Native Press in the Movement toward Self-Determination, 1867–1967." Paper presented at the International Association for Mass Communication Research Conference, August, Prague.

———. 1987. "Origination of State-Supported Entertainment Television in Rural Alaska." *Journal of Broadcasting and Electronic Media* 31.4:169–80.

Jenne, Theron, and Harry Mitchell. 1982. "Military Long-Lines Communication in Alaska." In *Telecommunications in Alaska,* ed. Walp. 12–19.

Johnson, Gerald W. 1970. "Technological Development of Nuclear Explosives Engineering." In *Education for Peaceful Uses of Nuclear Explosives,* ed. Weaver. 11–21.

Johnson, Robert David. 1998. *Ernest Gruening and the American Dissenting Tradition.* Cambridge: Harvard University Press.

Jungk, Robert. 1958. *Brighter Than a Thousand Suns.* Trans. James Cleugh. New York: Harcourt, Brace and World.

Kamenskii, Anatolii. 1985. *Tlingit Indians of Alaska.* Trans. Sergei Kan. Fairbanks: University of Alaska Press.

Kan, Sergei. 1985. "Russian Orthodox Brotherhoods among the Tlingit: Missionary Goals and Native Response." *Ethnohistory* 32.3:196–223.

Keith, Michael. 1985. *Signals in the Air: Native Broadcasting in America.* Westport, Conn.: Praeger.

KOTZ-AM. 1997. Program Narrative. National Telecommunications Information Administration: Public Telecommunications Facilities Program Grant Application, pp. 1–6.

Krauss, Michael. 1974. *Native Peoples and Languages of Alaska.* Fairbanks: Alaska Native Language Center.

———. 1980. *Alaska Native Languages: Past, Present, and Future.* Fairbanks: Alaska Native Language Center, University of Alaska.

Kreith, Frank, and Catherine Wrenn. 1976. *The Nuclear Impact.* Boulder, Colo.: Westview Press.

"The Land Is Ours" (videotape). 1996. Juneau: Aurora Films.

Langdon, Steve J. 1986. *Contemporary Alaskan Native Economies.* Lanham, Md.: University Press of America.

Lefebvre, Henri. 1991. *The Production of Space*. Cambridge, Mass.: Blackwell.

Lenz, Mary Jane. 1985. *Bethel: The First 100 Years, 1885–1985*. Bethel, Alaska: City of Bethel Centennial History Project.

Leuthold, Steven. 1998. *Indigenous Aesthetics: Native Art, Media, and Identity*. Austin: University of Texas Press.

Lidchi, Henrietta. 1997. "The Poetics and the Politics of Exhibiting Other Cultures." In *Representation*, ed. Hall. 151–208.

Littlefield, Daniel F., Jr., and James W. Parins. 1984. *American Indian and Alaska Native Newspapers and Periodicals*. Westport, Conn.: Greenwood Press.

Lukacs, John. 1966. *A New History of the Cold War*. Garden City, N.Y.: Doubleday.

Lule, Jack. 2001. *Daily News, Eternal Stories: The Mythological Role of Journalism*. New York: Guilford Press.

Martin, Calvin. 1987. "The Metaphysics of Writing Indian-White History." In *The American Indian and the Problem of History*, ed. Martin. 27–34.

Martin, Calvin, ed. 1987. *The American Indian and the Problem of History*. New York: Oxford University Press.

Martin, Calvin Luther. 1999. *The Way of the Human Being*. New Haven: Yale University Press.

Marx, Karl, and Frederick Engels. Edited and with an Introduction by C. J. Arthur. 1976. *The German Ideology*. New York: International Publishers.

Massey, Doreen, and Pat Jess, eds. 1995. *A Place in the World?: Places, Cultures, and Globalization*. Oxford: Oxford University Press.

McBeath, Gerald, and Thomas Morehouse. 1994. *Alaska Politics and Government*. Lincoln: University of Nebraska Press.

McIntire, Ted. 1984. "History and Current Management of State Provided Television Service." Prepared by Division of Telecommunications Services. December. Juneau.

McNickle, D'Arcy. 1973. *Native American Tribalism: Indian Survivals and Renewals*. London: Oxford University Press.

Melody, William. 1978. "Telecommunications in Alaska: Economics and Public Policy." Final Report to the State of Alaska.

Melody, William, Liona Salter, and Paul Heyer, eds. 1981. *Culture, Communication, and Dependency: The Tradition of H. A. Innis*. Norwood, N.J.: Ablex.

Meyrowitz, Joshua. 1985. *No Sense of Place: The Impact of Electronic Media on Social Behavior*. New York: Oxford University Press.

Michaels, Eric. 1994. *Bad Aboriginal Art: Tradition, Media, and Technological Horizons*. Minneapolis: University of Minnesota Press.

Miller, Susan. 1989. Sheldon Jackson biographical statement. In Finding Aid to Record Group 239. Presbyterian Church (U.S.A.) Department of History and Records Management Services, Philadelphia.

Mitchell, Donald Craig. 1997. *Sold American: A Story of Alaska Natives and Their Land, 1867–1959*. Hanover, N.H.: University Press of New England.

Mitchell, William. 1904. "Building the Alaskan Telegraph System." *National Geographic Magazine* 15.9 (September): 357–61.

Moore, Nellie Ward. 1997. Personal interview, June 12. Anchorage.

Morgan, Lael. 1988. *Art and Eskimo Power*. Fairbanks: Epicenter Press.

Morley, David. 2000. *Home Territories: Media, Mobility, and Identity.* New York: Routledge.

Murphy, James Emmett, and Sharon Murphy. 1981. *Let My People Know: American Indian Journalism, 1828–1978.* Norman: University of Oklahoma Press.

Naske, Claus-M., and William R. Hunt. 1978. "The Politics of Hydroelectric Power in Alaska: Rampart and Devil Canyon—A Case Study." Report prepared for the Department of the Interior, Office of Water Research and Technology, October.

National Public Radio. 1973. NPR Program Standards. Washington, D.C.

Nelson, Cary, and Dilip Parameshwar Gaonkar. 1996. *Disciplinarity and Dissent in Cultural Studies.* New York: Routledge.

Nelson, Richard. 1983. *Make Prayers to the Raven: A Koyukon View of the Northern Forest.* Chicago: University of Chicago Press.

———. 1986. *Hunters of the Northern Forest.* Chicago: University of Chicago Press.

Nelson, Russell. 1999. Personal correspondence.

Nichols, Jeannette Paddock. 1924. *Alaska: A History of Its Administration, Exploitation, and Industrial Development during Its First Half Century under the Rule of the United States.* Cleveland: Arthur H. Clark.

Northrip, Charles. 1985. Personal interview, August 29. Fairbanks.

———. 1998. Personal interview, January 27. Washington, D.C.

Northrip, Charles M., and Richard P. Dowling. 1972. Report on Mini-PTV Transmission: Local Public Television for Rural Areas. Submitted to Alaska Educational Broadcasting Commission, Corporation for Public Broadcasting, and the Federal Communications Commission. November. Fairbanks: University of Alaska Division of Media Services.

Norwood, Gus. 1961. "Wings over the Yukon." Rampart Action Committee. University of Alaska Anchorage Consortium Library. May.

Oberg, Kalervo. 1973. *The Social Economy of the Tlingit Indians.* Seattle: University of Washington Press.

Ong, Walter J. 1982. *Orality and Literacy: The Technologizing of the Word.* New York: Methuen.

O'Neill, Dan. 1994. *The Firecracker Boys.* New York: St. Martin's Press.

Oswalt, Wendell H. 1966. *This Land Was Theirs: A Study of the North American Indian.* New York: John Wiley and Sons.

———. 1990. *Bashful No Longer: An Alaskan Eskimo Ethnohistory, 1778–1988.* Norman: University of Oklahoma Press.

Patty, Stanton. 1971. "A Conference with the Tanana Chiefs." *Alaska Journal* 1.2 (Spring): 2–18.

Paul, Frederick. 1986. "Then Fight for It." Abridged version of unpublished manuscript. Alaska Historical Commission Studies in History No. 207. Loussac Library, Anchorage, Alaska.

Paul, William L., Sr. 1971. "The Real Story of the Lincoln Totem." *Alaska Journal* 1 (Summer): 2–16.

Pearson, Larry. 1990. "Communication Issues of the '90s." The Chugach Conference. October 5–6. Anchorage: University of Alaska/Anchorage Center for Information Technology.

Pearson, Larry, and Doug Barry. 1987. "Talking to Each Other, Talking to Machines:

Alaska's Telecommunication Future." A Report to the Joint Committee on Telecommunications of the Alaska State Legislature. January.

Peters, John Durham. 1997. "Seeing Bifocally: Media, Place, and Culture." In *Culture, Power, and Place,* ed. Gupta and Ferguson. 75–92.

Pittman, Theda Sue, and James S. Orvik. 1976. *ATS-6 and State Telecommunications Policy for Rural Alaska: An analysis of recommendations.* December. Fairbanks: Center for Northern Educational Research.

Pratt, Mary Louise. 1992. *Imperial Eyes: Travel Writing and Transculturation.* New York: Routledge.

Pratt, Richard Henry. 1964. *Battlefield and Classroom: Four Decades with the American Indian, 1867–1904.* New Haven: Yale University Press.

Price, Robert E. 1990. *The Great Father in Alaska: The Case of the Tlingit and Haida Salmon Fishery.* Douglas, Alaska: First Street Press.

Public Broadcasting Endowment Trust Fund. 1994. Minutes, April 7. Anchorage.

RATNET Council. 1981. Policy Guidelines Regarding the Use of the State of Alaska Satellite Television Project Adopted by the Rural Alaska Television Network Council. Adopted December 3, 1981, and amended February 17, 1984, and June 14, 1984.

Ricketts, Nancy J. 1994. "Matilda Kinnon Paul Tamaree/Kahtahnah, Kah-tli-yudt, January 18, 1863–August 20, 1955." In *Haa 'Kusteeyí, Our Culture,* ed. Dauenhauer and Dauenhauer. 468–502.

Riggins, Stephen. 1992. *Ethnic Minority Media: An International Perspective.* Newbury Park, Calif.: Sage.

Robbins, Bruce. 1993. *The Phantom Public Sphere.* Minneapolis: University of Minnesota Press.

Robinson, Gertrude Joch, and Donald Theall, eds. 1975. *Studies in Canadian Communications.* Montreal: Graduate Programme in Communications, McGill University.

Rogers, George W., and Richard A. Cooley. 1963. *Alaska's Population and Economy: Regional Growth, Development and Future Outlook.* Volume 2: *Statistical Handbook.* College: University of Alaska.

Rose, Gillian. 1995. "Place and Identity: A Sense of Place." In *A Place in the World?,* vol. 4, ed. Massey and Jess. 87–132.

Ross, Andrew. 1994. *The Chicago Gangster Theory of Life: Nature's Debt to Society.* New York: Verso.

Ross, Ken. 2000. *Environmental Conflict in Alaska.* Boulder: University Press of Colorado.

Schiller, Herbert. 1973. *The Mind Managers.* Boston: Beacon Press.

Schudson, Michael. 1978. *Discovering the News: A Social History of American Newspapers.* New York: Basic Books

Sheldon Jackson Papers. Record Group 239. Presbyterian Church (U.S.A.) Department of History and Records Management Services, Philadelphia.

Sinclair, Upton. 1906. *The Jungle.* New York: Grossett and Dunlap.

Smith, Philip. 1982. "Non-Profit Organizations in Rural Alaska Development: The Role of RurAL CAP." In *Alaska's Rural Development,* ed. Cornwell and McBeath. 101–11.

Smith, Valene, ed. 1989. *Hosts and Guests: The Anthropology of Tourism.* Philadelphia: University of Pennsylvania Press.

Snapp, Thomas. 1962. Personal correspondence with Henry Forbes, August 27.

————. 1983. Personal interview, December 17. Fairbanks.

Soja, Edward. 1989. *Postmodern Geographies: The Reassertion of Space in Critical Social Theory.* New York: Verso.

Starnes, Richard. 1963. "The Rampart We Watch." *Field and Stream,* August, pp. 12 and 64–65.

Stewart, Robert Laird. 1908. *Sheldon Jackson: Pathfinder and Prospector of the Missionary Vanguard in the Rocky Mountains and Alaska.* New York: Fleming H. Revell.

Stocking, George W., Jr., ed. 1985. *Objects and Others.* Madison: University of Wisconsin Press.

Sundborg, George. 1963. "From the Nation's Capital: The Weekly Newsletter from the Office of U.S. Senator Ernest Gruening." August 2. Archives, Alaska and Polar Regions Department, Rasmuson Library, University of Alaska Fairbanks. Gruening Collection, Box 4, M11H2, Folder: Public Works—Rampart—Native—1963–65.

Swanton, John. 1909. *Tlingit Myths and Texts.* BAE Bulletin 39. Washington, D.C.: Government Printing Office.

Teller, Edward, Wilson K. Talley, Gary Higgins, and Gerald W. Johnson. 1968. *The Constructive Uses of Nuclear Explosives.* New York: McGraw-Hill.

"They Never Asked Our Fathers" (videotape). 1980. KYUK-TV Productions. Bethel Broadcasting.

Tiepelman, Dennis. 1997. Personal interview, June 20. Kotzebue, Alaska.

Torgovnick, Marianna. 1990. *Gone Primitive: Savage Intellects, Modern Lives.* Chicago: University of Chicago Press.

Tuchman, Gaye. 1978. *Making News: A Study in the Construction of Reality.* New York: Free Press.

Tully, James. 1995. *Strange Multiplicity: Constitutionalism in an Age of Diversity.* Cambridge: Cambridge University Press.

Turner, Frederick. 1985. *John Muir: Rediscovering America.* Cambridge, Mass.: Perseus.

Twitchell, Peter. 1997. Personal interview, June 16. Bethel, Alaska.

————. 1999. Personal correspondence.

Udall, Stewart. 1963. *The Quiet Crisis.* New York: Holt, Rinehart and Winston.

Valaskakis, Gail Guthrie. 1992. "Communication, Culture, and Technology: Satellites and Native Northern Broadcasting in Canada." In *Ethnic Minority Media,* ed. Stephen Riggins. Newbury Park, Calif.: Sage. 63–81.

————. 1993. "Parallel Voices: Indians and Others—Narratives of Cultural Struggles." *Canadian Journal of Communication* 18.3:283–96.

————. 1996. "Negotiating the Meaning of Land in Native America." In *Disciplinarity and Dissent in Cultural Studies,* ed. Nelson and Gaonkar. 149–69.

————. 2000. "Blood Borders: Being Indian and Belonging." In *Without Guarantees,* ed. Gilroy, Grossberg, and McRobbie. 388–94.

Walp, R. M., ed. 1982. *Telecommunications in Alaska.* Honolulu: Pacific Telecommunications Council.

Weaver, Jace. 1997. *That the People Might Live: Native American Literatures and Native American Community.* New York: Oxford University Press.

Weaver, Lynn, ed. 1970. *Education for Peaceful Uses of Nuclear Explosives.* Tucson: University of Arizona Press.

Wenzel, George. 1991. *Animal Rights, Human Rights: Ecology, Economy, and Ideology in the Canadian Arctic.* Toronto: University of Toronto Press.

Widders, Terry, and Greg Noble. 1993. "On the Dreaming Track to the Republic: Indigenous People and the Ambivalence of Citizenship." In *Communal/Plural,* ed. Hage and Johnson. 95–112.

Williams, Raymond. 1962. *Communications.* Baltimore: Penguin.

———. 1977. *Marxism and Literature.* Oxford: Oxford University Press.

———. 1985. *Keywords: A Vocabulary of Culture and Society.* New York: Oxford University Press.

———. 1989. *Resources of Hope: Culture, Democracy, Socialism.* New York: Verso.

INDEX

aboriginal fisheries: ANB resolutions on, 66; conflict between commercial and, 50, 68; conservation and, 71–72; cultural materialism of, 46; historical and ethnographic context on, 45, 49–50; leisure time for cultural creativity provided by richness of, 48; relative noninterference in, 47, 52; reservations not seen as solution to, 70; topic for ANM magazine, 176

aboriginal land rights: Athabascan petition for land withdrawal pending resolution of, 104–5; Edwardsen's petition for, 77–78; effect of statehood and economic schemes on, 13, 15, 90; extinguishment of by ANCSA, 6; reservations not seen as solution to, 70; resolution of lodged in Congress by first Organic Act, 51; Rock's appeal for, 123; role of *Tundra Times* in struggle for, 82; statement of Inupiat Paitot on, 102; Tlingit decision to fight for, 45, 76–77; 123; topic for ANM magazine, 176

acculturation, 58

Active, John, 151, 163

Adams, David, 12, 28, 29, 63

Adorno, Theodor, 162

AEC Environmental Studies, 93

AFN Telecommunications Committee, 178–79

Akiachak, 192

Akiak, 192

Alascom, 177, 183

Alaska, 9, 35, 36, 40, 43, 68, 86, aboriginal fishing in, 40, 45, 47, 49–50; absentee control of, 64, 76; Armed Forces Radio Network in, 144; census of 1880 for, 51; community media in, 15–16, 137, 139, 140–42, 149, 154, 157, 159, 161–62, 194; on COMSAT footprint in, 147, 168; congressional passage of Second Organic Act for, 57; cultural politics in, 1, 140, 141, 155, 198–99; decline in fish market for, 57–58; development of corporate canneries and fisheries in, 41, 45, 51, 52, 54, 57; discovery of oil on North Slope of, 15; earthquake in, 131–32; on economic cycles of boom and bust in, 15, 83, 89, 143; on energy needs in, 134; English explorers in, 22; establishment of civil government in, 29, 35; extension of 1872 Mining Act to, 51; fishery reserves for, 69; geopolitical importance of, 13, 84, 143–44, 166; growth in salmon pack in, 52–53; Gruening's civil rights agenda in, 110; Gruening's hydroelectric agenda for, 114, 118; on home rule for territory of, 66, 73; indigenous peoples of, 1, 3, 4 17–18, 20, 22, 51, 159, 176–77, 193; influence of Presbyterian missions in, 58–60; influence of Russian Orthodoxy in, 58–60; influx of military personnel and jobs in, 84, 86, 88; Inuit Circumpolar Conference of Eski-

PATRICK J. DALEY is an associate professor of communication at the University of New Hampshire. He is a contributor to *Ethnic Minority Media: An International Perspective* (1992), and his articles have appeared in the *Journal of Communication*, the *Journal of Communication Inquiry*, the *Journal of Mass Media Ethics*, and *Journalism and Communication Monographs*.

BEVERLY A. JAMES is an associate professor of communication at the University of New Hampshire. She is a contributor to *The International Movie Industry* (2000), and her articles have appeared in *Media, Culture, and Society*, the *Journal of Popular Culture*, and *Critical Studies in Mass Communication*.

The History of Communication

The University of Illinois Press
is a founding member of the
Association of American University Presses.

Composed in 10.5/13 Adobe Minion
at the University of Illinois Press
Designed by Paula Newcomb
Manufactured by Thomson-Shore, Inc.

University of Illinois Press
1325 South Oak Street
Champaign, IL 61820-6903
www.press.uillinois.edu